They Never Gave Up

They Never Gave Up

Adventures in Early Aviation

MICHAEL WILKEY

ORCA BOOK PUBLISHERS

Canadian Cataloguing in Publication Data
Wilkey, Michael, 1935
They never gave up

ISBN 1-55143-077-0
Includes index.
1. Aeronautics—Biography. 2. Aeronautics—History. 3. Flight. 4. Paper airplanes.
I. Title.
TL539.W54 1997   629.13'0092'2   C96–910791–9

Library of Congress Catalog Card Number: 97-65298

Orca Book Publishers gratefully acknowledges the support of our publishing programs provided by the following agencies: the Department of Canadian Heritage, the Canada Council for the Arts, and the British Columbia Ministry of Small Business, Tourism and Culture.

Cover design by Christine Toller
Illustrations by Michael Wilkey
Printed and bound in Canada

Orca Book Publishers
PO Box 5626, Station B
Victoria, BC   V8R 6S4
Canada

Orca Book Publishers
PO Box 468
Custer, WA 98240-0468
USA

97 98 99 5 4 3 2 1

This book is written for two young men
who have been inspired by some of these heroes of aviation.
For my sons, Mitchell Lee and Benjamin Drew.

Acknowledgments

My thanks to Pat Phillips for the use of his poem "The Beginning."

Every writer needs a patient typist and a diligent editor. Most grateful thanks for these tasks I give to my wife Gwendolyn. Without her help and encouragement I might have given up!

Contents

Preface   ix

Introduction   xi

Daedalus and Icarus   1

The Wright Brothers   3

William Wallace Gibson   19

Airmail   35

First Across the Mountains   45

Trans Canada Mail Flight   67

Tom Fox   75

How an Aircraft Flies   87

Paper Airplanes   105

Index   112

Preface

Since 1909, when the first Canadian flew in his own country, there has been an ongoing process of development and adventure in aviation. On February 23, John McCurdy flew the Silver Dart from a frozen lake in Nova Scotia, but the aircraft was designed and built by an American, Glenn Curtiss. Since that day thousands of pilots and aircraft have contributed to our aviation tradition in hundreds of ways — on missions of hope, mercy, commerce and adventure. Some of these adventures stand out more than others, some aircraft have gained greater reputations than others, and some pilot adventurers have become legends.

The story of the Wright brothers of Dayton, Ohio, is of great importance. They built and flew the world's first powered aircraft, never giving up until they succeeded. But all of the aviators in this book were special in many ways. They represent the very best of those whose only desire was to serve aviation and their country the best way they knew how — by flying.

For a better understanding of what we sometimes take for granted, I have also included sections on the basic theories of flight and on how an aircraft is controlled in the air. Check out the chapter "How Aircraft Flies" for any aviation terms you might not know the meaning of while reading the stories.

Most importantly, it is the determination, the inventiveness and the courage of these flyers that I hope will inspire young people to greater heights in aviation, or in other endeavors, for a better quality of life.

Michael Wilkey
Victoria, British Columbia

Introduction

Aviation today is not the risky business that it was in the earliest days of flying. Early aviators risked their fortune, pride, reputation and their very lives each time they flew their flimsy machines. Aircraft were nothing more than frail frames covered with lacquered cotton fabric. They were difficult to control and sensitive to the slightest air currents. Gasoline engines were not as reliable as they are today, and even motorists had a chancy journey in the cars of the day. And, at that time there were not many properly trained mechanics to keep aircraft airworthy, so the pilots themselves often kept them going.

Flyers were never sure they would reach their intended destinations because maps usually only covered territory where pilots had already been. Pilots who flew into new territory were on their own. But they enjoyed the thrill of it all. The excitement of a new environment to conquer and earn a living in outweighed the fear of the unknown.

The great age of aviation dawned on December 17, 1903, at Kitty Hawk, North Carolina, when Orville and Wilbur Wright flew the first powered aircraft. Seven years later a Canadian farmer and storekeeper, William Wallace Gibson, who had developed his own ideas based on tests with model kites, flew his Gibson Twin Plane from a field in Victoria, British Columbia.

During the 1920s, many records were established in North America by men and women who flew the early path-finding routes. They were the airmail and bush flyers and they all had one thing in common — the determination to succeed. Some reached their goals while others failed in uncommon attempts.

Captain Ernie Hoy flew his Curtiss JN4, the famous Jenny, across the Rocky Mountains without any knowledge of air currents, by flying through the passes or around the mountain peaks. To reach his goal he also had to endure the promotions of businessmen and political gains by many elected officials associated with early aviation record attempts. He succeeded because he was determined to do so.

While establishing an airmail route across Canada, military flyers also pioneered the future passenger airline routes across the continent. They not only tested different flight paths and aircraft, but they also tested themselves.

Later, when fledgling airlines were established, aviators reached out in another direction. They flew north over the tundra and frozen lakes to expand airline services to isolated communities in Canada's northern territories. Tom Fox, who founded Associated Airways, demonstrated his determination to maintain his airline by retrieving an old World War II plane from a frozen river in the Northwest Territories. Even though the temperature dropped to -50°C (-58°F) he never gave up and flew his Anson aircraft back to Edmonton.

Few memorials stand to honor the pioneer aviators, but the inscription on the memorial to the Wright brothers at Kitty Hawk sums up the determination to succeed that most of the early aviators displayed. The memorial says simply:

In commemoration of the conquest of the air by the brothers Orville and Wilbur Wright. Conceived by genius, achieved by dauntless resolution and unconquerable faith.

Daedalus and Icarus

"The First to Fly": A Greek Legend

Daedalus, an Athenian architect, had designed and built a labyrinth for King Minos of Crete. A labyrinth is a huge maze or walk-through puzzle. Crete is a small island in the Mediterranean Sea. When the construction was finished, the king refused to let Daedalus and his son Icarus ever leave the island. Daedalus and Icarus couldn't bear to stay in the foreign land and thought about all the different ways they could escape from the island and return home to Athens, which is in modern-day Greece. They concluded that the only solution was to fly away.

Daedalus watched and studied how the sea birds soared and swooped around the cliffs of the coast. He then built two sets of wings, which were wooden frameworks covered with feathers. He attached the feathers to the frames with beeswax and warned Icarus not to fly too close to the sun because its heat would melt the wax.

When the day to fly away arrived, they climbed to a high tower on top of the cliffs and launched themselves into the wind as they had seen the birds do. The wings worked like modern hang-gliders and they flew into the sky above the blue waters of the Mediterranean Sea.

Thrilled by the experience of flying, Icarus became excited and grew careless. He soared higher and higher. Daedalus again shouted the warning about the heat of the sun, but his words were lost in the sounds of the wind and water. Icarus flew higher still, overjoyed by the sensation of flight.

Soon the sun's heat began to melt the wax just as his father said it would. By the time Icarus realized what was happening, it was too late. All the feathers flew away and he fell into sea, hundreds of metres below, disappearing without a trace. Daedalus flew on alone until he reached the island of Sicily. He landed a very sad and lonely man and never flew again.

The flight of Daedalus and Icarus is a legend, not a true story. But the daring exploits of these mythical figures from ancient times illustrate the early human fascination with the possibilities and practicalities of flight.

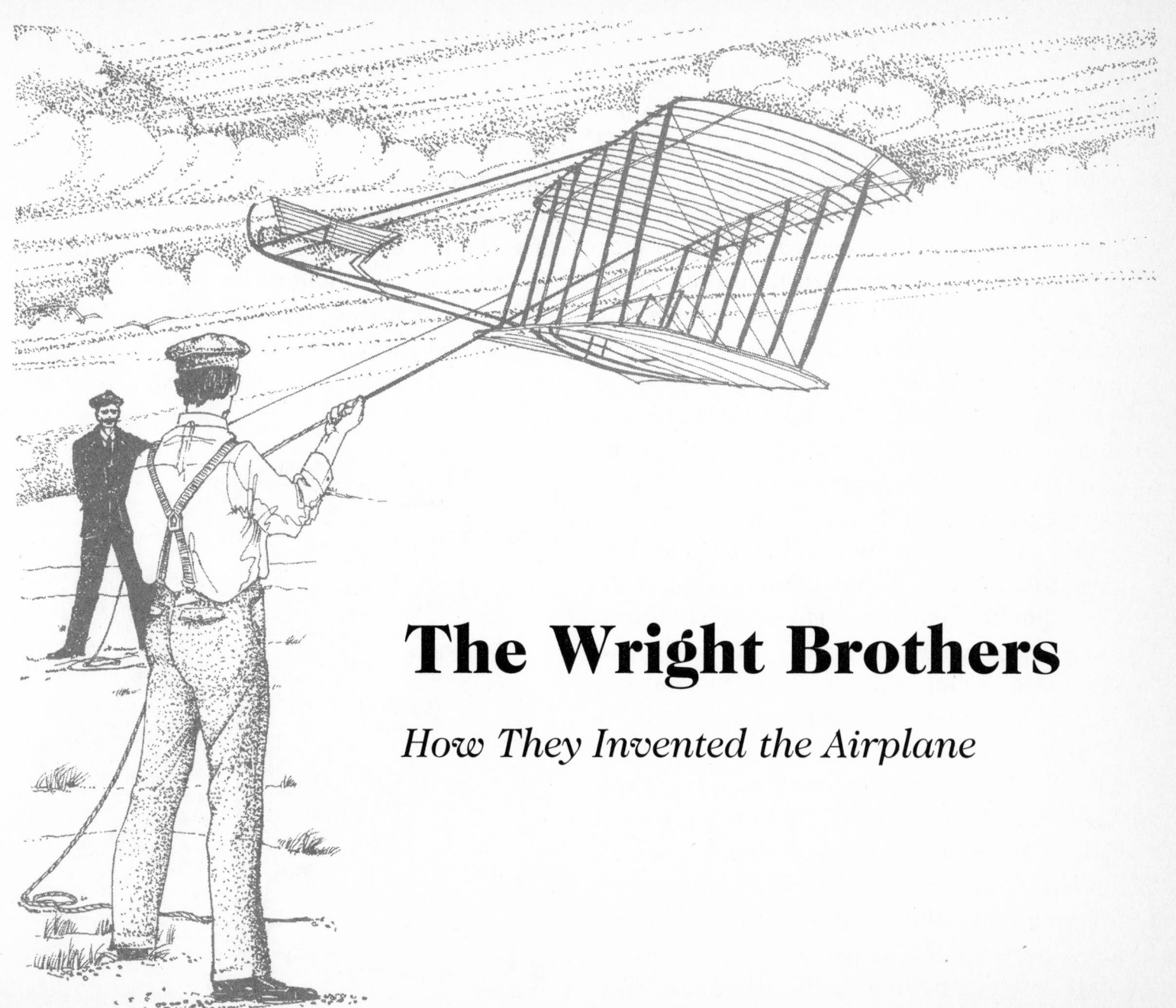

The Wright Brothers

How They Invented the Airplane

The First Flyer

Hawthorn Street in Dayton, Ohio, was very quiet in the late evening sun. Orville Wright walked from his home to the little workshop at the rear of his store on West Third Street. Inside the shop his brother was already busy working on a project that had taken all their spare time that whole summer. Each day after they finished working on the bicycles they were building, the two young bachelors spent their time reading. They read everything they could find about the efforts of inventors who were trying to fly powered aircraft and the theory of flying machines, although no one had succeeded in flying one yet.

The year was 1900 and only a few men had managed to fly even simple gliders. One man, Octave Chanute, had jumped from high hills into the wind with wings strapped to his body, not unlike today's hang-gliders. Orville and his brother Wilbur were sure that they could invent a real flying machine.

The Wright brothers had built many toys and gadgets and often tinkered with things around the house. When they were only twelve years old, Wilbur and Orville built a printing press and eventually went into the printing business. Their father, Milton Wright, a bishop in the Protestant Church, and their mother, Catherine, encouraged all five of their children to be as creative and inventive as possible. It was the two middle boys, Orville and Wilbur, who were destined to become famous. After the printing business they went into the bicycle business and sold, repaired and even built what was then called the safety bicycle. It was called the safety bicycle because it had two wheels of the same size instead of a large wheel in front and a smaller one behind, which was more usual at this time. The Wrights' best bicycle, called the Van Cleve after an ancestor who was killed on the old frontier, sold for $100, a

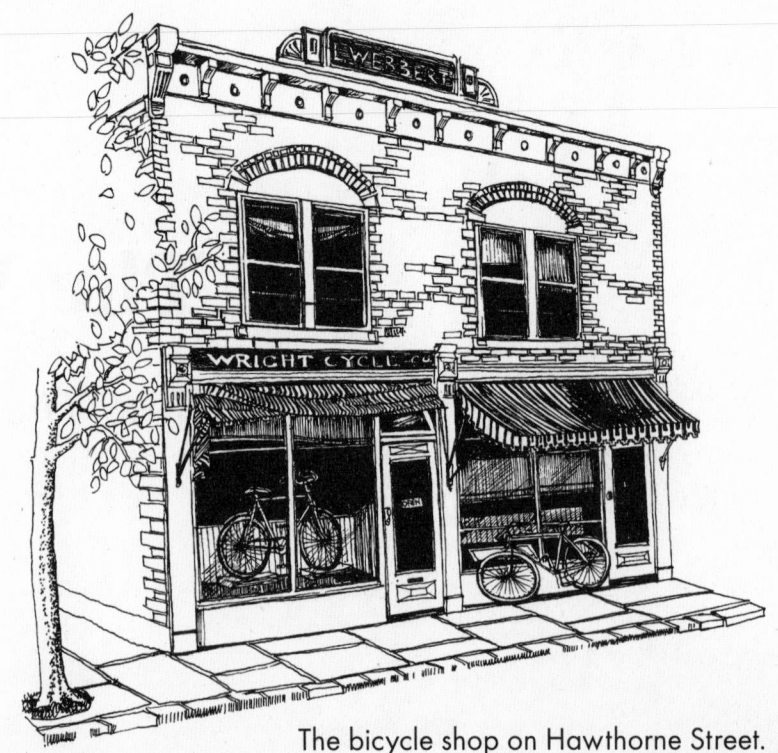

The bicycle shop on Hawthorne Street.

great deal of money in those days.

One day Orville entered the workshop and noticed his brother reading a letter from the United States Weather Bureau. Wilbur had written to find out where the strongest, most constant winds in the country could be found. He wanted the information in order to decide where to conduct flying tests on a glider that was partially complete in their workshop. The letter informed them that two of the best areas for flying were in California and Florida, both of which are a long way from Dayton. The third suggestion though was a tiny village on the east coast of North Carolina. The winds there were strong and were expected to be constant each fall.

The Wright brothers decided that this place, called Kitty Hawk, was the best location to test their glider. But like most of their efforts so far in their quest for flight, there was a problem with this decision. Kitty Hawk was very difficult to reach. The village is located on a 320-kilometre (200-mile) strip of sand that separates the Atlantic Ocean from the mainland of North Carolina. It would be very difficult to transport the glider to Kitty Hawk, but the young men never gave up. From Dayton they would have to take a train to the town of Norfolk, Virginia, then another train to Elizabeth City, North Carolina. Kitty Hawk is another 48 kilometres (30 miles) across a stretch of water called Albemarle Sound, which they would have to cross by boat.

Kitty Hawk was a small fishing village, and because the only hotel had recently burned to the ground, there was nowhere to stay. They would have to bring tents and camping equipment and hope they could find the other things they needed in the village. Wilbur wrote a letter to the operator of the telegraph in the village, which caused quite a commotion. Just about everyone in the area read the letter, and as a result, William Tate, captain of the lifeboat and husband of the postmistress, offered to help Wilbur and Orville.

The glider had two wings and was made of a spruce wood frame covered with silk fabric, all strung together with wires. The total cost of materials for the glider came to $15. Construction was well under way, but Orville and Wilbur decided to buy the spruce spars for the wings in Norfolk instead of taking the 5 metre- (16 foot-) long pieces with them. All the other pieces would be made beforehand and then assembled at Kitty Hawk. The finished parts of the glider and the tools they would need for the final assembly were all packed into boxes, ready for transport to the coast.

Wilbur left first to buy the wood for the spars in Virginia and make all the arrangements at Kitty Hawk. Twenty-four hours after leaving Dayton, he arrived in Norfolk, Virginia. He spent the next two days shopping for the spruce, but couldn't

Orville and Wilbur Wright in the workshop behind the bicycle shop.

find any. The only alternative to the spruce spars was 4.8-metre (15-foot) lengths of fir, which would have to do. Wilbur needed to get to Kitty Hawk as soon as possible so he left for Elizabeth City, North Carolina, deciding to adjust for the shorter wing spars after he arrived in the village.

Wilbur delivered all the new lumber, tools, supplies and all the separate parts of the glider on the dock at Elizabeth City to be loaded on the weekly freight boat to Kitty Hawk. The boat would arrive in another week and Wilbur was in a hurry to get to the sand dunes of Kitty Hawk.

For several days Wilbur tried to find transport to Kitty Hawk for himself, but no one seemed to know how to get there. Finally, he met a fisherman named Israel Perry who was willing to take him across the sound to Kitty Hawk. Israel's boat, the *Curlicue*, was old, uncared for and very dirty, not unlike Israel himself. Wilbur loaded his things onto the boat and they headed out into the sound. It would have only taken them a few hours to reach Kitty Hawk if there had been any wind. But as they moved into the sound, the sails flapped idly and the boat moved along slower than the two men could walk. Wilbur had come so far, but now he could only sit patiently and hope the wind would improve.

As the *Curlicue* slowly rounded the point into the open sound, the wind suddenly picked up, becoming a gale. Wilbur helped Israel take down all the sails except the jib, a small sail at the front of the boat. The boat rocked on the high waves and water splashed into it at an alarming rate. Wilbur bailed it out as fast as he could, barely keeping up with the water coming in. Finally they found their way into the mouth of the North River and, since it was already dark, decided to put down the anchor and land in the daylight of the next morning. Wilbur could not stand the smell or the cockroaches in the cabin below, so he huddled, cold and wet, under a blanket on the wooden deck.

Kitty Hawk is named after the birds that are seen in great numbers on the Outer Banks. The kitty hawk is really misnamed since it is not a hawk at all. Its name is derived from the local word "skeeter" (more correctly mosquito), on which the birds feed, and became skeeter (skitty) hawk. That night, Wilbur found out why so many kitty hawks were around. He woke up on the next morning, Wednesday, covered with mosquito bites and with a sore back from sleeping on the deck. The weather was not much better, so he and Israel spent another night on the boat waiting to land at Kitty Hawk.

Thursday morning, cold, wet, tired, stiff and sore, Wilbur knocked on William Tate's front door. He was also very hungry because he had eaten nothing for two days except a small jar of jam. Mrs. Tate welcomed him and, after he cleaned up, fed him a big meal of ham and eggs. She told

Wilbur he could stay at their house until Orville arrived with the camping equipment.

The next morning was warm and sunny, so Wilbur took Mrs. Tate's sewing machine outside and started sewing the seams of the wing covers he had adjusted to make up for the shorter wing spars. He was quite a curiosity to the villagers as he sat there sewing in the high starched collar and tie he always wore. The freight boat arrived two days later and Wilbur carefully unpacked the trunks and boxes containing the glider parts. The glider was almost assembled by the time Orville arrived.

The brothers erected their tent and made things comfortable. They had to tie the tent to an old oak tree to prevent the constant wind from blowing it away. The wind that was so necessary to their work often became their enemy at night, when they were forced to leave the warmth of their blankets to hang onto the tent until the wind died down a little. They soon settled down to a routine of living and working, Orville doing the cooking chores, Wilbur taking on the clean-up. They worked on the flying tests together.

By the end of September the glider was ready to fly. Just as they had planned, the brothers first flew it as a kite. Taking turns, one rode the tethered glider while the other held the ropes, assisted by the ever-present William Tate. The pilot lay flat on the bottom wing and manipulated the controls with his hands and feet. A small opening in the lower wing allowed him to drop his legs down when landing and run with the glider to a full stop. This procedure proved unnecessary because both brothers could land the craft very well while lying prone on the wing.

That fall, Orville and Wilbur only spent a total of ten minutes actually flying the glider with one of them on board, but they learned a great deal about flying. They made every adjustment they could at Kitty Hawk, but the major changes would have to be made when they got the glider back home.

Several flights were made with the glider at-

The first camp at Kitty Hawk.

tached to a derrick and the controls manipulated from the ground using ropes. They flew the glider up to 12 metres (40 feet) above the ground in 50 kilometres (30 miles) per hour wind. Wilbur was making some adjustments to the controls after one of those flights when a sudden gust flipped the glider over, causing extensive damage which took more than a week to repair. One night the wind blew so hard that the glider was buried in 60 centimetres (24 inches) of sand by the following morning. After more repairs and tests it was the middle of October and time to return home to Dayton. The Wright brothers had succeeded in making flights of up to 12 metres (40 feet) above the ground, lasting only fifteen to twenty seconds, but they had covered distances of up to 122 metres (400 feet). For the time being, they were content.

The Second Flyer

After Christmas Orville and Wilbur Wright resumed work in the little shop behind their bicycle store. The new flyer would be larger than the one they had experimented with in the fall at Kitty Hawk. They bought new wood, sewed new silk fabric covers for the wings and made many adjustments to their design of the previous year. During regular store hours the brothers worked in the bicycle shop, fixing and building their safety bicycles. Then, after supper, they went to work on the flyer, often working until quite late at night and returning home tired after each long day.

The glider finally began to take shape and

Orville and Wilbur test the first flyer as a kite.

started to look like an airplane. Wilbur and Orville checked and tested it as much as they could in the workshop, but they couldn't do any flight testing until it was transported to Kitty Hawk.

"Well, it's as ready as it can be," Orville said one

evening as they were putting on the wool suit jackets they usually wore.

"It will be fine, Orville, the best so far," answered Wilbur, as they locked the shop door.

The move to Kitty Hawk was easier in 1901 because Orville and Wilbur were now aware of all the problems. They arranged for William Tate to build them a wooden shack, which was a real luxury. Orville and Wilbur slept well at night because they did not have to worry about the wind. The shack soon took shape as a temporary home. Wilbur, who was very tidy, made the best possible use of the small space by building shelves to hold the food, cooking utensils, tools and spare parts for the flyer.

But the flying did not go well. The glider behaved erratically in the air, swooping and diving without apparent reason. The young men frequently redesigned small pieces and parts, but the adjustments didn't make the glider perform as it should.

"Man will never fly in a thousand years," Wilbur said to his disappointed brother, but he never really believed it.

The weather was not in their favor either. It rained so often that it was impossible to fly very

The interior of the shed at Kitty Hawk.

much, but the brothers continued to adjust the glider's control surfaces, all without much success. At the end of October Wilbur and Orville decided to redesign the flyer completely when they returned to Dayton. Although they were very disappointed with the larger flyer and its performance at Kitty Hawk that fall, they were still determined to be the first men into the air under power.

At home they thought a great deal about the new glider they were going to build. Orville also wrote more letters to everyone who was working on the same problem and read everything available on the subject. At that time not much had been written simply because no one knew very much about flying or flying machines.

The Wind Machine

The major problem the brothers faced was that they couldn't test the flying machine in the wind out on the dunes until it was finished. Orville and Wilbur spent a great deal of time thinking about how to overcome the problem. Then, one day Wilbur received some information about a device called a wind tunnel that might help them. But where would they find such a machine? With their usual enthusiasm, Orville and Wilbur decided to use their technical skills and build the wind tunnel themselves. They concluded that the time it took to build it would be well spent if it helped them build a successful flying machine. So they began both projects in the spring.

The wind tunnel was a wooden box which was 1.8 metres (6 feet) long and open at both ends. One end was fitted with a fan blade driven by a small motor that produced a large volume of air to be directed down the tunnel and out the other end. The amount of air could be controlled to come close to wind speeds of up to 50 kilometres (30 miles) per hour. Wilbur and Orville made scale models of the parts of the glider they wanted to test and placed them inside the box. By watching the action of the model in the wind tunnel they were able to test the part before they manufactured the actual large piece. It was much easier, cheaper and quicker to do this than to wait all summer to fly the real glider in the fall at Kitty Hawk.

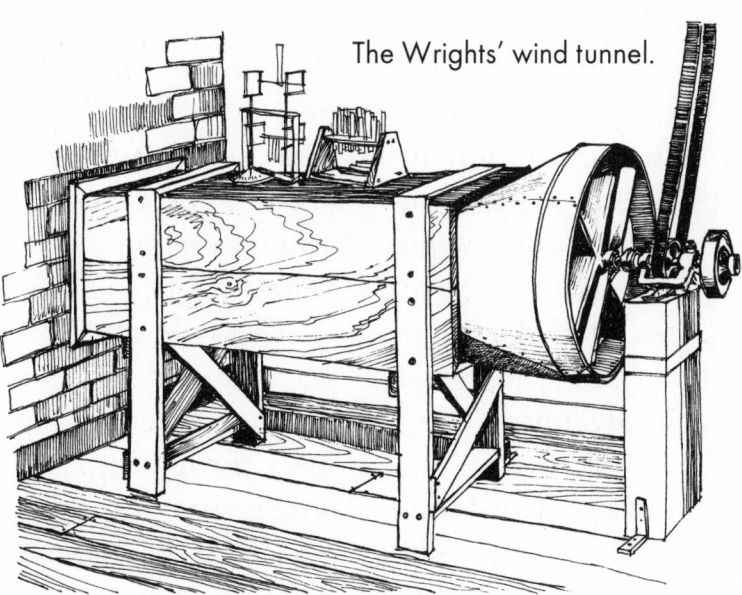

The Wrights' wind tunnel.

Using the wind tunnel, they discovered that the glider flew much better when they added a tail to give it stability in the wind, and redesigned the wings with less of a curve. The new wing shape also gave the glider more lift so that it needed less wind to fly.

Wilbur and Orville's wonderful wind tunnel even showed them that the wings could be used to control the direction of the aircraft. When they twisted the wings up at the tips, air flowed over them a bit faster, producing more lift than at the center of the wing. If they twisted one tip up and the other tip down, the aircraft would tilt and turn in the direction of the twisted down wing because the up twisted wing moved through the air faster than the down wing. With the help of their new wind tunnel, the Wright brothers had come to a greater understanding of flight and aircraft construction. Now it was time to return to Kitty Hawk.

The winds were right and the weather was perfect when they arrived at the Kitty Hawk shack in the fall of 1902. The brothers went to work as soon as they were able to get organized. The glider was a success. Both of them flew the machine in many different wind conditions and it behaved exactly as their scale models had done in the wind tunnel, except for one problem. About once in fifty flights the aircraft went into a tail slide that the young men called "well digging," because when the flyer hit the ground, it dug quite a deep hole in the sand. Orville stayed awake for an entire night trying to solve the puzzle of the well digging. He finally concluded that a tail that could move sideways like a ship's rudder would correct the spin. The following morning he modified the tail and connected it to the wing warping control. Now when the wings tilted, the tail rudder also turned. Orville solved the problem because he never gave up until he found a solution that worked.

Orville and Wilbur went on to make over one thousand flights all over the sands that fall, and they went home convinced that they would take a motor-powered flying machine to Kitty Hawk the following year.

The Wright Flyer

The problems with the framework of the aircraft were solved, but now Wilbur and Orville had a new difficulty to overcome. Where would they find an engine to power their aircraft? Nothing of the sort existed at that time. There were automobile engines, but they were too heavy to be suitable for powered flight.

The only solution the brothers could think of was to build their own motor. They also had to manufacture their own propellers to move the flyer through the air. In spite of all these challenges, they never gave up.

Well into 1903, the engine was assembled and tests were carried out. Results from the tests showed that the engine gave out about twelve horsepower, four more than the originally expected eight horsepower. (Horsepower is an old Imperial unit based on the hauling power of a large draft horse.) The engine weighed a little more than 55 kilograms (120 pounds) without oil or water.

Expectant Wright Brothers wait for better weather to fly the Wright Flyer.

Propellers for the flyer gave Orville and Wilbur a lot of problems. At first they worked with information based on a ship's propeller, but this got them nowhere. So they had to start from the beginning again and invent a new propeller that would work against the air.

"It was a matter of cut and try, and if it did not work, cut and try again," Wilbur said later.

From that trial and error they produced the propellers, or props. There were two props driven by the single engine and they were more efficient than any of the marine propellers of the time.

Success

Towards the end of September 1903, the Wrights took their flyer to Kitty Hawk. This aircraft differed greatly in design detail from their previous gliders. Instead of bending ash ribs to construct the wings, they built the ribs by sawing the wood, then gluing and nailing them together. The wings were covered in fabric on both the top and the bottom surfaces, the first time that wings had ever been constructed in such a way. Control of the machine stayed the same as it had been on the 1902 flyer.

To gain more flying experience, the brothers also took the rebuilt 1902 glider with them to Kitty Hawk and built a shed for it. Orville and Wilbur assembled the old glider and flew it as far as 120 metres (400 feet) before the new flyer arrived. It was shipped separately because there wasn't enough room for all the freight in one trip.

While they waited for the freight boat to deliver their flyer, Orville and Wilbur set about building the shed to house the new machine. They used bad weather days to finish the shed and flew the old glider when the weather was good. At last the freight boat arrived, the big boxes and crates were carefully emptied and the bits and pieces of the flyer were assembled. The new aircraft had to be rushed into the shed when a fierce windstorm suddenly blew up. The strength of the gale reached hurricane force and the Wrights were almost flooded out of their quarters before the weather changed.

At last it was time to test the new airplane. The Wright brothers primed and checked the engine with their usual care and attention. Eventually, the motor burst into life and the propellers turned. Unfortunately, there was half a turn of movement in the propeller shafts before they turned the propellers. The brothers considered this to be a bit of a worry, but not a danger. However, when they ran the power up to flying speed, the shafts twisted because of this slack fitting and the motor had to be shut down.

The only solution was to send the shafts back

to Dayton where their machinist, Charlie Taylor, could rebuild them. It took two weeks for Charlie to fix the shafts and send them back. In the meantime, Orville and Wilbur flew the old glider again and fixed the damage from the storm.

On an unusually warm day at the end of November the shafts arrived back in Kitty Hawk. Two days of replacing and testing them revealed another disappointment when tiny splits in the hollow tube shafts began to enlarge. New shafts were necessary, but they had to be made of higher quality, solid machine steel. It had taken so long to get the old tubes replaced and shipped back that they decided Orville should return to Dayton and remanufacture the shafts completely with Charlie Taylor. He would then bring them back to Kitty Hawk himself. Ten days later he was back, fitting the new solid shafts to the flyer with his brother.

While Orville was away, Wilbur tested the efficiency of the propellers and found that his initial estimate of a friction loss of seven percent was wrong. Friction loss is the amount of pushing power lost to the propellers before the aircraft moves forward. The results of his test showed a loss of only five percent, which showed how well the propellers worked. The props bit into the air more strongly than expected, producing more stress on the shafts that connected them to the motor.

At last everything was ready for the first powered flight, or so they thought. But when the sprocket wheels that guided the chains to the propellers were under full power of the engine, they vibrated the securing nuts and bolts loose. No matter how tight the brothers pulled on the wrench, nuts and bolts failed to stay put. As a desperate last ditch attempt to overcome the problem, Wilbur suggested trying the glue they normally used to hold the tires of their bicycles to the wheels. They heated up the glue, spread it on the threads of the nuts and bolts that held the sprocket wheels to the shaft, and pulled them down tight. It worked, and they never had to face that difficulty again.

William Tate, who had been such a good friend and helper to the Wrights during the previous years, suddenly became disenchanted with the project. After an unfortunate disagreement with Wilbur and Orville over firewood, he left the Kitty Hawk camp, forfeiting his chance to witness history being made.

The first attempt to fly the new machine was made on the fourteenth of December, but a small handling mistake at the start of the test caused slight damage to the aircraft. The flyer rattled down the rail that was positioned on the side of Big Hill to get more speed, lifted slightly, then suddenly pitched up. Wilbur, who won the coin toss to try first, had to push the control down hard and the flyer came down very quickly. One

Success — the first to fly.

of the landing skids broke when it crunched into the hard-packed sand. It was all over in three and a half seconds and the Flyer had travelled almost 30 metres (100 feet). Even though the Wright brothers did not consider it a true flight, they were excited about the prospect of success on the next test. But first they had to make a new landing skid and repair the cracked wing rib.

Three days later the Wrights were ready for their second test. They had built an 18-metre (60-foot) monorail track in a slight depression in the flat ground about 30 metres (100 feet) west of the camp. A small two-wheeled trolley supported the airplane on the track. The skids of the flyer rested on the trolley. When the aircraft sped along the rail, it would be guided by a bicycle wheel hub at the front of the machine.

During the early hours of the morning of Thursday, December 17, 1903, the wind rose to about 43 kilometres (27 miles) per hour, as indicated by the wind speed measuring device the brothers brought with them. By the time the rail was put in place, John Daniels, Adam Etheridge and Will Dought from the Kill Devil Hills lifeboat station had gathered to watch the flight.

Orville climbed aboard the craft and the engine was started. There was no aviator clothing for these flyers. As usual, they were dressed in business suits, starched collars, ties and wool caps. Orville slipped the restraining rope from the machine, and with Wilbur holding on to the wing tip, the flyer rolled down the track at a ground speed of only 11 kilometres (7 miles) per hour. At that speed Wilbur was able to keep up quite easily until he let go at the end of the track. The Flyer then shot into the air at about 48 kilometres (30 miles) per hour. That speed was calculated by measuring its rate over the ground, then adding the known wind speed. The aircraft travelled a distance of 37 metres (120 feet) at an altitude of 3 metres (9 feet) and landed on a spot slightly higher than the takeoff point. The entire flight took only 12 seconds.

To record the attempt, Orville had set up a large plate camera on a tripod and instructed John Daniels how to shoot a photograph. Daniels did exactly as he was told and provided the world with a great picture of the first successful powered flight. "The first in the history of the world," Orville wrote in an article in *Flight Magazine* in 1913.

Four more flights were made that day and each one went further, higher and longer than the first. The brothers' measuring equipment was just as ingenious as the flyer itself. A wind speed indicator called an anemometre, a revolution counter and a stopwatch were all installed on the aircraft and were set to start simultaneously. The hard landings jarred the stopwatch back to zero, but Wilbur was able to record the time using another watch.

After their initial success, the Wright brothers knew it would only be a matter of more practice to be able to fly further and higher before landing. They discussed the possibility of using up the 13 or 14 litres (3 gallons) of gasoline left in the fuel tank by flying the 6.5 kilometres (4 miles) up to the Kitty Hawk weather station. Mr. Dosher, the telegraph operator, worked there, and he would be able to send the news of their accomplishment to their father in Dayton.

A trip of this length would give the brothers all the flying practice they needed. While they stood discussing whether they should eat lunch first and then go to the weather station, a sudden gust blew up. Although John Daniels was holding the flyer at the wing tip, the wind was too strong and flipped the aircraft. John became the first aviation casualty when he was badly bruised by the mishap.

The Wright Flyer, having earned its name, was too badly damaged to fly again, but the Wright brothers from Dayton, Ohio, had finally accomplished their ultimate goal. Orville and Wilbur Wright were the first to complete a powered flight because they never gave up.

William Wallace Gibson

Flash in the Sky Man

Early Attempts

In Canada we have given time, energy, resources, and even lives to the quest for the freedom of flight. Today as we travel, seemingly without effort, through the sky in a variety of private and commercial aircraft, it is hard to imagine the problems that early questers experienced. But it was only in the lifetimes of our great-grandparents that successful journeys into the air were made from the ground. Before this, flying was not considered possible, and those who meddled with the idea were often considered to be a little weird, just as were those in the fifteenth century who thought the earth was round. "The world is flat," most people said, and sometimes actually punished the visionaries who thought that our planet was a globe.

Orville and Wilbur Wright struggled for more than three years to get the Wright Flyer into the sky over Kitty Hawk in North Carolina. Fueled by the success of the Wrights, a group of Canadians met in the home of Dr. Alexander Graham Bell, the scientist who invented the telephone. Dr. Bell lived in a large, beautiful house in the small fishing village of Baddeck on Cape Breton Island, Nova Scotia. The group came together to form an organization called the Aerial Experiment Association (AEA). At the meeting were two young, idealistic friends who were recently graduated as engineers from the University of Toronto. Frederick "Casey" Baldwin and John A.D. McCurdy wanted to build the first airplane to fly in Canada. Mrs. Bell listened to her husband and the two earnest young men talking about how they would design and fly the aircraft. She was so impressed and so sure they would succeed that she gave them the money to finance the experiments.

Building the airframe was not too difficult, but finding an engine to power it proved to be more of a problem. Dr. Bell suggested they contact Glenn Curtiss who lived in Hammondsport, a town in New York state. Curtiss made motorcycle engines and was interested in flying. In fact, he was so interested that he became a member of the AEA and got everyone organized to build the aircraft in his workshop at Hammondsport.

The framework of the aircraft was constructed with wood and covered in red silk, so earning the name Red Wing. Red Wing was powered by a forty-horsepower engine. (The Wright Flyer was a success with an engine of only twelve horsepower.) Although Red Wing flew for the first time on March 16, 1908, it was not in Canada. It lifted off the ice of the frozen Lake Keuka, New York, piloted by Casey Baldwin, and covered three times the distance of the Wright brothers' first successful powered flight at Kitty Hawk. Unfortunately, Red Wing was destroyed in a crash on its second flight.

John McCurdy waits on the ice at Bras d'Or Lake to fly the Silver Dart.

A second aircraft, White Wing, was built with wood and white silk and flew successfully in Hammondsport. A third aircraft, named June Bug, also flew well. June Bug was altered slightly and renamed Loon. By this time the AEA members decided it was time to fulfil their dream to fly an aircraft in Canada. The Silver Dart, the fifth aircraft built in Hammondsport, was transported to Baddeck. John McCurdy flew the Silver Dart off the ice of Bras d'Or Lake in Nova Scotia on February 23, 1909. McCurdy was the first Canadian pilot and the eighteenth pilot to receive an aviator's license in North America.

Western Canadians were also anxious to build and successfully fly the first Canadian machine. Krugerville, Alberta, no longer exists and is barely even remembered today, but in 1907, the sons of John K. Underwood built a flying machine. John Underwood was an inventive farmer who lived in Krugerville. He developed the multi-disc plow that still makes the work of plowing much easier than it used to be.

Underwood's sons, George, John Junior and Elmer, inherited not only the farm but also their father's inventiveness. The boys had been interested in the possibilities of flight for years, and as youngsters had built kites to fly out on the prairie pastures. As they grew older their kite flying became more serious and they designed and built them as practical flight experiments. The

brothers dreamed of one day building a kite with its own motor that would carry one of them up into the western skies.

The Underwood boys read everything they could about flying, but not much reached Krugerville in 1907. One article that did reach them was written by a Nova Scotia mathematician who theorized that it was impossible to fly. He obviously had never heard of the Wright brothers. The Underwoods ignored his pessimism and set about designing an aircraft according to their own ideas.

The brothers began experiments with a kite

The Underwood brothers experiment with a kite.

The Underwood flying saucer is left neglected on the farm when the brothers can't afford an engine.

in May 1907. The kite was a 3-metre (9-foot) tail less rectangle. All of the Underwoods' designs are called flying wings, meaning they had no fuselage. Flights were made with a number of designs, some of them up to a distance of 50 metres (165 feet). Their final design, a "flying saucer," weighed about 200 kilograms (440 pounds) and was 12 metres (40 feet) wide and 8 metres (26 feet) long. The saucer-like wing carried a platform under-neath it, which acted both as the engine mounting and the pilot's seat. The landing wheels were attached to the platform's four corners.

By mid June the major work on the flying saucer was complete and the Underwoods were asked to display their machine at the Stettler Agriculture Exhibition. They still had not attached the undercarriage to the airframe, so to get their precious invention to the exhibition, they had to drag it 16 kilometres (10 miles) on a sled pulled by a team of horses from the farm. It became the centre of attention and the main attraction at the fair. Newspaper reporters across the area described the machine in strangely different ways. Some called it an airship, others referred to it as a five hundred horsepower airplane.

Like the Wrights before them, the Underwoods tested their machine as a kite. It was attached to a 21-metre (70-foot) rope. After flying successfully with 160 kilograms (350 pounds) of sacked wheat, the youngest of the three, John Junior, pleaded with his brothers to let him ride the kite. They gave him the privilege and for fifteen minutes, he became the first Canadian to ride a Canadian-built tethered kite. It was harvest time on the farm by then, so the kite was put away until the following spring.

Buoyed by their success, the Underwood brothers added a four-blade propeller powered by a seven-horsepower motor to the flying machine. In preparation for flight, they cleared and leveled part of a meadow on their farm, creating the first airstrip in Canada. It was small by today's standards, measuring only 91 metres by 97 metres (300 feet by 320 feet) of packed bare earth.

It turned out that the engine was not powerful enough to lift the saucer, so the brothers began a search for a more powerful motor. They tried to buy a motorcycle engine from Glenn Curtiss in Hammondsport, but they couldn't afford the cost of $1300 so they continued to fly the machine as a kite. One day that summer they became careless and the kite crashed to the ground. The Underwoods might have become the first Canadians to build and fly an aircraft but for the cost of an engine. They walked away from the damaged saucer never to touch it again.

William Wallace Gibson

A short time before the Underwoods began their experiments, another boy was also flying a kite he had built. William Wallace Gibson, a small boy with a big name, was riding his pony across the northern prairie of present-day Saskatchewan and trailing his kite instead of watching his father's cattle.

William was born 40 kilometres (25 miles) northeast of the city of Regina in what, at that time, was the Northwest Territories. The Gibson family farm was close to the Piapot Reserve ruled by the Cree chief Kisikaw Wawasam. The chief's name in English means "flash in the sky man." Young William's playmate was the chief's grandson, so the two boys often played near the chief's house. One day Kisikaw Wawasam looked at little William and told him that he too would be a great chief. Instead of ignoring the remark of an old man, William took it to heart and tried all his life to fulfill that prediction.

William continued to design and build better and better flyers. As he grew older he became more serious about flight and decided to one day design and build a kite big enough and strong enough for him to ride up into the endless blue of the prairie sky. Eventually, William inherited the farm and became a good farmer. He grew quite wealthy and, with credit in the bank, decided to expand into the general store business. When his first store was successful, he opened two more stores in the surrounding settlements. His main store and his home were in the village of Balgonie. By this time, in 1905, the territory

Young William and his kite on his father's farm on the prairie.

had become the Province of Saskatchewan.

All this time William had also continued to study the theory of flight. His models became more sophisticated, larger and stronger, and flew very well. He began powering his gliders with elastic-driven propellers that he hand-carved and balanced by making the two blades exactly the same weight. Later, he devised an ingenious motor made from the spring of a roller blind, which he attached to a twin-winged model that he tested in secret. William was not afraid that his ideas would be stolen, but did worry that people might think he was crazy. He particularly did not want his banker to find out what he was up to because he thought that the man might not extend his loans at the bank.

Early one Sunday morning William climbed to the roof of his general store and set up the launching device for his newest powered glider. The polished wooden ramp was like the ski jump decks of today's aircraft carriers that launch Harrier jets. He wound up the spring and the metre-(3 foot-) long model sped into the air. It flew very well, all the way across the street and over the railroad station buildings before it crashed into the top of a box car and was badly damaged. Both disappointed and elated by these results, he packed up the launch platform and went home.

Later in the day William was visited by the local physician, a Dr. Kaulbfleisch, who wanted to discuss the strange, large, blue bird he saw William trying to catch on the roof of his store. The doctor was on his way home at 5:30 a.m. after attending to an emergency earlier that morning, and was concerned when the strange bird flew over his buggy and disappeared behind the railway cars. Dr. Kaulbfleisch had a strange look on his face and a twinkle in his eye while William told the story. William thought he had better confess his obsession, so he told the doctor all about his experiments and begged him to keep it a secret. There was no need for him to worry because Dr. Kaulbfleisch never told anyone, but often dropped by to visit and talk about "the experiment."

A Full-Size Flying Machine

William carried on with his work and his hobby until the time came, as it eventually does to all model makers, to build a full-size flying machine.

He knew it would be expensive, but the farm and the stores were doing well, so he went ahead with the project. He particularly wanted to keep this project a secret so he worked on it in a large barn on his farm, 6.5 kilometres (4 miles) from the village.

Since a motor for his flying machine would be difficult to find and very expensive, he decided to build one himself. The aircraft was well on its way in 1905 when the railroad building boom hit the province. Hoping to make a small fortune, William took a contract with the Grand Trunk Railroad to build 32 kilometres (20 miles) of track, and later took on another 32 kilometres. But he knew nothing about building a railway and fell so far behind in the schedule that he couldn't finish the line and had to pay a large penalty of more than $40,000. Now all he had left was his farm, for he had to sell his general stores to pay the penalty. But William was a man of resolve. He had been rich once and he would be again, so he rented the farm and took his wife and family as far west as he could go, to Victoria on Vancouver Island, British Columbia.

William and his family landed in Victoria with practically nothing and with no prospects, but he was lucky enough to meet Locky Grant. Locky was also down on his luck financially and was trying to sell a gold mine. William decided to take the risk and bought a 5-metre (16-foot) boat to

26

get to the mine on the west coast of Vancouver Island at a place called Elk River. He figured the trip might take two days in his small boat, but he knew very little about the Pacific Ocean. The trip was terrible and took eight days, with rough seas and the rocky coastline making the journey almost unbearable. William was ready to give up several times, but Locky Grant wanted his money for the mine and kept him moving.

After he and Locky landed at Elk River, grateful to be alive, William took a short rest before going to work as a gold miner with his usual enthusiasm. Locky Grant worked with him all summer and then they took the dreadful boat ride back down the coast to Victoria. They took the results of their summer's work to the gold dealer and found they had more than $1000 worth of gold. William was ecstatic, but he also knew he did not want to be a miner. He promptly sold the mine for $10,000 and became a rich man again.

William used some of his money to begin building another aircraft. Even though he had exceptional skills as a businessman and possessed great creative ability, he had received little education in his youth and was never trained in the science of aeronautics. The theories he developed were formulated from his experiments with the kites and models he made. There were no kits, no examples to copy and no people to talk to about his ideas. William knew the Wright brothers had flown a machine in the eastern United States, but he had never even seen a picture of the Wright Flyer.

Pictures and models of William's designs show that his approach to flight was quite different. They did not look at all like those of the Aerial Experiment Association in Baddeck, nor like those of the Wrights. Although William knew nothing about drafting and certainly had no engineering skills, perhaps his experience fixing broken-down farm implements in the blacksmith's shop on his farm had some effect on his ideas. Building an airplane without any scientific education would certainly be unthinkable today. But William thought carefully about his problems and solved them simply.

Victoria has a beautiful park on the edge of the ocean which is a wonderful place to fly kites and models. William soon discovered the hill overlooking the Juan de Fuca Strait in Beacon Hill Park. He was not the only visitor to that particular part of the park, and many people saw the grown man flying kites alone on windy days. His friends used to smile and make remarks about the "bird man," and strangers would imitate a bird flapping its wings when they saw him on the street or flying his kites in the park. He ignored people's remarks, though, preferring to go along with his experiments, totally consumed by the idea of flight.

William Wallace Gibson and a kite model of his Twin Plane at Beacon Hill Park, Victoria.

A lot of power would be needed to lift his heavy machine into the air, so William designed a motor that was revolutionary for the time. It was a six-cylinder, in-line engine that worked on the same principle as today's lawnmower engines. Called a two-cycle system, the engine is fueled by a mixture of oil and gas. The oil in the gasoline lubricates the moving parts of the engine while it is used up as fuel. Most automobile motors use a four-stroke cycle, in which the engine burns gasoline for fuel and has a separate oil reservoir to lubricate its moving parts. William's big engine was air cooled, meaning that it did not have a radiator through which water was cooled and recycled back through the engine. His motor was cooled by the air flowing over it, the same way modern aircraft piston engines are cooled today. He arrived at this overall design after building a four-cylinder engine that he said "jumped about like a chicken with its head chopped off when it was run up to operating speed."

William took his engine design to a machine shop in Victoria and discussed it with Dan Hutchinson, one of the two machinist brothers who ran the shop. Dan insisted the design was crazy and impractical. He said it was impossible for a six-cylinder motor to operate on a mixture of oil and gasoline and, being air cooled, it would surely overheat. William listened without comment until Dan exhausted all the reasons why the motor would not work, but he stuck solidly to his ideas. He insisted that it would not only work, but would also be better than the conventional engine. Dan was still doubtful, but he took William's plans anyway and built the engine. He did an excellent job and the new motor worked perfectly.

William's other great innovation was his arrangement of the propellers. He fixed a propeller on either end of the engine, each one turning in a different direction. This solved a problem called engine torque, in which the motor produces a force that wants to twist the whole engine over in the direction in which it is turning. A propeller turning in the opposite direction at the back of the engine slows down the force of the torque movement by producing its own rolling movement in the other direction. One force cancels the other. The front propeller was 2 metres (6.5 feet) long. The rear propeller was shorter, only 1.5 metres (5 feet), but it rotated twice as fast as the one in front. William achieved this variation in speed by inventing a simple gear system. Many of today's ultra light engines and propellers are geared the same way.

The motor was finished in March 1910 and William took it back to his own workshop to assemble and test before attaching it to the airframe. His ground tests were satisfactory, and he found that he could rely on the engine to produce at least fifty horsepower. It also ran very smoothly, contrary to Dan Hutchinson's prediction. When the engine was fully assembled and ready to be fitted onto the airframe, it weighed only 95 kilograms (210 pounds).

While Dan was building the engine, William made the hundreds of metal fittings he needed to assemble his aircraft. He made them all by hand in a smithy he set up at his home. The time he spent in the blacksmith's shop as a youngster was now paying dividends.

The aircraft itself was as unique as the engine. It was designed with two wings, one behind the other, each measuring 7 metres (23 feet) from tip to tip. The wings were covered in beautiful bright blue silk. Each wing span was a wide "W" shape, which we now call a gull wing. This shape was used for many years after William's aircraft was built. The main spar, a support for the wings, was also unusual because it was placed across the top of the wings instead of running through them.

The aircraft's movement was controlled by two devices, unlike modern aircraft which have three movement controls. The up-down motion (pitch) is controlled by what we call an elevator, since it moves the airplane up and down. Sideways motion (yaw) is controlled today by the pilot's feet moving the rudder from side to side, like the rudder of a boat. The modern control that William didn't have is the one that makes the aircraft's wings move (roll). When the right wing goes down, the left wing goes up. William could move his Twin Plane up and down with the large wooden elevator in front of him. He could turn the aircraft sideways using two rudders controlled by a harness attached to his shoulders, merely needing to twist his shoulders in the direction he wanted to turn.

Lift Off

All the controls worked well on the ground and in tests, but would they really work in the air? The only way for William to find out was by flying the Twin Plane. On September 8, 1910, William decided his invention was ready to fly. He took the aircraft apart in his workshop and transported it to a large meadow on the farm of his friend Mr. Dean, near Mount Tolmie in Victoria. Today that meadow is the playing field of Lansdowne Junior High School. It takes its name from the commercial airfield it became ten years after William used it. Many people thought that Lansdowne Field should really have been named Gibson Field.

When William was satisfied that his Twin Plane was ready to fly, he started the engine and the propellers began to turn. With the engine running and several men hanging onto the aircraft,

William and Farmer Dean discuss the conditions of the field
near Mount Tolmie in Victoria before his first take-off.

he climbed into the pilot's seat he had made by strapping a horse saddle to the cross brace of his airplane.

William lifted off from Dean's field briefly and then landed quickly. The weakest part of his aircraft was its undercarriage, which consisted of four bicycle wheels fastened to metal tubes attached to the main airframe. The wheels had no shock absorption except for the air that was in the small tires and the whole undercarriage collapsed when the aircraft hit the ground.

He did not consider the first lift-off to be a flight and his Twin Plane was grounded for another two weeks while he repaired the undercarriage. On September 24, he moved the blue-winged airplane back out to Dean's farm. At five o'clock in the morning, William was ready to fly again.

His helpers held onto the aircraft while he started the engine and then climbed into the saddle. On his signal, they let go and away he went. The Twin Plane was in the air and flying beautifully, but drifting a little to the right. All William had to do was lean left into the harness that controlled the rudders to bring it back on course. Somehow he forgot and leaned the wrong way, pulling the plane further to the right and straight towards a stand of Garry oak trees at the end of the field. After pushing down on the elevator, he shut off the motor and made a beautiful level landing. The plane didn't have brakes, but the small wheels and long grass should have stopped it short of the trees. For some reason the heavy aircraft kept on rolling and rolling and William was thrown clear just before it smashed into the stand of Garry oaks. He only suffered minor cuts and bruises, but his Twin Plane was badly damaged.

William had intended to fly his airplane all the way across the Strait of Georgia to Vancouver. As it was, he managed to fly his machine up to an altitude of 15 metres (50 feet). His forward movement through the air was not recorded, but it was estimated afterwards that he flew further than 60 metres (200 feet). William was satisfied that his invention worked and that his design was good enough to try again. Since it was a little late in the season, he gave up for the year, now able to claim he had flown the first entirely Canadian aircraft.

One Last Try

The following year, with the success of the Victoria flight behind him, William set out to build another aircraft. He read the theories of a British inventor who thought that more wings were better for lift and believed that Hiram Maxim knew what he was talking about. The next Gibson design would be the Multi Plane. His little workshop once more became a hive of activity and slowly a new aircraft took shape.

William was anxious to avoid any more oak trees, so he accepted the invitation of the Lieutenant Governor, Thomas Paterson, to complete the Multi Plane on his farm in Ladner, on the Lower Mainland near Vancouver. It was a good place to fly from since the country was very flat and treeless. The construction and ground testing took almost six weeks, but flight tests were not possible until the ground dried so that the narrow wheels would not sink into it.

In Vancouver that year, a large and important exhibition was held to show off Canadian-made goods to the rest of the world. William Wallace Gibson was known well enough by the organizers to be invited to show off his new aircraft. While waiting for the dryer ground and the flight testing, he agreed to enter his invention in the exhibition that was named "Made in Canada."

Because the weather did not improve much, William decided to travel to a drier part of the province. He chose a racetrack in Kamloops as the test location and shipped the Multi Plane there by railway freight. The aircraft was assembled but never flown, partly because of more bad weather and partly because William was pestered by a crooked promoter who wanted to make money for himself by advertising the flight. For William, flying was not about money so he moved on again, this time to Calgary, Alberta.

Alex Japp had been hired to fly the Multi Plane because William's wife was afraid he might crash again. Alex made several short hops in Calgary before taking the airplane up for the last time. The Multi Plane took off and flew perfectly, but at 15 metres (50 feet) Alex saw that his landing area was pitted with badger holes. The aircraft came down before he could do anything about it and was completely destroyed in the landing.

William had spent well over $20,000 on his experiments and finally ran out of money. Had he been able to continue, he might have become one of the premier aircraft designers in Canada. Instead, he gave up aviation completely and moved to southern California in 1912.

In 1948, William returned to Canada for a vacation and to visit old friends in Saskatchewan. At a very special ceremony on the Piapot Reserve he was made an honorary chief, fulfilling the old chief's prediction. The name that William was given was Kisikaw Wawasam, "Flash in the Sky Man."

Airmail

First Flights in the East

The First Airmail in Canada

Captain Brian Peck of the Royal Flying Corps (RFC) was training flyers at Leaside Aerodrome in northeast Toronto. He had not seen his family for a long time but it would be a while before he would get leave. So Captain Peck went to his commanding officer, General C.G. Hoare, and suggested that the RFC should do some flying displays over Montreal like those performed over Toronto. The RFC was in need of recruits and this might increase its numbers. General Hoare thought this was a good idea and gave the young captain permission to do so.

On Friday, June 20, 1918, Captain Peck and his passenger, Corporal C. W. Mathers, checked over the aircraft they would fly to Montreal. The plane was a Curtiss JN 4 that was widely used as a training plane because it had a strong airframe and a reliable engine. The Curtiss JN 4 was an aircraft designed by the Glenn Curtiss Company formed after the successful flights of his aircraft built with the Aerial Experiment Association. Known as the Jenny, this American-designed plane was built in Canada under a special licence from the Curtiss Aircraft Company of the United States. The Canadian manufacturer of the JN 4 was Canadian Airplanes Limited of Toronto.

Early that morning Captain Peck had chosen Jenny number 230 from the regular lineup of trainers. The ground crew prepared the plane and fueled it for the flight to Montreal. The weather was poor for June, with a strong cross wind sending the low, dark clouds scudding across the sky. Captain Peck was forced to fly almost sideways in order to maintain a true directional heading, but the flight went well and he stopped at Deseronto for fuel before going on to Montreal.

The final landing site was the Polo Grounds at Bois Franc, on the outskirts of the city. After making a circuit to check the surface, he put the trainer down without mishap. Once on the ground the two airmen made sure that everything was tied down securely for the night and left the Jenny in the capable hands of the guards from the Military District Number Four, Montreal.

Captain Peck and Corporal Mathers had planned to give an exhibition the next day, but the bad weather persisted, so flying was postponed. The demonstration flight was never made and the flyers' return to Toronto on Sunday was also canceled. Captain Peck was able to spend two days with his family as continuous rain prevented any flying displays.

In Montreal at that time there were two businessmen who were thinking of promoting flying through the mail delivery business. George Lighthall and Edmund Greenwood were members of the Aerial League of the British Empire,

Captain Brian Peck talks with George Lighthall and Edmund
Greenwood at the polo grounds in Montreal. Corporal
Mathers stands on his left without a jacket.

Montreal Branch. They were familiar with flying activities and, in particular, with the aircraft tied down in the rain at the Polo Grounds. They decided to ask Captain Peck if he would deliver some mail to Toronto. Captain Peck was thrilled. Since he had not been able to make his demonstration flights, he thought that General Hoare might be happy with a mail delivery instead.

Lighthall and Greenwood talked to the Deputy Postmaster, who agreed to authorize the trip. Instead of issuing the usual post office stamp, he issued a special "Air Mail" rubber stamp to cancel the postage stamps. Greenwood randomly selected 120 letters from the Toronto mail and stamped them all twice with the special cancellation.

At this time many Canadian provinces were observing the prohibition of alcohol, but not Quebec. Captain Peck thought that a case of Scotch whiskey, which could be purchased legally in Quebec, would be just the thing for the officers' mess in Toronto, as Ontario was one of the "dry" provinces. So Monday morning, Corporal Mathers sat on a case of whiskey and clutched the sack of 120 letters on his lap, awaiting takeoff.

All the cargo and the full load of fuel added up to a great deal of weight for the little JN 4 to lift into the air from a relatively short runway inside the Polo Grounds. Peck started the engine and pushed the power lever all the way forward, but the extra weight held them down for a long time. When they finally lifted off, the pilot had to make a sharp turn to miss the telegraph wires and poles at the south end of the Polo Grounds. Captain Peck was able to fly 3 or 4 metres (about 12 feet) above the railway lines until a bridge appeared in his flight path and again he banked the aircraft as sharply as he could to avoid it. He turned again and flew over the river toward a place called Lake of Two Mountains. The Jenny floundered on for almost 10 kilometres (6 miles) before Peck finally gained enough altitude to turn overland toward his destination. He was only 15 metres (50 feet) high by this time, but was headed in the right direction and slowly gaining altitude.

The bad weather that kept Captain Peck from making the demonstration flights was still in the area and strong head winds prevented him from getting as far as the refueling stop in Deseronto. But he did make it to Kingston in Ontario and landed safely in a farm field before running out of gas. The flyers were only able to purchase automobile gasoline, so they half-filled the tank and took off.

With the Liberty engine hitting and missing because of the low-grade automobile gasoline, Peck and Mathers finally reached the base at Deseronto. Here they drained the tank, then filled it with proper aviation fuel. From there they made good time in good weather and arrived at Leaside by 4:55 p.m. Having taken off at 10:30 a.m., they were not breaking any speed records.

Captain Peck delivered the first sack of airmail in Canada to the postmaster at the General Post Office in Toronto. He was given the sack as a souvenir of the event. The officers' mess was grateful for its case of Old Mull whiskey and a celebration of the day's flight was rightly observed.

Katherine Stinson

Further west later that same summer, a young American woman was making exhibition flights around country fairs in the Calgary area. Her name was Katherine Stinson and she was the fourth licensed woman to fly in North America. Two years before, in 1916, at the age of only twenty-five, she flew tours over England, Japan and China in a Laird Looper airplane rented from the manufacturer. Her younger sister Marjorie — the youngest woman to receive a licence to fly at age twenty — was an instructor to the Royal Flying Corps in Ontario. Before Marjorie's twenty-second birthday, she had trained more than one hundred military pilots.

The Stinsons were a flying family. Encouraged by their mother, two sons and two daughters became pilots, enabling the family to found the Stinson Flying School in San Antonio, Texas. Marjorie and her brothers instructed at the school while Katherine raised money by stunt flying. She became the first woman to fly a loop in 1915. Later she added a snap roll at the top of the loop to put female pilots ahead of the men in the science of aerobatics.

During WWI, the Stinson sisters tried to enlist in the air corps, but were restricted to recruiting tours and fundraising flights.

Katherine had completed a contract to make exhibition flights around Calgary at the end of June and planned to do the same kind of flights over Edmonton. She thought it would help pay for the flight north if she carried letters with her, so she made arrangements with Postmaster King in Calgary. Katherine had already carried mail from various points in Montana to Helena, becoming the first woman to fly mail in the United States.

Katherine put the mailbag containing 259 letters in the cockpit of her single-seat Curtiss biplane and took off for the City of Edmonton, 292 kilometres (181 miles) from Calgary. But engine problems and poor visibility caused by low clouds forced her to land midway and wait for the weather to improve. The trip took seven and a half hours, although Katherine was in the air

Katherine Stinson accepts mail in Calgary for Edmonton.

for little more than two hours and five minutes. Still, the long wait did not deter the citizens of Edmonton from giving Katherine Stinson a noisy western welcome. A whole civic reception was waiting for her when she landed, and the crowd cheered deafeningly when she handed over the mail to Postmaster Armstrong.

The First International Airmail

There were a lot of flights in Eastern Canada during the early days of aviation. Slowly the activity was moving west, but the great obstacle of the Rocky Mountains was more than physical, it was also a psychological barrier. Some flyers were afraid of the unknown air conditions in the mountains.

Things were happening on the West Coast, and the Aerial League in Vancouver and Victoria would be part of the continuing advances. After all, the first Canadian built and flown aircraft lifted off from Victoria in 1910. Nine years later, former military pilots Captain Ernest Hall and Captain Alfred Eckley were about to keep the tradition going.

These two members of the Vancouver branch of the Aerial League prepared a Curtiss JN 4 aircraft — a Jenny — for what was then a dangerous flight across the Strait of Georgia to Victoria. The aircraft they chose was a conventional wheel-equipped trainer incapable of landing on water, which is what made the flight so dangerous. It was going to be the first flight to Vancouver Island.

Every detail of the Jenny's airframe and engine was checked by the mechanics and then again by the flyers. When everything was ready on May 13, 1919, Captain Hall climbed into the front seat and Captain Eckley squeezed into the rear cockpit. They fired up the Jenny's engine. Captain Hall pushed the power lever all the way forward and gave the rudder bar a little right pressure to keep the aircraft in a straight line for takeoff. Slowly at first, then gathering speed, the little cream-colored trainer lifted off from the solid earth of Vancouver and headed out over the water. From an altitude of 800 metres (2600 feet), the young men were able to see the Gulf Islands ahead of them. In the early morning mist they pointed the nose of their aircraft straight at the top of Mount Tuam on Salt Spring Island.

The flight was uneventful and the flyers were grateful for the work put in by their ground crew. They flew southeast around the mountain and followed the coast of the Saanich Peninsula south, all the way to Victoria. They landed on the airfield to the northeast of the city, just where the University of Victoria stands today. There was no large crowd to welcome Hall and Eckley, but

Captains Ernest Hall and Alfred Eckley at the airfield in Victoria.

coat. The flight home was also uneventful and the flyers were met with just as quiet a reception when they landed. But this record-breaking flight inspired the Victoria branch of the league to set some records of its own.

One week later on May 18, Lieutenant Robert Rideout and Lieutenant H. Brown, both former military pilots, set off from Victoria for Seattle in a wheel-equipped Curtiss. They carried a letter, an invitation from the Mayor of Victoria to the Mayor of Seattle to attend the May 24 celebrations in the British Columbia capital city. Their aircraft had the name "Pathfinder" painted down its side. Rideout and Brown left at 1:00 p.m. in bright sunshine, but by the time they were out over the waters of Juan de Fuca Strait they ran into very low cloud cover and the turbulent air that sometimes accompanies it. The flyers agreed to put down at Coupeville, on Whidbey Island, and wait out the weather. Late in the afternoon the weather cleared enough for them to take off and head for Seattle, where they arrived at 6:00 p.m. The dignitaries who had waited for Rideout and Brown earlier in the day came back to the field to shake their hands and receive the letter of invitation. The flyers were given some mail to carry back to Victoria on the return leg of the journey, but because it was not officially sanctioned by the post office, the flight was never recorded as an airmail flight across Puget Sound.

a few members of the Aerial League were on hand along with the usual reporters and photographers.

There is a wonderful photograph of the airmen standing beside the Jenny just before they left for the return trip. Both men look happy and quite relaxed, with Captain Hall dressed in flying overalls and Captain Eckley in his military over-

Boeing and Hubbard

On March 3, 1919, Eddie Hubbard flew Bill Boeing from Vancouver to Seattle in a Boeing C3 seaplane. Bill Boeing was the man who started the huge Boeing Aircraft Corporation that builds the B747 airliners today. This internationally important flight was an American success because the aircraft and the pilot who delivered the mail were from the United States.

The flight had begun earlier from Lake Union, as a ferry flight which means they did not carry any mail as the post office wanted the official mail flight to be made from Vancouver to Seattle, Washington. Then they stopped to refuel at Anacortes. Large waves and gusty winds outside the harbor damaged the tail controls of the aircraft and a launch had to tow them ashore. The plane was repaired and the flight resumed on February 27. Once again, poor weather delayed the flight. The following day, Hubbard and Boeing finally crossed the Juan de Fuca Strait and landed at Coal Harbour in Vancouver.

Later Eddie Hubbard made several spectacular flights over the city, performing aerobatic maneuvers. On one of the flights he carried a passenger, Mrs. Jimmie Patterson, the wife of a wealthy businessman, who enjoyed the aerobatics but said afterwards only that, "it was awfully cold."

Vancouver Postmaster Bob McPherson provided a brand new mail sack for the mail flight which contained sixty letters. He personally handed up the mail to Bill Boeing from a small boat in the harbor. The flight was supposed to pass over Victoria, but poor weather forced Hubbard and Boeing to refuel in Edmonds, Washington, instead. They landed on Lake Union two hours and ten minutes after taking off from Vancouver. The surviving letters they carried in the new canvas mailbag are very valuable to collectors today, and may well be worth over $200 each.

Eddie Hubbard later set up a company to fly mail between Victoria and Seattle. He flew between the harbors of Victoria and Seattle in a Boeing C3 two-seat aircraft on floats. The inaugural flight took place on October 15, 1920, when Eddie carried five sacks of mail to Victoria. Some of the mail was transferred to a Japanese ship, the *Africa Maru*, which was just about to leave Victoria harbor for the Orient. Hubbard's flying time over the 135 kilometres (84 miles) from Seattle was only fifteen minutes. His return trip, in the dark and against a strong headwind, took an hour longer.

Eddie Hubbard logged an amazing number of flights as an airmail pilot before going on to do other things. In total, he recorded 560,000 kilometres (350,000 miles) of flight on the Victoria–Seattle airmail run.

Postmaster Bob McPherson hands up the sack of mail to Bill
Boeing at Coal Harbour, Vancouver.

First Across the Mountains

Captain Ernest Hoy

Early in 1919, the British Columbia branch of the Aerial League of the British Empire based in Vancouver made plans to fly an aircraft across the great natural barrier dividing British Columbia from the rest of Canada — the Rocky Mountains. At this time in aviation history the airplane had only been flying for ten years. Although the more recent designs were proving to be capable machines, their altitude limits were very low, making any flight over the Rocky Mountains virtually impossible. The Curtiss JN 4 aircraft, or Jenny, was only capable of operating up to an altitude of 2000 metres (6500 feet). Some of the peaks in the Rocky Mountains are more than 3600 metres (12,000 feet) high, making for an interesting and dangerous flight so the route would be flown at as low an altitude as possible and take a path through the mountain passes because of the Jenny's flight capabilities.

The Aerial League organized the attempt with the support of some of the area's newspapers, which reported the event and donated money to make it possible. The *Vancouver Daily World*, *Calgary Herald*, *Lethbridge Herald* and the town of Golden, BC, all contributed money to the adventure. The newspapers thought that the dramatic headlines would sell more papers whether the flight was a success or a failure. The town of Golden expected to reap financial benefits from being reported in all the publicity, so it too had much to gain.

Many airmen were available to make the flight, so how would the Aerial League choose? All the flyers were capable young men and well qualified as pilots and navigators. Every one of them wanted to make the flight and further the cause of aviation in Canada. League members decided to write the names of all qualified pilots on small cards and place them in a hat. The one drawn from the hat by the president of the league would make the flight.

Captain Ernest Hoy of the Canadian Air Force was the name that came out of the hat. Captain Hoy was a decorated hero, having been awarded the Military Cross with an army unit during the early part of World War I. He was later wounded in battle and sent back to Canada.

After his recuperation Hoy wanted to get back to the war. He took pilot training and returned to France with the Royal Flying Corps. In late August of 1918, only two months before the war came to an end, his Sopwith Camel aircraft was forced down during a dogfight. He crash-landed behind enemy lines and was taken prisoner. For his gallantry in the air Captain Hoy was awarded the Distinguished Flying Cross, a high honor still given to deserving military pilots in action.

After the war the Royal Flying Corps became the Royal Air Force in Britain and the Royal Canadian Air Force was established as a separate unit.

The ninety horsepower aircraft Captain Hoy chose for his flight had also distinguished itself during World War I, but as a two-seat training aircraft for military pilots, not as a fighter. Manufactured by the Curtiss Aircraft Company, the JN 4D was more a product of trial and error than of inspired design. Its OX-5 engine was temperamental and difficult to keep from overheating. Much of the engine cover had to be cut away simply to achieve an efficient cooling system. Its short exhaust tubes spat fumes and flames towards the pilot throughout the flight and occasionally set fire to the nitrate paint called "dope," covering the fabric of the fuselage.

The Jenny's thin wings were braced with wooden struts and cross-laced with wires kept taut by a series of turnbuckles. These devices are used to adjust the tightness of the wires. The undersides of the wings were protected from poor landings by wooden hoops fixed under the wing tips. Pilots thought of the Jenny as a good airplane, but mechanics sometimes described it as "a bunch of spare parts flying in formation and held there with wire."

The only modification for the mountain flight that was made to Captain Hoy's aircraft was the addition of a secondary fuel tank. The new tank fit into the space made in the front cockpit after the seat was removed. It gave the airplane an extra 54 litres (12 gallons) of fuel, increasing the total capacity to 181 litres (40 gallons). This extra fuel made the Jenny capable of flying for four hours at a cruising speed of 122 kilometres (75 miles) per hour. Captain Hoy would be able to fly almost 500 kilometres (310 miles) without refueling.

A False Start

By August 4, 1919, all the arrangements had been made, reconsidered and revised. The racetrack on Lulu Island near Vancouver was chosen as the starting point. The track, called Minoru Park, had been the site of many air displays in the previous two years. Captain Hoy, suitably dressed in leather flying gear for the early morning flight, sat in the rear cockpit waiting for the decision to go. The sky was overcast with low rain clouds, but all the organizers were satisfied that the weather would clear as the Jenny flew east. They decided on a "go."

At 4:30 in the morning a mechanic swung the great wooden propeller and the OX-5 engine burst into life. Ernie Hoy ran the power up to make his checks and when he was satisfied that all was well, he waved the wheel chocks away. His mechanic stooped under the wings, pulled the wooden chocks from in front of the wheels and

Captain Ernest Hoy takes off from the muddy field in Chilliwack.

gave his pilot the thumbs up signal. Captain Hoy opened the throttle and the JN 4D rolled over the wet grass of the infield and smoothly lifted into the air. When the aircraft disappeared into the clouds and light rain, the onlookers ran for the shelter of the clubhouse and a hot breakfast.

Captain Hoy banked the little aircraft onto a course that put him over the Fraser River, which he would follow all the way to Kamloops. Instead of getting better, the weather became steadily worse and he had to fly lower and lower in order to get out of the rain clouds. After an hour of bumpy flight and with the wet clouds so close to the ground, he decided that it was too dangerous to continue. Having flown only about 100 kilometres (60 miles) of his adventure, he throttled back the engine and landed in a farm field near the town of Chilliwack.

Captain Hoy contacted his friends in Vancouver by telegram and found overnight lodging in the farmer's house on whose field he had landed. He rose early the next morning and walked down to the field dressed in his heavy leather flying coat. Although the morning sky was not clear, there was little evidence of the rain storm he had flown through the previous day.

He walked around the Jenny, cleaning and drying it and checking that all the control surfaces were operating efficiently. Then he checked the fuel tanks to see if rain water had got into the fuel. Satisfied that all was well with the aircraft, he found some wooden blocks and taught the farmer and his son how to swing the propeller and take away the chocks. The farmers were quick to learn and pleased to help the distinguished pilot.

Captain Hoy pulled the big propeller through a few times to make sure that there was fuel and oil in all the right places. Then he climbed into the cockpit and gave his last instructions to the temporary crew. When Hoy said, "Contact," the farmer swung the propeller, once, twice, and on the third try the engine started. He then waited for Ernie to check his instruments. As the engine revolutions slowed, the captain called, "Chocks away!" and the farmer's son dove under the wings to pull the makeshift wheel chocks away. Smiling and swinging the wooden blocks in one hand, he gave the captain a thumbs up signal. He was sure he had done everything right, but the airplane would not move, even when Captain Hoy gave the OX-5 full power. The Jenny was stuck in the soft surface of the wet field. Captain Hoy, realizing what had happened, shut down the engine and climbed down to see what could be done.

"Not too bad," he said, "seen lots worse in France. All we need to do is push the old girl forward enough to get her clear of the rut she's made for herself. Come on boys, push."

They soon had the aircraft clear of the ruts and went through the starting drill again. The OX-5 started on the first try and the young man pulled the chocks away. Again a big grin appeared on his face as he held up his thumb. When the aircraft moved forward he began waving an enthusiastic good-bye. He and his father stood in the wet grass of the meadow and watched the airplane rise into the gray sky over the Fraser Valley. They stood there until the Jenny was out of sight, then went home to the morning's farm chores.

Meanwhile, Ernie Hoy was swinging round from a southerly heading to a westerly one that would put him on course for the racetrack on Lulu Island. He had decided that the aircraft needed to be thoroughly checked before he attempted to fly all the way up the river. He landed smoothly, as he usually did, shut down the engine and gave instructions to his ground crew to check the Jenny over. After the ground checks were made the crew put the aircraft into the hangar to wait for better weather.

The Great Adventure Begins

The seventh of August dawned clear and bright, and the aircraft was taken out of the hangar and rolled to the end of the infield at 4:00 in the morning. Captain Hoy looked into the early morning sky and saw it was CAVU, "Ceiling And Visibility Unlimited." This is what flyers call a perfectly clear sky. Ernie talked to his crew and to the officials of the Aerial League. This time there were no doubts about the decision to go. He climbed up into the cockpit and gave the thumbs up sign to his mechanic to start the engine. The big propeller was turned a few times and then swung quickly. A cloud of smoke puffed from the exhausts and the engine roared to life.

Sitting in the rear seat made it quite difficult for Captain Hoy to see directly in front of the aircraft, so he had to lean sideways to see his mechanic. He waved the chocks away with the usual signal and was ready to resume his great adventure. The captain pushed the throttle lever forward and the little Jenny began to move ahead. Faster and faster over the grass it went until he was able to bring the tail up. Once the tail skid was off the grass, the aircraft moved more quickly to the takeoff speed of about 70 kilometres (45 miles) per hour. Then the main wheels left the grass and he was flying at last. This is the time when a pilot feels free of the earth and in his own element.

Ernie Hoy felt this exhilaration and grinned his usual grin. He checked all the settings for climb and sat back waiting for the Jenny to get to her best cruising altitude. The field was far below him now as he turned to his heading using the big brass compass in front of him. He would soon be flying back over the Fraser River and Chilliwack and wondered if the farmer and his son would look up and recognize him as he passed overhead.

The farmer's son now looked up at the sound of every aircraft engine. It was five o'clock in the morning and the farmers were also beginning their long day as Captain Hoy flew over the farm. The young man saw him and waved his arms. Although it was difficult to see the field far below, Ernie imagined him to be there, wishing him luck.

The weather was good, the aircraft was behaving well and Ernie settled down to the routine of navigation. He checked off the landmarks he expected to see along the way and constantly checked his direction by the big compass. The flight went smoothly until he entered the narrow Fraser Canyon, where the warming air of the valley rose up, causing the small aircraft to bounce a little. This kind of turbulence is normal, although it can be uncomfortable if it gets too rough. Captain Hoy was an experienced pilot and able to endure all the rough air because he knew exactly what was causing it. On he went, trying to fly higher to find smoother air.

Eventually, as he gained a little more height, the air became smooth and he enjoyed the view of the dry country at the point on the map where the South Thompson River joins with the North Thompson to become the Fraser River. This was one of the points where Ernie had to change directions. He checked the compass to make sure he was headed in the right direction, although the network of rivers was quite clear and pointed him due east towards the little country market town of Vernon.

The land below Captain Hoy was becoming greener and the large open ranges of the cattle-ranching country gave way to the little fields of mixed farms. It was time for him to begin his descent into the Vernon field by Lake Okanagan, which he could see quite clearly in the early morning light. Captain Hoy circled the north end of the lake and saw the field where he would refuel. There were a few people down there and he wondered if they had remembered to bring the gasoline. As he flew lower he saw the gas cans lined up by a little Ford Model T truck and he thought how pretty the little vehicle looked in the early morning light.

Down the captain went, lining up the Jenny for landing. The difficulty of seeing ahead over the nose of the plane was more critical during landing than on takeoff, and once his tail was down, Ernie couldn't see ahead at all. He leaned sideways out of the cockpit, twisting first left and then right to get a clear view. Eventually, he brought the aircraft to a halt and switched off the engine. As the propeller came to a dead stop, all was quiet. After sitting behind the engine and propeller in an open cockpit for the past three hours, Ernie appreciated the silence for a few moments. He pulled off his leather helmet and goggles, rubbed his ears and eyes and thought about the rest of the flight over the mountains. He looked at his watch and then made an entry in the notebook called a pilot's log. It was 7:18 a.m.

The arrangements made by the Aerial League for refueling the aircraft were followed dutifully by the ground crew. Captain Hoy had become a celebrity even before he landed in Vernon and so had to endure what he thought was worse than the turbulence in the canyon. He was obliged to get down from his aircraft and meet all the local dignitaries. He rummaged through the package of forty-five letters he had been given in Vancouver to find the one addressed to the mayor. It was one of the first airmail letters to go that far east from the West Coast. Ernie spent a great deal of time talking to people at the airfield and he was anxious to be on his way.

At last he was able to climb into the cockpit. He smiled at the dark-suited, bowler-hatted politicians, and businessmen and their wives and children. He looked for the familiar faces of the ground crew. Seeing their captain's discomfort, they cleared the crowd from the front of the aircraft and started the engine. The noise and the wind from the propeller soon moved the crowd well away from the Jenny, and Captain Hoy, no longer smiling at the crowd but concentrating on his work, set the aircraft in motion. As the bumpy motion of takeoff ceased and the little aircraft lifted into its element, Ernie began to smile again. He smiled for himself and his plane, gliding smoothly into the warming sky of the Okanagan Valley.

The captain never glanced back at the ground because he was too busy checking all his instruments and the big compass. The Jenny was running well and Captain Hoy was once more on course for the adventure. A shadow of a frown crossed his face for a moment as he thought about all the stops for fuel he had to make and all the hands he had to shake before he got back to Vancouver. If he could only do it all in one go it would really be a triumph, he thought. But, being an officer and a gentleman, he also knew he had to do his duty.

From Vernon Captain Hoy flew on a compass bearing that would take him to the town of Grand Forks, southeast of Lake Okanagan. The country looked dry again with lots of ponderosa pine trees and he knew he was not too far from his next stop, on the border with the United States. Grand Forks is at the southern end of Christina Lake, on the Kettle River, which flows into the

Columbia River about 30 kilometres (20 miles) further south in the state of Washington. As he looked ahead he could see the water of the lake to his left. All he had to do was fly down the lake, keeping the settlement called Christina Lake on his port (left) wing and looking for the town of Grand Forks on his starboard (right) side. (Aviators use these nautical terms for left and right, too.) Ernie found it easy to remember because left is a four letter word, just like port, so right must be starboard. He learned this technique during his early flying lessons with the Royal Flying Corps.

All of his little worries about fuel and hand-shaking disappeared when it was time to set up for his landing. He was a professional pilot who did things the right way so he was able to put everything else out of his mind when he cut the throttle and made his final approach to the field. The field was quite busy with horses and buggies, automobiles, men, women, children and dogs. Ernie liked dogs, but not when they were running loose on airfields. He had seen a friend badly injured in a takeoff accident caused by a large dog.

"If they keep them under control," he said to himself and the Jenny, "everything will be all right."

Captain Hoy watched closely for animals when he landed but came to a stop without incident. After shutting off the motor he took off his goggles and helmet. Six hours flying time was beginning to make his eyes a little sore, but he had put in longer days before. He wrote down the time in his log book. It was 10:34 a.m.

Ernie swung over the cockpit and took a few steps to stretch his legs before the dignitaries arrived. He looked around for the refueling crew and saw them walking towards the Jenny with the big red cans of gasoline. At this stop they let him supervise the refueling before the hand-shaking began. The mayor introduced himself, and then the town council and one or two local business people shook his hand and wished him luck for the next leg of the flight.

Captain Hoy was away from Grand Forks in record time and was happy enough to give the people below a wave as he circled the field overhead. The compass told him that his heading for Cranbrook was due east along the border to Creston, at the bottom of the Kootenay River Valley. From Creston he had to turn to a new heading that would take him all the way to Cranbrook, a little town situated in the Columbia River Valley. His map indicated that the Columbia crosses into Canada from Lake Koocanusa in Montana, flowing north. It continues down the broad valley on the west side of the Rocky Mountains all the way up to Golden, where Ernie would refuel on the return flight. The river

The captain hands down the mail to an airforce mechanic at Cranbrook, British Columbia.

makes a big bend 232 kilometres (144 miles) north of Golden, swings west, then south and flows back through Washington and out to the Pacific Ocean in a big 500-kilometre (800-mile) horseshoe. The captain thought it might be fun to fly the Columbia some time from its source to the sea, but for now he was on his way to Cranbrook.

Cranbrook is nestled in the Purcell Mountains and sits at an elevation of more than 900 metres (3000 feet). As he approached these mountains, Captain Hoy looked out over his port wing and saw the Rockies rising high above him in the distance. Their peaks had a permanent covering of ice and snow and reached well over 3000 metres (10,000 feet) into the sky. Ernie shuddered a little as he thought about flying through them. He saw the water of Moyie Lake to the starboard side and checked his compass.

Captain Hoy could not yet see the town in the valley, but as he turned further to the north the steep roofs of the little houses became clearly visible. He looked for the field on the west side of town where the fuel would be waiting. He was thinking that nothing had gone wrong so far into the flight and he began to worry again. Would the fuel be there? Would there be dogs or, even worse, children running across his landing path? He checked everything twice this time. Fuel, oil pressure, engine revolutions, air speed and altitude were "all in the green," as pilots say if everything is all right. This expression comes from the fact that most aircraft instruments have green and red sections in their gradations. It is all right to operate when the gauge needles show the reading in the green section of the scale, but it is dangerous when they flicker in the red area.

"All set, throttle back, watch the air speed, nose up just a bit, level out," Captain Hoy said. "Great, chop the throttle and we're down, a perfect landing for all those people who came out to see me. They deserve the best."

The Jenny rolled to a stop quickly when the tail skid came down and dug into the grass of the meadow. Ernie flicked the ignition switch with a flourish, killing the motor.

"At least nothing ran across me on landing," he said, still speaking to himself aloud. He looked up into the friendly face of a mechanic who smiled and nodded his head.

"No, we've got it all under control here, sir," he said. "Did you have any trouble anywhere, Captain?"

The big man held out his hand to help Ernie from the cockpit. "Welcome to Cranbrook," he said. Ernie could only smile in thanks, not really hearing what was said. The propeller and the engine noise still rang in his ears even though he had packed cotton wadding into them before taking off from Grand Forks. He asked what time it was, then checked his own pocket watch against his mechanic's. He recorded the time 2:05 p.m. in his log book.

Captain Hoy scrambled out of the rear seat and over the side of his aircraft to shake more hands and answer more questions. The letter for the mayor of this town was tucked away with a package of *Vancouver Daily World* newspapers. He handed these over and looked back at his aircraft. Ernie was happy to see the big mechanic filtering the gasoline through a chamois leather into the large funnel resting in the fuel tank filler. It was essential that the gasoline be as free from impurities as possible. The pilot did not want an engine failure during the next stage of his flight, which would take him to Lethbridge, on the other side of the Rocky Mountains. The real adventure started here.

The hand-shaking and smiling was over and Captain Hoy was back where he really liked to be — the friendly rear cockpit of the Jenny. He reached for the rudder board with his feet and felt the familiar pressure of the wire and the rudder itself. He moved the stick forward and sideways, looking out at the aileron and elevator responses at the same time. These were the key components that guided the aircraft where he wanted it to go. Ernie felt the worn smoothness of the wood as he slid his hands from the stick.

It was time to go. Captain Hoy reached under the seat, found his helmet and gloves and put them on with care. He pulled the seat's safety straps tight around his body. The last thing he wanted was to be thrown from the aircraft in the mountain turbulence he expected to encounter. His gloved hands pulled the goggles down over his eyes and settled them comfortably on his face. He had double-checked every last detail.

"What could go wrong?" the apprehensive little voice inside him asked.

The professional pilot took control and answered aloud, "Nothing will go wrong. There are lots of things that could go wrong but nothing will." He said this confidently, really believing that all would be well.

"Switches off," he answered to the same words from the mechanic.

"Fuel on," he responded to the question from the big man at the front of the aircraft.

"Contact."

The engine burst into life. Captain Hoy's mechanic stepped away from the front of the propeller and watched from a safe position at the side of the Jenny as Ernie completed his instrument check. He saw his captain look up and wave away the wheel chocks. Down he went to retrieve the big wooden blocks and stepped back, bringing his right hand up to his cap in a smart military salute. Captain Hoy returned the salute, then stuck up his thumb confidently in the universal, "all is under control and ready to roll" signal.

Ernie pushed the throttle forward as smoothly as he could, putting the Jenny in motion and beginning his takeoff roll into the wind. He watched the ground in front of him as well as he was able until the tail came up, improving his view ahead. The needle on his airspeed indicator showed almost 70 kilometres (45 miles) per hour as the wheels left the grass and the Jenny was airborne

Looking back in a quick sideways glance, Ernie saw all the people on the ground and wondered how many of them would prefer to be with him, winging towards the mountains. His compass showed him the course he must take and he pushed on the rudder bar with his right foot. At the same time, he put the stick over to the right a little and the Jenny banked, dipping her right wing low to help in the turn. Captain Hoy leveled the wings and centred the rudder as he gently pulled back the stick to bring the aircraft to a straight and level flying attitude. (Attitude is simply leveling the aircraft so that the line through the nose and tail are at the best angle to the air flow over it. It is not necessarily perfectly level.) He trimmed back the throttle to a level that would give him the fastest airspeed for the least fuel consumption and settled down for a long flight.

Through the Mountains

Crouched behind the tiny glass windscreen of the JN 4D, Ernie felt the cold wind blowing off the snow-covered ledges. He looked around, glad that he was wearing the fleece-lined, leather flying suit and the leather helmet, goggles and silk scarf that kept his head and face well protected from the cold. The sky was clear blue, providing a contrast to the white snow that blanketed the higher peaks and ledges. To keep his wings level he had to keep his eyes trained on the most distant line of peaks for a reference point. In order not to fly into a ridge or a sharp shoulder, he had to keep constantly alert and also look closer to his aircraft. This exercise of moving his visual attention from near to far and back again was difficult because the aircraft kept bouncing up and down.

Air currents forced the Jenny up and down as much as 120 metres (400 feet) at a time. These mountain downdrafts were more dangerous than the air currents forcing them up. A downdraft could suck the aircraft into a rock face with enough force to smash it into small pieces. Captain Hoy had to be alert to all the movements of the air around him without being able to see them. Although he tried to force the Jenny higher to prevent being sucked into the rocks, the airplane was flying as high as it possibly could

Captain Hoy flies his Jenny, bearing his old WWI squadron insignia, through the narrow passes of the Rocky Mountains.

and none of his pilot skills could make it gain more altitude. He was forced to steer the aircraft through the valleys, rather than over the peaks.

The air currents became more of a problem when he had to fly through Crawford Pass, with only 30 metres (100 feet) separating his wheels from the rocks below. As the ground rose up to meet him he could clearly see the thin, stunted spruce and balsam trees below and thought how close they were to the delicate, fabric-covered wings. Looking north along his port wing, Ernie could see the permanent snowfields and was pleased that he had chosen this route through the southern part of the Rocky Mountains.

Before setting out on the journey, Captain Hoy had planned the route as carefully as he could. Using the maps of the time was a little risky because a thorough survey of the mountains had not been made. The railroad builders had more reliable maps of the two areas of the mountains when they planned their routes through them. Ernie was taking the lower route and when he looked at the maps, he wondered what the terrain was like in the large areas of blank space on them. The officials of the Aerial League had decided he should fly through the passes that were known.

Now here he was, flying east through Crawford Pass towards Calgary. On the way home to Vancouver he would take the surveyed route of the Canadian Pacific Railway and follow the railroad tracks all the way west. For the moment though, he had to give all of his attention to the rocky peaks around him.

Captain Hoy's courage, his good physical health and his superb flying abilities eventually brought him to a point where he was able to see through the main mountain valley onto the rolling woodland of the eastern foothills. As he came out of the mountains down a stream bed that started high up on a glacier, Ernie saw the flat lands of the prairies stretching away into the distance. Even if he had been unable to see that far ahead, he would have known he was flying out of the mountains because the turbulence suddenly subsided and the air became calm and smooth.

Ernie Hoy was happy with the gentler ride after almost three hours of buffeting and bumping. The sky was still blue, but it was almost 6:00 in the evening when he finally cleared the mountains. Now he could see the ranch land and hay fields that seemed to go on forever to the east. As he neared Lethbridge he was able to pick out the landing field easily. It looked as if the entire population of the town had turned out to watch him land. He sat in his tight cockpit and thought about his success.

Captain Ernest Hoy, DFC, MC, was now the first pilot to fly an aircraft across the Rocky Mountains. He spoke aloud to his aircraft. "We did it, you and I, Jenny. We crossed the great divide

Captain Hoy sees the field near Lethbridge, Alberta, after a turbulent flight through the Rockies.

together. Thank you old girl."

He leaned forward to give the top of the cockpit a gentle pat with his gloved hand.

"Although we did not actually fly over these rocks, we threaded our way through them," he said, with only the Jenny to hear him. "We did make it. I wonder if we will ever be able to fly over them? We were the first and there is Lethbridge ahead."

Ernie kicked the rudder bar and pushed the stick over to bring them round. The Jenny banked, immediately putting her nose into the wind for the landing. Captain Hoy cut the power by pulling back on the throttle quadrant and the roar of the OX-5 settled down to a gentle purring sound. The wind whistled through the struts and wire as Ernie spoke aloud again.

"Wings level, air speed right on the nose and the Jenny's flying attitude dead on. We are making a perfect approach for all these people. They want to see a professional pilot. They'll see one today."

The captain's great fear was that someone — perhaps a child — would run out in front of his aircraft at a time when he was unable to do anything about it. There were a lot of excited people waiting for him to land but the crowd kept still as he made his approach. The wheels touched the grass and when the tail skid came down, the aircraft came quickly to a halt. The wooden propeller flicked to a stop as his wheels stopped rolling.

The crowd rushed up on Captain Hoy's aircraft in an enthusiastic welcome, voices raised in congratulations. Some shouted, "Bravo Captain Hoy!" while others yelled, "Well done Ernie!" But they all came up in a wave that scared the young flyer. Ernie sat in his rear seat wondering what to do and feeling tired. It had been ten hours since he took off from the racetrack on Lulu Island and he still had more flying to do. All he wanted to do was leave right away so he could get to Calgary before it got dark. Sitting there amidst all the cheering hurrahs, Captain Hoy's thoughts, as usual, were on the refueling that needed to be done quickly. It was 6:22 p.m. when he made the entry in his log book.

There were letters and newspapers to hand over to the town's officials, hands to shake, people to smile at and yet more hands to shake. Most importantly, the Jenny needed fuel and a thorough check by the mechanics. The three hours of bumping and shaking in the mountains might have jarred some small part loose. Ernie had to find the mechanics, so he tried to smile at everyone and shake all the hands that were offered while looking for the ground crew who would help him get away.

Two red-coated Mounties came to his rescue. They pushed through the crowd, clearing a way for the mechanics, and then made a space for the small truck carrying the gasoline. The ground crew quickly filled the tanks and walked around the Jenny with the captain to see if anything had shaken loose. They climbed up into the cockpit and wiped away all the oil and soot from the windscreen and the cowling. They cleaned the glass of the instruments, being especially careful with the compass. The flight to Calgary would take about an hour, but Captain Hoy did not know the few landmarks on the prairies and would have to fly on a compass heading.

The crew knew that if he did not get away soon, Ernie would have to land in Calgary in the dark. The chief mechanic commented on how well the Jenny had stood up to the flight so far.

"Everything is all right, sir," the man reported as he firmly guided Ernie towards the rear cockpit. "Best be off right away, sir," he said. "The light is beginning to fade, captain. You had best be aboard. We'll clear the way for you to get into the wind."

"Almost an hour," Captain Hoy said to himself. "I had better be on my way."

The mechanics and the Mounties had recruited another six men and were gently moving the crowd back from the aircraft. When the townspeople saw the resolve on their faces, a way was cleared very quickly and the Jenny was moved into the wind for takeoff.

"Contact?" came the question. "Contact," was the reply and the big curved propeller on the front of the OX-5, swung expertly by the chief me-chanic, spun the engine to life. After Ernie pulled down his goggles, he waved the chocks away and the second mechanic ducked under the wing to retrieve the wooden blocks. The mechanic signaled the wheels clear and the Jenny rolled into the evening wind.

Full throttle lifted the tail into a level flying attitude, enabling Captain Hoy to see ahead of the aircraft. He glanced quickly to port, then to starboard before fixing his gaze straight ahead. The wheels separated from the turf and he was airborne again. It was 7:20 p.m.

On to Calgary

Without turbulence or large obstacles it was an easy sixty minutes of smooth flying to Calgary for Ernie and the Jenny. The aircraft was behaving well and even though Captain Hoy was very tired, he knew he would stay awake. His one anxiety was that the light was fading fast. Dusk on the prairies seemed to pass quickly and the sun over his port wings was already setting behind the mountains to the west. When the captain neared the airfield in Calgary the light was almost gone. A red glow of sunset lit the sky to the west, but to the north it was dark.

The finale to the eastern odyssey was to be at

Bowness Park, and in the settling gloom Ernie could make out the landing site. It was marked by gasoline flares set out by the Air Board people as well as the headlights of hundreds of automobiles. The drivers of the cars wanted to welcome the courageous flyer by marking his way to the park. Although he had made night landings before as an air force pilot, it had always been with the help of gas flares. The lights that shone for him that night were the best he had ever seen and he made a smooth-as-silk landing right down the centre of the strip.

Captain Hoy could not see beyond the lights of the cars when he landed but he knew a lot of people were present and tried to estimate the number of vehicles and passengers. What he could not see, or even guess at, was a crowd of more than five thousand men, women and children who had turned out on this warm August night to see a hero.

"What an adventure it has been," he thought. "And only halfway over."

When Ernie climbed out of the cockpit he was picked up and carried shoulder high through the crowd. It was only then that he realized how large the crowd was. The captain was embarrassed by all the attention he was receiving for doing something he really enjoyed. Looking back at the little Jenny, he was relieved to see a group of air force mechanics already taking her away to a safe place. He hated to think that she might be damaged by the unchecked enthusiasm of the large crowd of well-wishers. As he turned again he managed to see that it was 8:55 p.m. He would remember to write that in his log book later.

It was time for the civic welcome. Captain Hoy thanked everyone for being so hospitable and the drivers for their helpful headlights. What else could he say? Ernie wasn't very good at making speeches, but he did remember the letters to be given to the mayor. He said a few words about the first airmail flight across the Rocky Mountains before handing the letters over. Ernie displayed the Vancouver newspapers from the previous day and the first edition of the current one, which the crowd enjoyed. He smiled and waved, shook hands and smiled some more. The captain was very tired and wanted to climb into a warm, comfortable bed and sleep.

Captain Ernie Hoy had set off from Vancouver sixteen hours and forty-two minutes earlier in order to make the crossing. Most important to him, of course, were the twelve hours and thirty-four minutes he had actually been in the air. The four hours difference accounted for the time he took at all the refueling stops. Ernie was aware that he had achieved something extraordinary, and he was proud to have crossed the great stone barrier of the Rockies.

He was grateful too that nothing had gone seriously wrong on the long journey. Before Captain Hoy went to bed that momentous night, he made arrangements with the air force mechanics to go over his Jenny very carefully. He also planned to check their work himself, but it was not because he mistrusted them. They were well trained and always did their job well.

Captain Hoy stayed in Calgary until August 11, making sure that the Jenny was mechanically ready for the trip back to Vancouver and planning the route for his return. This time he was going to fly a northern route over Banff, Golden and Revelstoke, and then go south to the coast. He would fly through the Rocky Mountains again and be the first airman to fly over the Selkirk Mountains that gave the builders of the Canadian Pacific Railway so many problems. Ernie planned to follow their rails from Golden to Revelstoke, through the famous Rogers Pass, before heading south.

Captain Hoy took off on the first leg of his return trip to Vancouver on the eleventh of August, at 9:50 a.m.

The End of the Odyssey

"So much for an early start," he grumbled as he circled up to 2000 metres (6500 feet) and made the turn west on a heading from the big brass compass. Captain Hoy encountered good weather all the way through the Rockies and on to the eastern ridges of the Selkirks. He again had to thread his way through canyons and high valleys because the jagged mountain peaks were much higher than he could fly the JN 4D. As he looked up to the peaks above him and down to the valleys below, he realized that he was the first person to view these mountains from such a vantage point. Ernie was awed by the experience, but also felt grateful for the calm winds and bright sunshine, speculating that "there was little danger of encountering a cloud with a rock in it."

As he lined up for a landing at Golden he checked the altimetre and saw that the town is more than 1000 metres (3200 feet) above sea level. Landing is more difficult at this high an altitude because the air is a little thinner. At least he was not carrying a full fuel load, so the aircraft was quite light. Originally, the local agricultural show grounds were chosen as the landing site but they turned out to be too small and Ernie opted for a small hay field beside them. It wasn't as smooth a surface as the show grounds but he landed without difficulty at 12:30 p.m. Ernie took care of the small crowd as quickly as he could, even if it seemed to go on forever.

Two hours later Captain Ernest Hoy lined up the fuel-heavy Curtiss JN 4D into the wind and

Ernie Hoy landing at Golden on the return flight from Calgary, Alberta.

opened the throttles wide. Just as he was about to pull back on the stick to climb away from the hay field, all his worst fears came true. All through the journey Ernie had worried about animals or, worse, people getting in his way as he landed or took off. Now, two small boys ran onto the field in front of him and he was forced to bank the Jenny very steeply to avoid flying into them. A large cotton-wood tree was now directly in his path and he pulled the stick further over to the left to avoid hitting it. He dodged the tree but lost 2 or 3 metres (6 to 10 feet) of badly needed height. As Ernie continued to turn, his port wing struck the ground, breaking off the tip in a cloud of splinters and dust.

The brave pilot crawled from the

The dreadful end of an odyssey and a good aircraft.

downed aircraft uninjured, but after checking the faithful Jenny, he realized that she needed extensive repairs. There were no mechanics or airframe fitters in Golden to do the job for him. He would not be able to complete the odyssey by air. Telegrams were sent to and from Vancouver and he was advised to ship the aircraft there by rail and then return with a small pouch of letters by train as soon as possible.

Ernie Hoy was deservedly honored in Vancouver for his courageous first flight. It has gone into the records of Canadian aviation as a tremendous success. He was only sad that the Jenny was eventually lost because the aircraft was not rebuilt or displayed for her part in the great adventure.

De Havilland DH9 registered G-CBYF dwarfs the tall pilot,
Colonel Arthur Tylee, at the emergency landing in Revelstoke.

very large British biplanes were powered by a four-hundred-horsepower American Liberty engine. Aircraft G-CYAJ was flown out of Winnipeg by Captain C. W. Cudemore with Sergeant Young as his passenger. They landed in Moose Jaw without incident.

Pilot number two was Captain Home-Hay, who was accompanied by Lieutenant Colonel Arthur Tylee in the passenger seat of G-CYAN, although the colonel was also a very good pilot. They made it as far as Regina in terrible weather and had to make a forced landing because of engine failure. The spare airplane that was supposed to be used in an emergency had been wrecked in a landing accident, so the Cudemore-Young plane was flown back to Regina to continue the attempt. Arthur Tylee jumped in the back seat with the mail and Cudemore flew off without effort to Calgary.

The Calgary landing was made at Bowness, out on the open prairie to the west of the city. Here Lieutenant-Colonel Tylee became the third pilot and was joined by navigator Captain G.A. Thompson as they changed planes to the now-famous G-CBYF which had been shipped to Calgary from eastern Canada. It was October 13. Although not superstitious men, they checked the De Havilland over very carefully before taking off at 11:55 a.m. for a flight all the way to Vancouver.

Weather reports for the mountain leg of the journey were not good, with clouds and rain almost down to ground level. But these flyers had come so far and overcome so many difficulties that they were determined to carry on.

They made it through the Rocky Mountains and then through Kicking Horse Pass, where the Trans Canada Highway runs today. But the weather went from bad to worse. While flying through Rogers Pass in the Selkirk Mountains, they encountered a hurricane-force wind as they passed over the little railway town of Revelstoke. Even worse weather was to come as they headed for Vernon. Blinded by snowstorms, they turned around reluctantly and landed on a farmer's field near Revelstoke to wait out the weather.

Bad weather plagued Thompson and Tylee for two more days, but their forced stay was quite entertaining. Mayor Walter Bews of Revelstoke thought that the mail flight was a great undertaking, so he organized parties at his home for the airmen. Townspeople drove out to see the airplane and many photographs were taken.

At about noon on October 15, Tylee and Thompson lifted off in the DeHavilland and flew under the clouds to Merritt. The bad weather persisted, keeping the airmen in Merritt until the seventeenth, when they decided to chance the trip through the Coquihalla Valley where the highway runs today. After a really rough and exciting flight, the Fraser River finally came into view through patchy clouds. The last part of the flight down the Coquihalla Pass weaved through steep-sided cliffs, finally twisting out into the open of the Fraser Valley near Hope. As the flyers came out into the valley sunshine, they hoped for a safe ending to the dangerous journey and landed on a smooth field in Agassiz.

After a short delay to check over the De Havilland, it began to rain again. It looked like Tylee and Thompson would have to fly the last leg in driving rain. Never being ones to give up, they lifted off the field at about 10:00 a.m. and flew west towards Vancouver. They were tired and very wet when they saw the racetrack at Brighouse Park in Richmond, cutting the power to drop down and check the surface of the infield. Even though it too was rain soaked, it looked inviting to the weary pilots and they landed perfectly in front of a small but enthusiastic crowd. Vancouver city officials honored Tylee and Thompson for their great accomplishment.

To end the flight correctly, Arthur Tylee and George Thompson decided at the last minute to fly the De Havilland across the Strait of Georgia to Victoria, completing a true coast-to-coast flight. They had covered 5226 kilometres (3247 miles) in forty-five hours of flying, over a ten-day span.

Tom Fox

The Anson Clip Wing

In 1933 A.V. Rowe Aircraft Company, known as Avro, designed a twin-engined aircraft for the British airline Imperial Airways. The small airliner, known simply as the Avro 652, was powered by two 330-horsepower, Armstrong Siddeley "Cheetah" engines. By the time the aircraft was built and tested in 1936, there was a threat of war in Europe and the Avro 652 was pressed into military service as a reconnaissance aircraft and aircrew trainer. It became known as the Anson. In 1940 a decision was made by the British and Canadian governments to build 11,000 Ansons in Winnipeg, Manitoba. They were constructed entirely of wood and covered with a linen fabric before they were painted.

The Canadian planes used 320-horsepower Jacobs radial engines. They are called radials because the pistons are arranged in a circle around the centre drive shaft, a very different design from automobile engines. The Ansons were nicknamed "Annies" by the Canadians and were used by the Royal Canadian Air Force to train air crews for operational bombers. Ansons had a wingspan of 17 metres (55 feet) and were 14 metres (44 feet) long. It was capable of flying at 290 kilometres (180 miles) an hour up to an altitude of 3000 metres (10,000 feet). This is the story of one of those Ansons and a very special Canadian pilot.

In 1945, Tom Fox took his discharge as a trans-Atlantic ferry pilot from the Royal Air Force in Britain and returned to Canada. He bought a two-seat ex-military trainer, the De Havilland Tiger Moth, which he registered with a civil registry of CF-BEN. He also bought a larger, eight-passenger De Havilland Dragonfly and registered it as CF-BZA. Tom intended to start an airline in northern Alberta to fly people and goods out of Edmonton to more remote locations further north. These planes became the initial fleet of his airline, Associated Airways. It was a two-plane, two-person operation. Tom Fox was chief pilot, chief engineer, chief accountant and, as he put it himself, chief janitor. His wife, Clara, was ticket agent, ground stewardess, and odd-job person.

Eighteen months after Tom purchased the planes, the airline was fairly well established and he added an Anson Mark V to his fleet. The ex-military Anson, which was registered CF-EKD, was put on skis for the winter of 1947. On January 23, it left Edmonton with supplies for the Hudson Bay post at Chipewyan Lake. The newly hired company pilot, Spence Addeman, flew 400 kilometres (250 miles) due north. On route he encountered a low cloud layer so he climbed and flew above it, looking for a "hole" in the clouds.

After a while, deciding there might be not be one, he throttled the Anson back and let down through the clouds, not knowing that the aircraft had picked up a load of wing ice on the way down. This condition is caused by the moist atmosphere

Tom Fox and Maury Danes try to keep warm on the frozen surface of Chipewyan Lake. Behind them is the warming cover over the chipped wing tip.

depositing a layer of condensation on the wings that freezes as the temperature goes down. The starboard wing stalled because it was icier than the port wing. Ice disrupts the smooth flow of air over a wing and destroys its lift. As the Anson hit the ice of Chipewyan Lake, 2.9 metres (9 feet) of the wing broke off, sending splinters of spruce across the ice. Addeman managed to taxi the Anson across the frozen lake to the Hudson Bay post and unload his cargo. But what next? Luckily, another pilot on his way south saw the damaged aircraft and landed to see what had happened. He picked up Addeman and flew him back to Edmonton.

Tom Fox could not afford to lose the aircraft left on the ice, and it had to be recovered before the spring thaw. There were no roads to Chipewyan Lake so the aircraft had to be flown out. But how? Tom questioned the pilot in detail to learn the extent of the damage. Then he went to work figuring out how he would retrieve the Anson.

Tom worked out what the wing-loading on the aircraft might be if he cut off a corresponding length of the port wing. Wing-loading refers to the weight of an aircraft that the wings can bear during flight. If the wing area is reduced by removing part of the wing and the weight of the aircraft and its cargo remains the same, the load on the shortened wings is increased. Tom calculated that the resulting wing-loading would not be much higher than that of some of the maximum loads they had flown previously. He decided to fly the Anson out, taking Maury Danes, one of his pilots, with him to fly their ski-equipped Taylorcraft CF-DBY loaded with tools and materials to help do the "clipping."

To the Rescue

At 1:30 the next afternoon they took off from Edmonton in the small aircraft with the dope and fabric they would need to patch up the wing tip. They landed on the ice three hours later and taxied to the Hudson Bay post. Maury and Tom were dismayed when they saw the damaged Anson. As well as a broken-off wing tip, half of the starboard aileron was shattered in the crash, but even worse, the rear wing spar was also damaged. The wing spars are the main support for the whole wing and it was broken about halfway. After they repaired the aileron by fastening the broken pieces together with screws, they realized the spar would have to be extended to carry it. The biggest problem for the men was not the repair, but finding materials to do the job. But they didn't give up.

Fox and Danes didn't bring spruce or any other airframe material with them in the Taylorcraft.

A search only turned up some unused maple flooring left over from the construction of the post. The two cold airmen then set about squaring off, or clipping, the broken wing and re-installing the repaired aileron on the wing-spar extension. This took several days because the temperature was hovering near -50°C (-58°F). In this temperature, covering the clipped wing with fabric and doping the cotton were slow and difficult tasks. Gasoline stoves placed under the wing made the process possible, but there was always the danger of fire. After they finished, the port wing was clipped to match.

It was January 30th by the time the work on aircraft was complete. The airmen sat down in the warmth of the post's kitchen to reassess the work they had done and consider what entries could be made in the Anson's log book. Tom Fox had a difficult decision to make. Tom had two licences issued by the Canadian Department of Transport (DOT). One was his pilot's licence and the other was his flight engineer's licence. He had to list all the repairs in the aircraft's log book and sign the entry as the person responsible, either as pilot or engineer. If he signed off the aircraft as air worthy and flew it, it was possible that the DOT would revoke his license as an engineer because the alteration to the Anson was not authorized by the DOT. On the other hand, if he signed off the Anson as unfit for flight, the same DOT would probably pull his pilot's licence for flying an unsafe aircraft. There he was up in the far north with an aircraft that, as an aircraft engineer, he knew would fly but which the DOT would not certify for flight in its altered configuration. Fox decided he needed his engineer's licence because he had the only one in the company, so he wrote, "not airworthy and not fit for flight" in the Anson's log. His pilot's licence might have to be sacrificed to get the aircraft home.

Starting Home

It was time to fly the Anson to Edmonton. They fired up the gasoline stove heaters to warm the 450-horsepower Pratt and Whitney radial engines for starting. The big Wasp Junior engines, which had replaced the 320 Jacobs, started up with the usual puffs of smoke, and then Tom taxied the aircraft about 2 kilometres (1 mile) down the lake and turned into the wind. He applied power and ran the airplane on its skis almost all the way back down the lake without taking off. Tom then turned, taxied back to the starting point again and put the power to the R 985 engines. This time he flew the aircraft about 1 metre (3 feet) above the snow to see how EKD would handle in its new clipped-wing shape.

A takeoff and circuit gave him the answers he needed. The Anson required a lot of power to reach the new takeoff speed. Tom finally lifted off at just over 120 kilometres (75 miles) per hour. He found that the cruising speed was extremely low, even when he applied power to climb. Control of the aircraft with its new wing and shortened aileron configuration was very "Sloppy," is how Tom described it, but the Anson flew, as he knew it would. What is more, it would fly all the way to Edmonton. They would take off the next day.

Preheating the engines in extremely cold temperatures is always a chore, but warming three engines at -36°C (-33°F) takes a lot of time. The Anson needed special care checking all the repairs and the moving parts of the wings before takeoff. It was 1:15 p.m. when Tom Fox lifted off from the ski tracks he had made the day before, flew a circuit round the Hudson Bay post and headed southeast ahead of the single-engined Taylorcraft. Tom flew towards Fort McMurray while Maury Danes turned the Taylorcraft south to Edmonton.

Tom had flown a gradual climb to 700 metres (2300 feet) when he noticed the fuel gauge for the starboard tank was dropping drastically. He opened the cross-feed valve so that the starboard engine could draw fuel from the port wing tank. But after a few seconds the engine began to misfire and it was obvious that something was wrong. Fox switched to the starboard tank again. He tried the cross-feed valve two or three times, but it did not work. The inter-tank fuel line was frozen.

Tom then remembered Pat, the pilot of an Anson from another company who dropped down onto the lake when he and Maury were working on the port wing. Pat was low on fuel due to terrible headwinds and borrowed 200 litres (45 gallons) from EKD's starboard wing tank. The next day on his flight north he returned the gas, but because they were working on the starboard wing, he put it into the port wing. So even though Tom was flying with lots of gas he had no way to use it. The gauge showed red and he was still 32 kilometres (20 miles) west of Fort McMurray. Deciding he couldn't make it, he flew lower over the big bend of the Peace River where it heads east to the fort. Then the starboard engine quit. Tom feathered the dry radial's prop and pulled back power to the port engine. Feathering a prop is turning the prop blades at an angle so that the wind flowing over them would not turn the blades like a windmill. He knew the aircraft would not be able to reach Fort McMurray on a single engine. A forced landing on the river was his only alternative.

Tom tried to radio Fort McMurray but had no luck and went down just past the bend where there was a straight stretch for about 2 kilometres (1 mile). It was there, close to the north bank,

Maury Danes finds his boss Tom Fox and lands the
Taylorcraft next to the Anson on the frozen Peace River.

that he put the Anson on the ice. Just before shutting down the engine, Tom made another attempt to contact someone on the radio. He failed, but was able to make a blind transmission, that is, a broadcast, to anyone and everyone within radio distance rather than to a specific radio station. It was 2:25 p.m. when he cut the power.

After draining the engine of oil to prevent it from freezing and putting on the engine covers, Tom gathered together some supplies and set off on snowshoes down the river towards Fort McMurray. He left a written message in the Anson saying he was going to walk to the town. But he didn't get far. The snow was too powdery and he kept sinking quite deeply, even on the snowshoes, so he turned around and retraced his tracks to the aircraft. He tried again to use the radio but had no luck. After making a fire to heat the little stove on which to cook up soup and tea, Tom tried to make himself comfortable using the wing covers as a mattress on the floor of the Anson. It was very cold and the poor weather prevented him from seeing very far. He went out to cut more wood but the axe handle broke so he had to gather small pieces that he could break by jumping on them. It was getting colder so Tom took the little tin stove into the aircraft and put the chimney through a hole he broke in the Plexiglas astrodome on top of the Anson's fuselage. He then put on all the clothes he could find, including his flying boots, and crawled into his sleeping bag.

At 8:00 a.m. on Sunday, February 2, Tom woke up with his face frozen to the sleeping bag and had to warm his cheek with his hands to detach it. It started to get warmer by the afternoon. He had just made tea and soup at about 4:30 p.m. when he saw the Taylorcraft CF-DBY overhead. Maury Danes had flown back to look for his boss. Fifteen minutes later, after sharing the tea, they took off for Fort McMurray. After a bath and supper, Tom sent a wire to Associated's office in Edmonton asking for a drum of gas and a proper engine heater. He also asked that someone contact his wife Clara to let her know what had happened. When Associated's second Anson arrived from Edmonton, he learned from pilot Doug Ireland that an all-time low temperature record had been established in the Yukon Territory. Tom had just experienced an estimated -56°C (-68°F) at his Peace River landing site.

Back on the river, Tom, Maury and Doug filled the starboard fuel tank and preheated the engines. When the engines roared to life, Doug Ireland took off in the second Anson, making ski tracks for EKD to lift off more easily. They all arrived safely at Fort McMurray. Tom wired Associated again, this time asking for the hangar doors to be opened when he landed in Edmonton so that he could taxi straight in. The last thing he wanted was to draw attention to the clipped-wing aircraft.

Home

In Fort McMurray, on Wednesday, February 5, Tom had the skis removed for the flight back and found that without them he could easily maintain an airspeed of 160 kilometres (100 miles) per hour. He made it without mishap, even though EKD's controls were less responsive and he had to move them continually to keep the Anson straight and level during some extreme turbulence en route. He taxied the modified aircraft right into the company hangar and the doors were closed behind him.

Home safely and out of sight! he thought. Tom climbed out of the Anson and ran his hands over the repair with pride before walking to his office. Just as he sat down in his swivel chair, glad to be home, the door burst open and in roared Jock Currie. Mr. Currie was the district Department of Transport's engineering and maintenance superintendent. He was livid and shouted at Tom, "What sort of contraption was it that just flew over my house?"

Currie demanded to be shown the aircraft, its log books and, in particular, the entries Tom had made. Tom had to do what he asked. Jock Currie also demanded that Tom give him both his pilot's and his engineer's licence. He stormed out saying that no responsible person would fly a contraption like the one in the hangar.

The next day, Tom had to meet with the district superintendent of air regulations, Ken Saunders. Mr. Saunders told Tom that he disapproved of the unauthorized modifications and that he was sending Tom's licences to DOT's head office in Ottawa with the recommendation they be "suspended forthwith." Tom spent a mixed week, receiving both congratulations and sympathy and trying to figure out what he would do without either of his licences. By the end of the week he was almost at his wits end when his licences were returned by mail from Ottawa without suspension or comment. He was back in business, but he never knew who had returned his papers or why. Tom Fox never gave up, and as a result, Associated Airways eventually grew into one of Alberta's largest airlines.

Tom Fox was inducted into the Alberta Aviation Hall of Fame in 1983 for his contribution to aviation in Alberta and Canada. The infamous Clip Wing Anson was mentioned at the ceremony without fear of retribution from Transport Canada (Air), as the Department of Transport is currently known. The Anson CF-EKD did not survive and was eventually taken apart and used for spare parts for Associated's other Ansons. Tom spent his retirement riding cutting horses in Cave Creek, Arizona. That was after a "retirement career" in auto racing which he began at sixty years of age. He retired from racing at age sixty-eight as Canadian National Road Racing Champion.

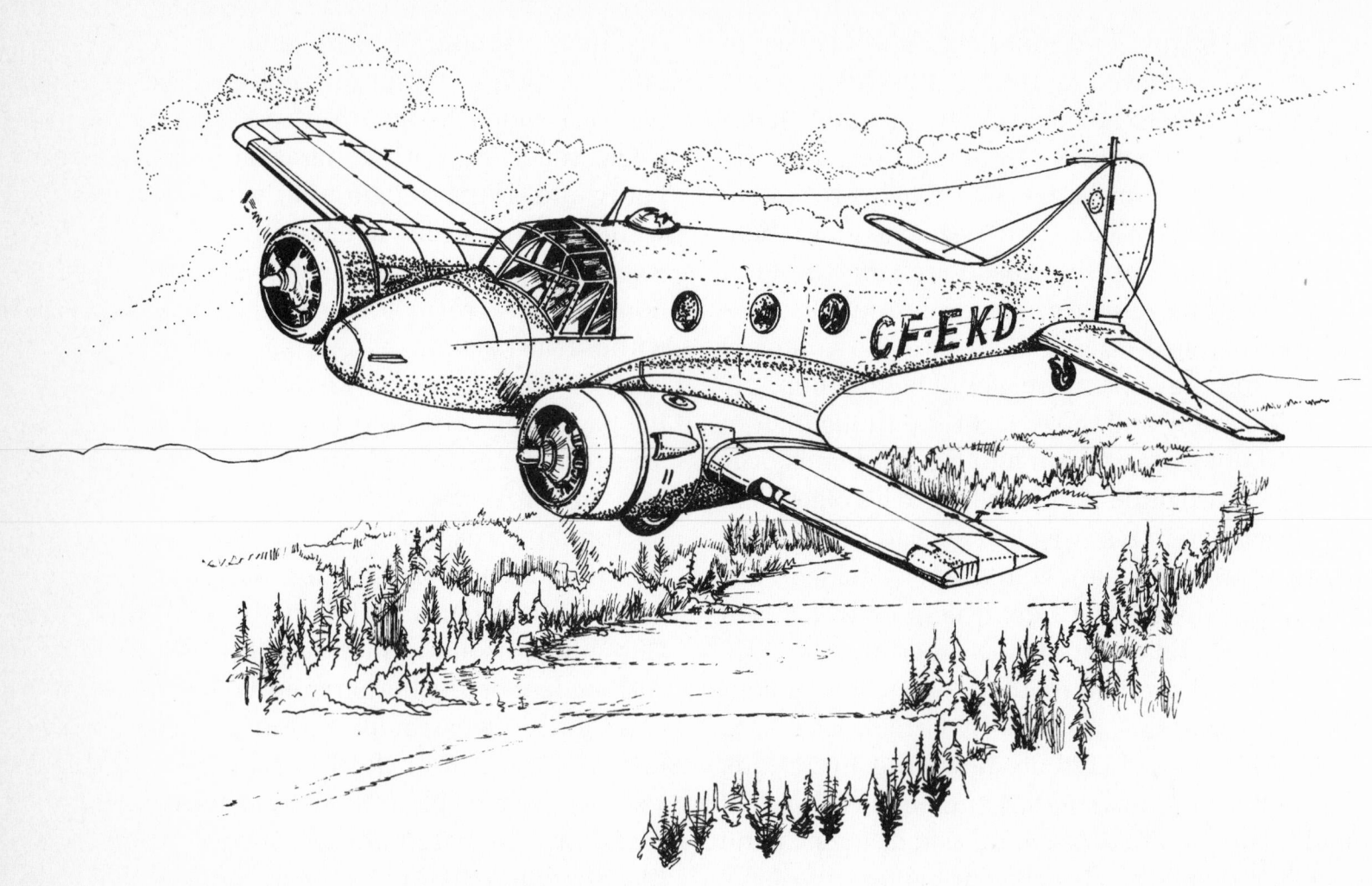

The clipped-wing Anson looks a little odd with its stubby
wings flying from Fort McMurray to Edmonton.

Conclusion

The story of aviation's first attempts does not end with Tom Fox. There are men and women who continue to make attempts to improve on existing records and some who will establish new ones. As aircraft change so do the conditions under which pilots and engineers work. Many different types of piston- and jet-engined aircraft, ultralight aircraft, and even strap-on flying machines exist, creating opportunities for new achievements and records to be established. Men and women keep on flying further, higher, and faster. They pilot aircraft that carry hundreds of passengers for thousands of miles, while others have established airlines and designed and built aircraft.

Aviators have been to the edge of space and men and women have been beyond, into space itself. However, like their predecessors, they have and will continue to succeed only because they have great determination, and no matter what the cost, will never give up.

There is a wonderful silver trophy called the McKee Trophy awarded each year to individuals who have stimulated aviation in Canada. It was introduced in 1927 and was at first only awarded to pilots. Later the rules were revised to include anyone or any group of people who have contributed to the advancement of aviation. To read the lengthy list of winners is to witness the spirit of aviation and the determination of winners who never gave up.

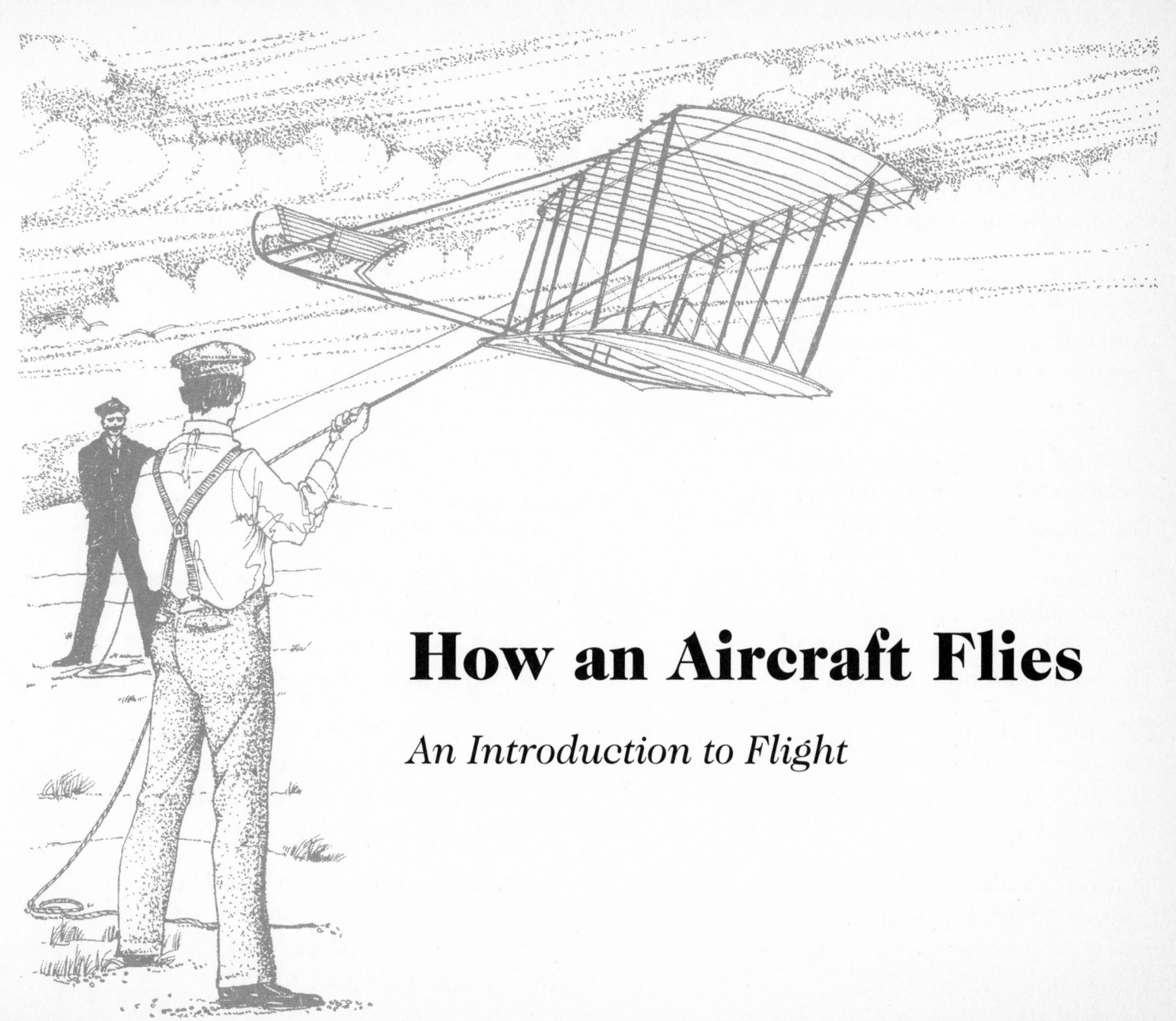

How an Aircraft Flies

An Introduction to Flight

The Beginning
by Patrick J Phillips

They say if men were meant to fly
Then babes would come with wings,
If this is true, then why's the sky
So full of flying things?

I'm told it started long ago
When folks still used their feet,
Until one day a thinking man
Thought flying would be neat.

So to his shop he carried forth
The stuff that makes our dreams,
He laboured long 'til he had formed
The first of flying machines.

Its lines were crude, the engine weak,
For strength he strung steel wire,
Then high atop a wind swept hill
The man did mount his flyer.

The prop was spun, the engine roared,
The ship soared into space
But since the man had never flown,
He landed on his face.

This failure did not stop him there,
For once more did he try,
And as you know from looking up,
The man did learn to fly.

Success complete, he struggled on,
His vision now seemed clear,
Of graceful ships to sail the sky
While friends looked on with fear.

Then to the craft he added struts,
A rudder shaped the tail,
In place of skids he mounted wheels
The ship no longer frail.

The years passed by, the craft refined
For nothing did it lack,
On board he mounted mighty jets
A washroom in the back.

The airports grew in size and noise
Which made the people frown,
And that's why runways to this day
Lie thirty miles from town.

The man felt sad among the crowd,
His dream was just to fly,
But now frustration seemed their mood
"Lost baggage" was their cry.

So from the airport did he walk
While jets flew over top,
Then as I watched, he smiled at me
And headed for his shop.

Introduction to Flight

Since photography was not invented until the middle of the nineteenth century, there are not many visual records of our historical attempts to fly that can be checked. There are a few written, medieval accounts and several drawings of men jumping from towers with wings strapped to their bodies. Most of these experiments ended tragically and in many cases fatally.

In the fifteenth century the Renaissance genius Leonardo da Vinci studied the flight of birds by watching how they moved their wings, tails and bodies. He wrote many notes with intricate drawings (since he was also a great artist) to illustrate how birds used the air. He reasoned that the movement of their wings against the air was as great a force as the movement of the air against their wings. Da Vinci was correct in this theory, but he did not really understand the basic theory of flight.

For more than forty years Leonardo designed and built flapping wing machines, but human beings were not strong enough to power these contraptions, and all of da Vinci's efforts failed. He did have a very good understanding of how birds' wings are constructed. If he had made his wings rigid, so they would glide, he might have succeeded. Unfortunately, Leonardo always split

the wings in two and tried to flap his way off the ground. He never gave up, but he was never successful.

In the sixteenth and seventeenth centuries, early scientists and dreamers built wings and even complete suits with which to jump from high towers — only to injure themselves severely, or worse! There are written accounts of dreamers wrapping large, loose cloaks around themselves, with strut devices to spread the fabric rather like a bat's wing. They usually jumped to their death.

In England, an aristocrat named Sir George Caley spent a lifetime and a great deal of money trying to fly. He knew more than da Vinci about the movement and pressure of air and wrote many papers on the subject. He even designed a glider in 1804 that flew very well as a small-scale model. But he was not taken very seriously at the time, even though his work on flight was accurate and practical.

Eighty-three years after Caley, a German scientist by the name of Otto Lilienthal built the first man-carrying glider. He spent years learning about double and single wings before running down a hillside and jumping into the air strapped to his successful glider. His wings were very similar to those of Leonardo's, but were of a rigid, fixed construction. He made more than two thousand glides with his wings, which looked very much like a modern hang-glider. Lilienthal tried

A page from Leonardo da Vinci's notebook on flight experiments.

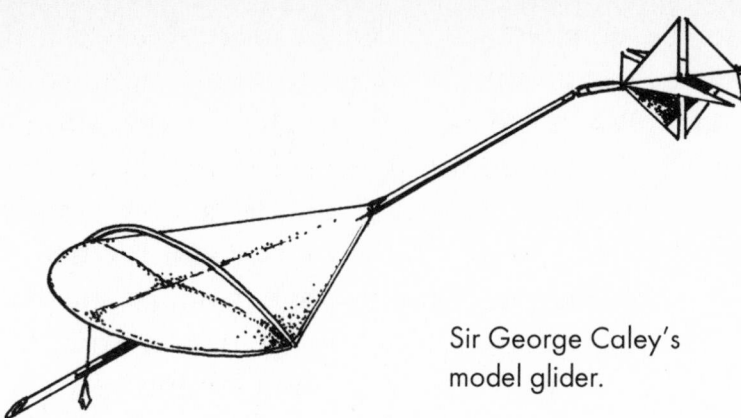

Sir George Caley's
model glider.

body movements that, he theorized, would control the direction of the glider, and they worked. Later, he was severely injured when his wings stalled in the air and he crashed to the ground. He died the next day in a Berlin hospital, but it was his research and influence that helped the Wright brothers fly successfully in 1903.

Daniel Bernoulli and the Theory of Flight

The theory of flight was not genuinely understood until the early part of the sixteenth century. Daniel Bernoulli, a Swiss mathematician, was studying fluids in motion when he accidentally discovered the theory of flight. Bernoulli's name is given to the scientific discovery, a very simple theory, that states "the faster a fluid travels over a wing, the pressure of the fluid decreases over it." Before we get too involved and confused with the theory, though, let's look at its practical application.

Since Professor Bernoulli was working with fluids, let's use water. You can see the effects of the speed of water by turning on a tap. The more water released by the faucet, the faster the water flows. Find a tablespoon and hold the rounded back of the spoon against the water flow. You would expect the force of the water to push the spoon away from the flow. But, if you hold the spoon as shown in the diagram, you will feel it being sucked into the tap water's flow.

Air is also a fluid and that is why Professor Bernoulli was able to formulate his theory of flight. You'll need two sheets of smooth paper to perform a paper test. These can be pages from your notebook or sheets of copy paper. Fold them about one-quarter of the way down the long side of the sheet, across the short side. Stand these two sheets on edge about 4 centimetres (1.5 inches) apart at the fold with the short fold facing you. Hold the closest edges firmly, blow gently into the space between the pieces of paper and watch their trailing edges move closer together. The air that you blow between the sheets can

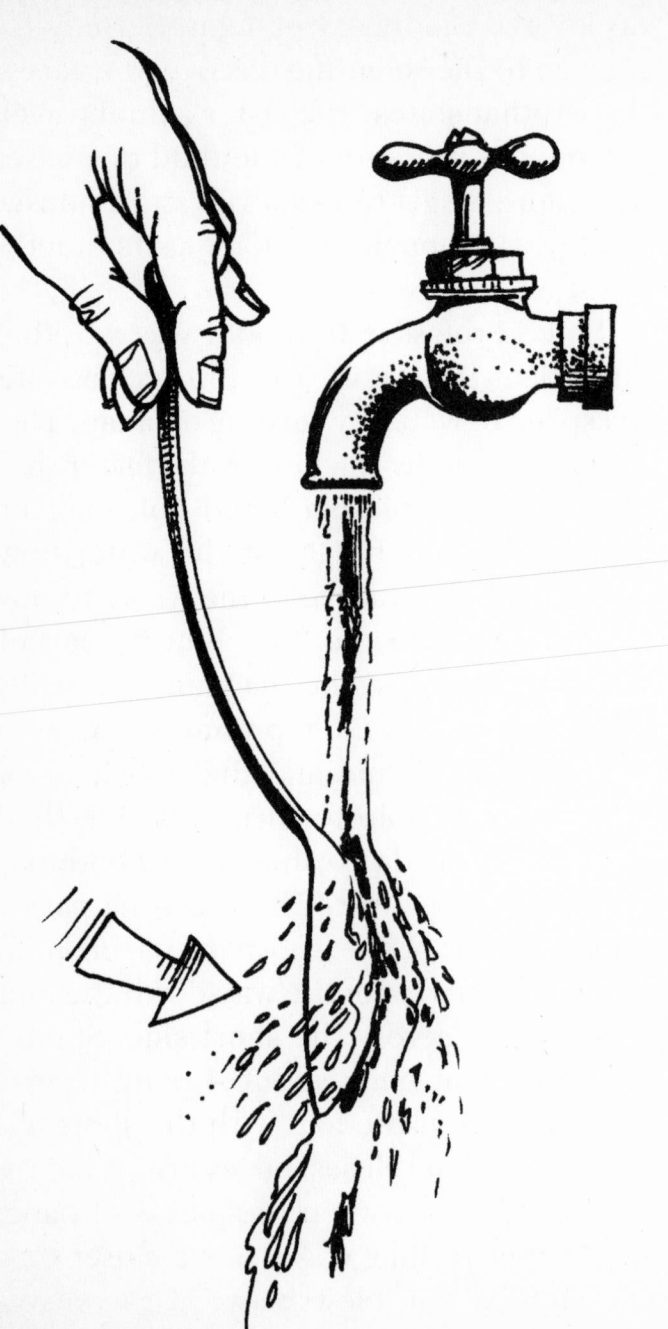

not be compressed or made more dense, so it has to travel quickly to get through the narrow space. When the air moves faster the pressure is reduced between the sheets, allowing the papers to move closer together. This is a very simple method of seeing Professor Bernoulli's theory work in practice. You may have to adjust the distance between the pieces of paper and the distance of your lips from the opening between the sheets for the experiment to work effectively.

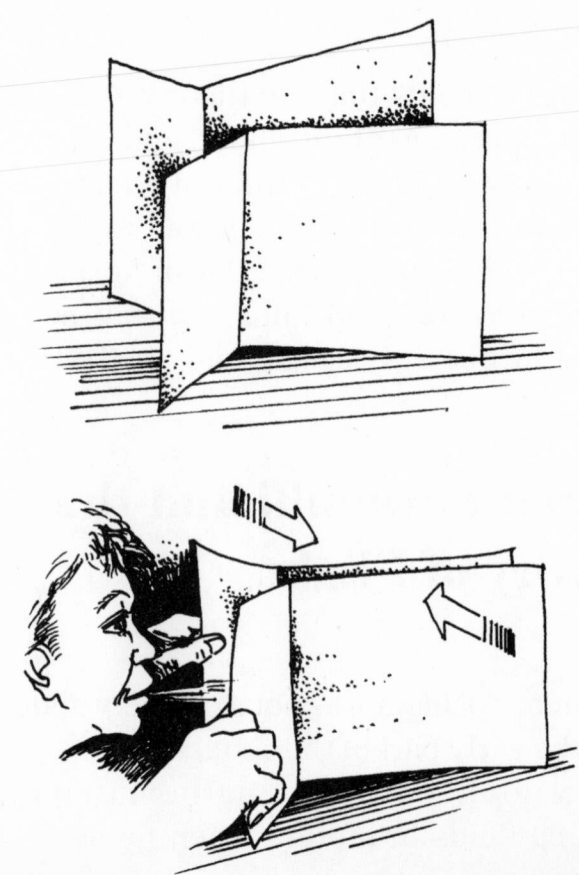

Another example of the theory can be shown by a slightly more complicated method. You will need one sheet of copy paper, two drinking straws or one straw and a pencil and scotch tape. Cut a strip of copy paper to measure 4 centimetres by 12 centimetres (1.5 inches by 5 inches) and tape one of the narrow sides to a drinking straw or a pencil. Then, using another drinking straw, blow gently over the top of it and watch it lift.

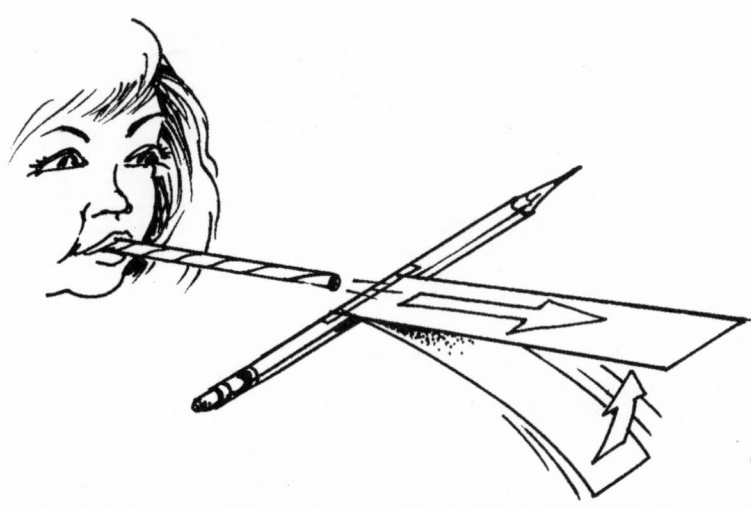

The air moving over the curve of the paper illustrates the basic principle of flight. The curved back of the spoon you used in the water experiment and the gentle curve of the paper taped to the pencil are very similar to the shape across a bird's wing or the shape you see looking at the end of an aircraft's wing. This upward curving shape has a special name in aerodynamics (the study of flight). It is called an AIRFOIL.

To make a simple airfoil, cut a sheet of paper to measure 8 centimetres by 12 centimetres (3 inches by 5 inches). Using a straight edge or ruler, score the paper by pressing down hard with a ball point pen down the centre of the paper. Then fold one edge of the sheet gently over to the other edge and tape it down. Do not press down the score mark before you fold it, or you will not see the airfoil shape clearly. To keep the airfoil shape, you could glue a drinking straw against the inside edge of the fold before you tape it down. This will keep the leading edge more rigid. Look at the diagrams to be sure you are doing it correctly. If you make two of these airfoils and make the bottom of each one flat instead of curved and

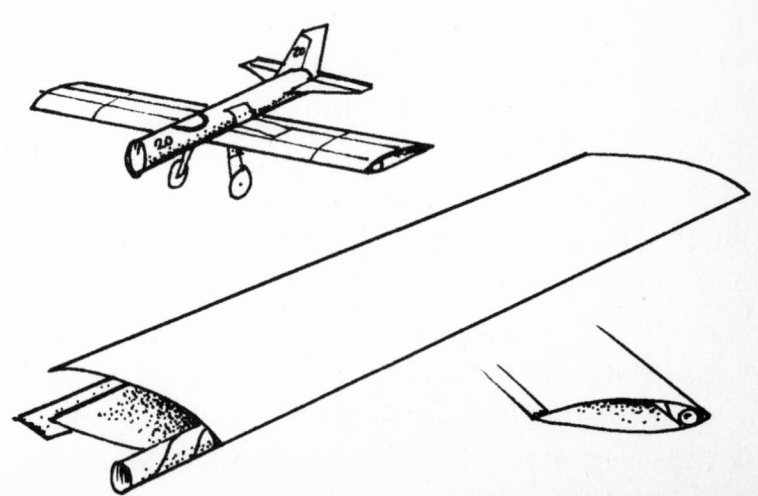

then tape them to each side of a roll of paper, you will see the beginnings of an airplane shape.

We know that all elements have a density, which is simply the weight of the element. Air has a density that changes slightly with its height above sea level. At sea level, air has a density of 14.7 pounds per square inch (101.52 millibars). If we measure the air at 3,000 metres (10,000 feet) above sea level, we find a tremendous drop in air pressure of almost one-third. This is why passenger aircraft have pressurized cabins for our comfort when they fly at altitudes of 10,000 metres (30,000 feet) or more. The cabin pressure is kept at a constant level by a kind of air conditioning unit so that we are able to breathe easily and not be overcome by changes of pressure as the aircraft climbs and descends.

Air pressure is the most important aspect of flight. As air flows over an airfoil, similar to the one you made, it is split by the leading edge of the wing. The air flowing over the wing has to travel faster than the air traveling under the wing because it has further to go. By traveling faster, we know from what Professor Bernoulli found out

that the air pressure is less above the airfoil, enabling the wing to move up into the denser air. This is called creating LIFT for the wing. When lift is created, we are flying. Look at the diagrams and see how the spoon and the airfoil you made relate to the section across the bird's wing, which is an airfoil too.

The airfoil and the spoon are similar shapes.

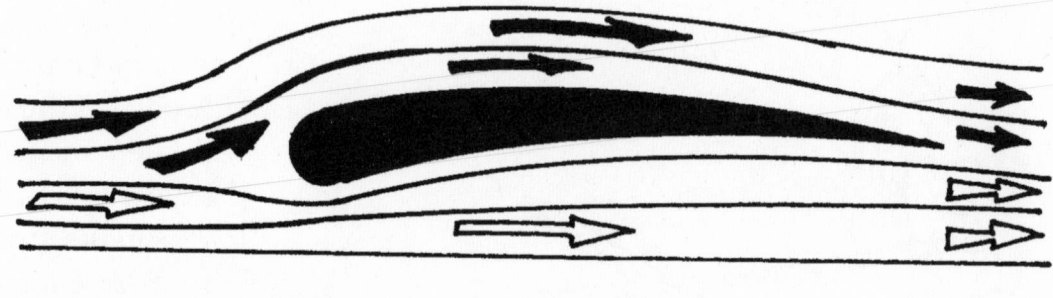

In a way, flying is like riding a bicycle because you need forward motion to keep your balance. Look at the next diagram and you might see the similarities more easily. The direction in which you are traveling by pedaling the bike is the THRUST against the stable air. Your weight is really the gravity that holds you in contact with the ground. The force of the wind you feel on

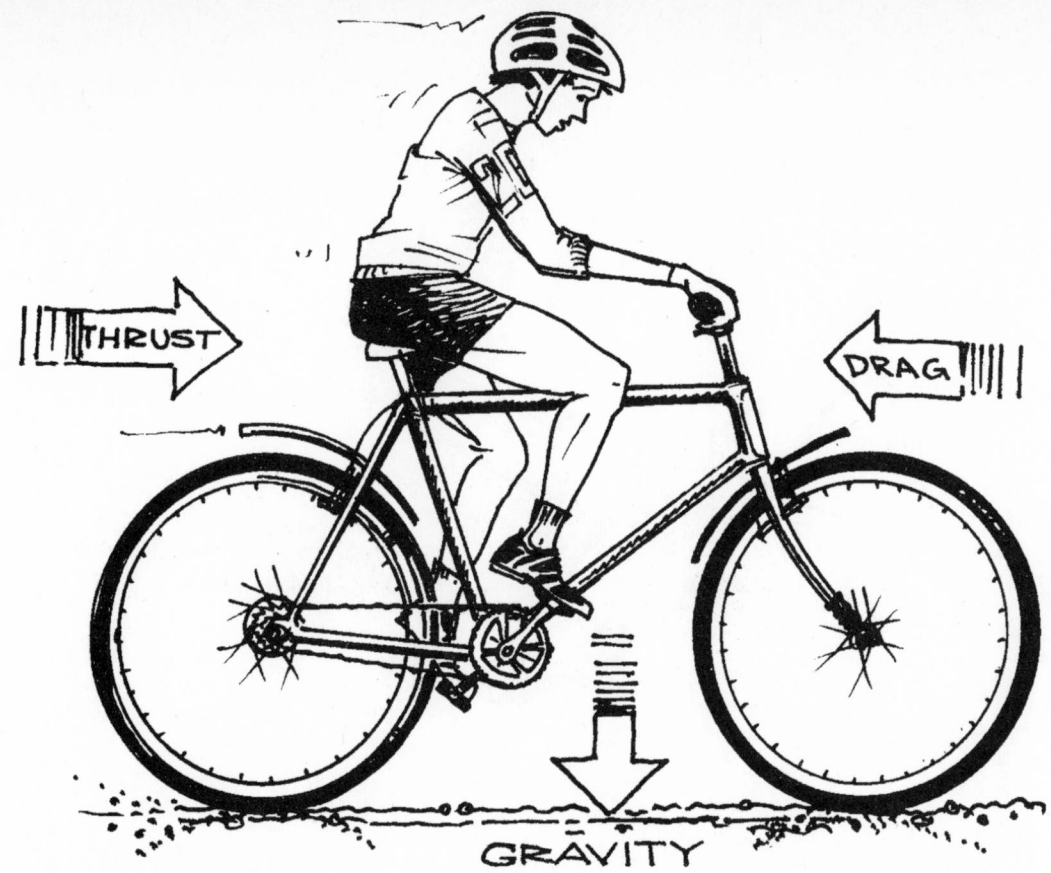

THRUST

DRAG

GRAVITY

Have you noticed that some aircraft have differently shaped wings? Birds do too. Seagulls have long, tapered wings and robins have short, wide wings. Sail planes have wings like a seagull because they fly in much the same way, by soaring. Jet aircraft often have triangular or DELTA shaped wings because they have a great deal of power to speed them along.

In aerodynamics, the distance across the wing from front to back is referred to as the CHORD. The relationship (or ratio) of the length of the wing to the chord is called the ASPECT RATIO. Seagulls and sail planes have a high aspect ratio, while robins and delta-wing jets

your face as you move forward is the pressure you are exerting against it. This is called DRAG. The LIFT that is created by this movement is created on your sides because the air is split around you and flows on both sides of you. One side is equal to the other because you are not shaped like an airfoil. An aircraft flies in a similar fashion, only LIFT is created on the airfoil because of its special shape.

have a low aspect ratio. Wing chords also differ a great deal in their shape. The first aircraft wings were curved like a bird's and were quite thin across the chord. As designs improved

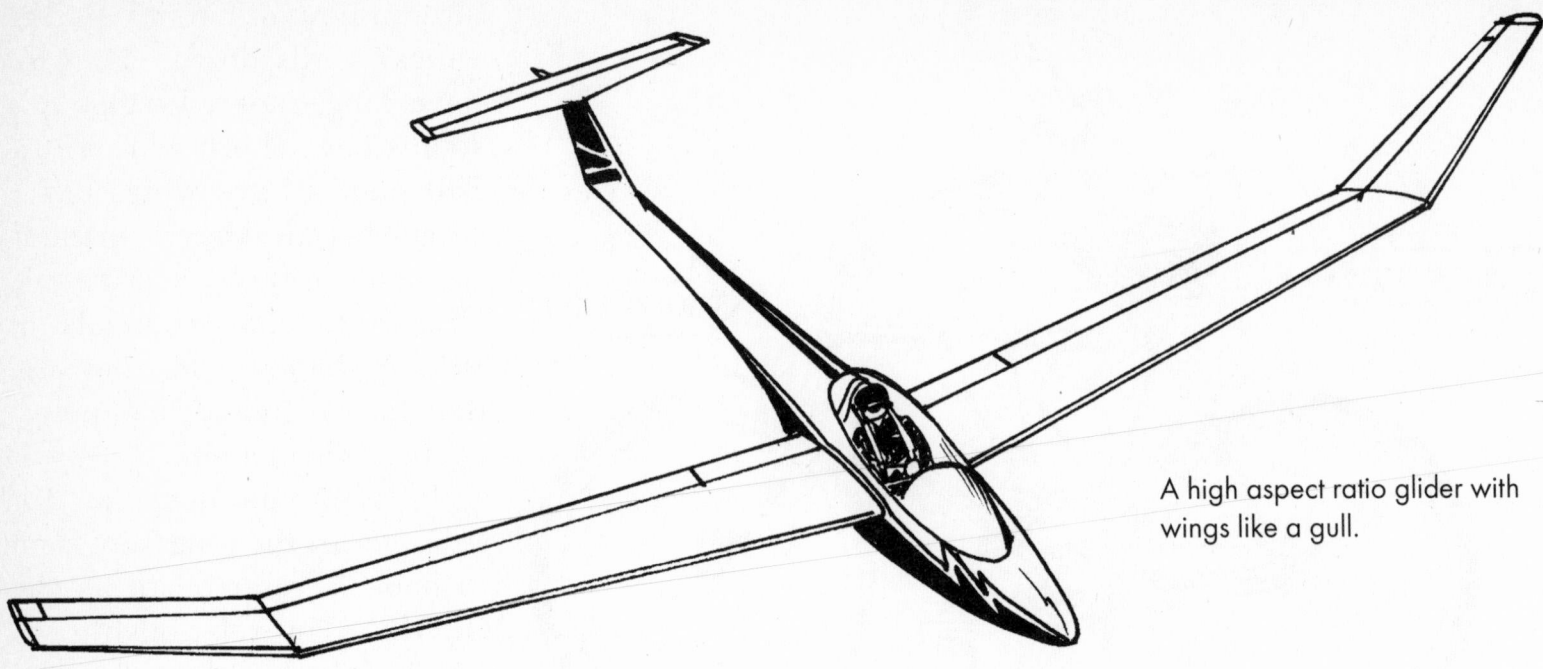

A high aspect ratio glider with wings like a gull.

there was a change to thick, short chords. They flew very well at the low speeds aircraft were then capable of flying. However, as airplanes were given better engines and flew faster, the chord was changed to what we refer to as a LAMINAR design. This thin, or narrow, chord enabled the airplane to fly faster but was less stable at low speeds. So there is an average chord shape that provides good stability at the fast speeds of en route flight and the relatively slow speeds for take-off and landing.

Let's take a look at an airplane now. Many parts make up the whole aircraft and even though there are many different kinds of aircraft, these main parts are common to all of them. They all fly the same way no matter how they might be powered or, in the case of a sail plane, not powered at all.

Parts of an Aircraft

1   Fuselage

2   Identification Letters

3   Horizontal Stabilizer

4   Elevators

5   Rudder

6   Vertical Stabilizer

7   Strobe Light

8   Flaps

9   Ailerons

10   Fuel Tanks

11   Navigation Lights

12   Engine Mount

13   Lower Cowling

14   Steerable Nose Wheel

15   Nose Cowling

16   Propeller

17   Spinner

18   Top Cowling

19   Engine

20   Main Gear

21   Fuel Filler Cap

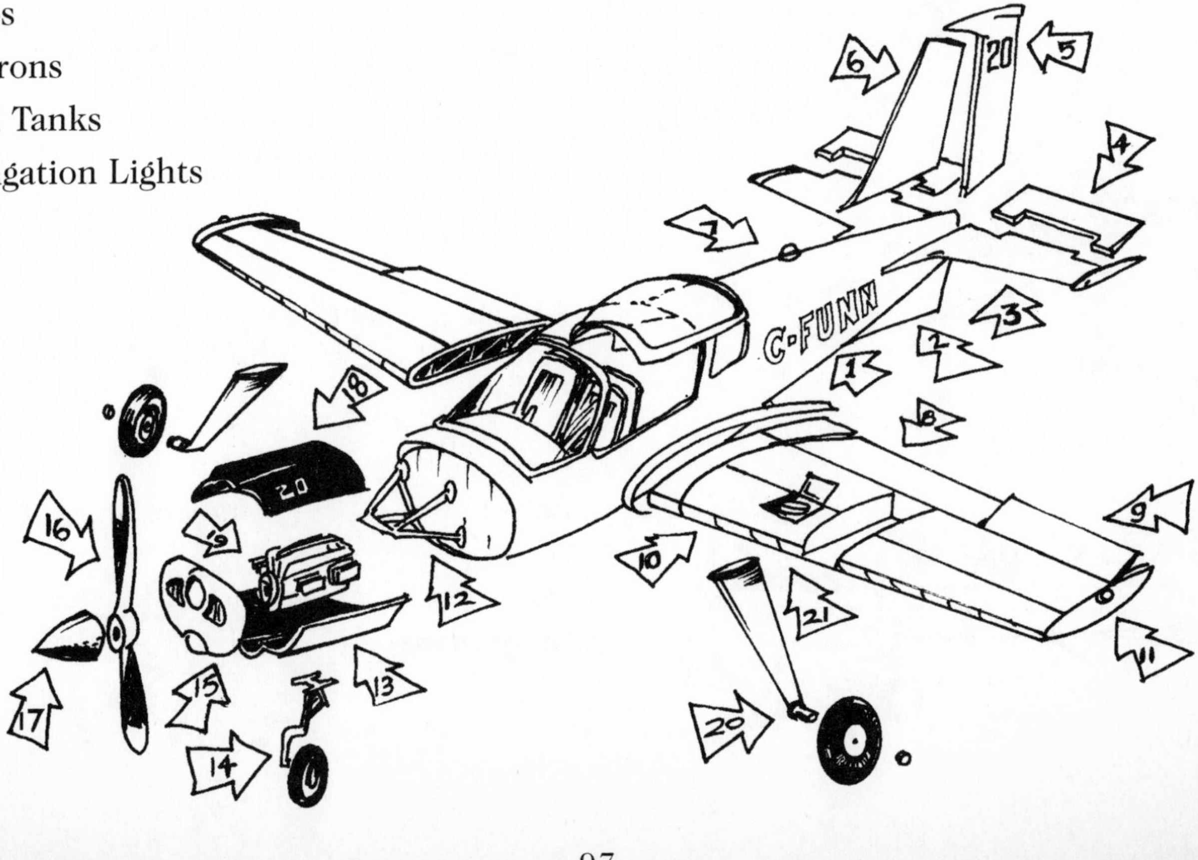

Aircraft Controls

ELEVATORS work together. Both up — both down. Control is the stick moving forward (down) and backward (up).

elevators down

elevators up

flaps down

FLAPS work together. Both up — both down. Control is a separate flap handle or electric switch.

RUDDER turns left and right. Control is foot pedals.

AILERONS work together. One up — one down. Control is the stick moving left or right.

Wings

The illustrations clearly show similarities to each other. Wings are the parts of the aircraft that create the lift. As you have already discovered, wings can be almost any shape and they can be placed almost anywhere on the fuselage of the aircraft.

CONSTANT CHORD wing shapes were the earliest designs used because so little was known about flight at the beginning of this century. These wings have a general purpose shape usually seen on the smaller, slower, older aircraft we fly for fun.

TAPERED wings are usually seen on small aircraft that can fly a little faster and turn a little faster than most other types of aircraft. Today we see wings like this on championship AEROBATIC aircraft.

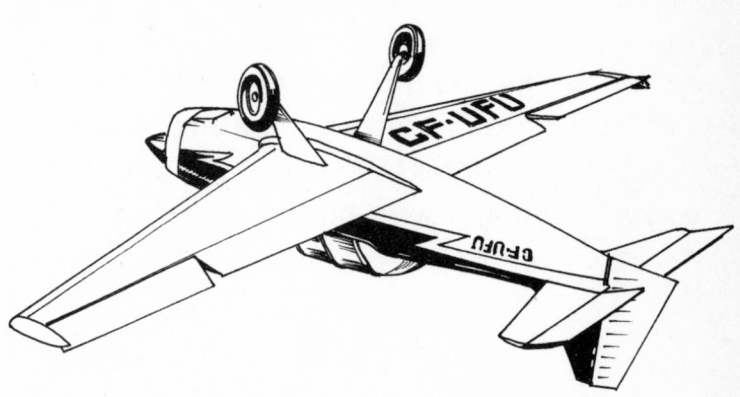

SWEPT wings are found on jet TURBINE-engined aircraft, which can fly higher and faster than most small aircraft. We see them on small private jets as well as on the large passenger jets. Many military jets also have wings shaped like this.

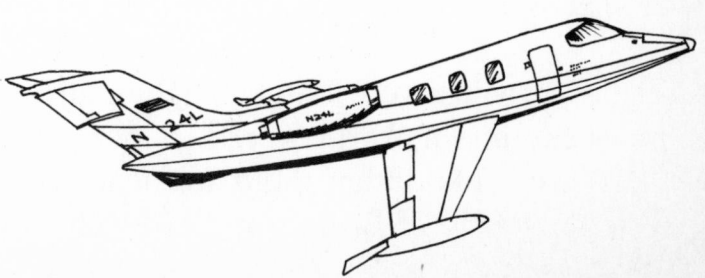

The DELTA wing is a design that was used in the early development of fast, military jet fighters in the 1960s. Although they are seldom seen on modern fighter aircraft, delta wing designs are still used on aircraft as famous as the Space Shuttle and the Concord. The delta wing functions exceptionally well at very high speed — over three times the speed of sound, or MACH 3 — and it is very stable at low landing speeds of around 200 kilometres (125 miles) per hour. Delta wings have a greater wing lift than the swept wing

wings enabled the fighters to turn, climb, and dive very easily and quickly. We do not see many elliptical wings today.

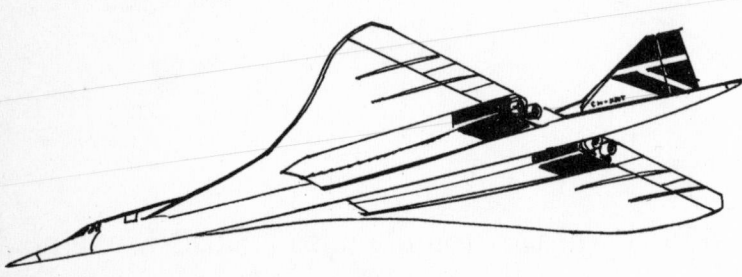

which provides better handling at lower speeds. Many new jet fighter aircraft have the capability to fold back the swept wings to a delta configuration for high speed flight, then open them for lower speeds and landings.

ELLIPTICAL wings were found on fighter aircraft at the beginning of World War II. Supermarine Spitfires used this design to great effect during the famous Battle of Britain in 1940. Elliptical

STRAKE or CHINE wings are the latest development on very fast and maneuverable aircraft. They use a small, narrow wing that flows into a larger swept wing or a delta shape and spans almost the entire length of the fuselage. Modern strike fighters used in the Gulf War, such as the F14 Tomcats, F15 Eagles, F16 Falcons, and F18 Hornets of the United States and Canada, as well as the Jaguars and F3 Tornadoes of Britain's Royal Air Force, all have chine or strake wings.

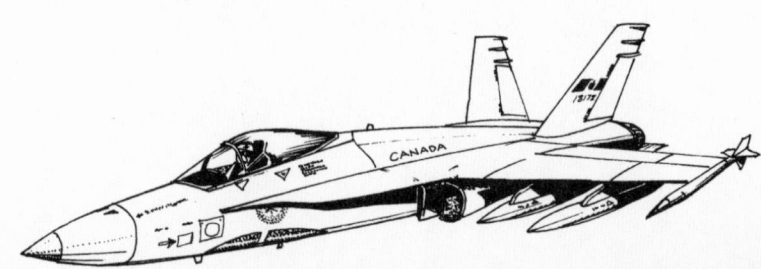

CANARD wings are wings that are on backwards. The main wing is at the back of the aircraft and the tail plane is at the front. The name canard comes from the French word for duck. These wings were given this name because ducks have wings far back on their bodies. The first powered aircraft to fly successfully in 1903, the Wright Flyer, was a canard design. Many of the early aircraft had wings shaped like this.

Wings can be set on the fuselage in a variety of ways.

There can be two complete pairs of wings on an aircraft, one above and one below the fuselage. We call this arrangement a BIPLANE.

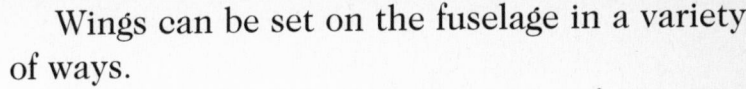

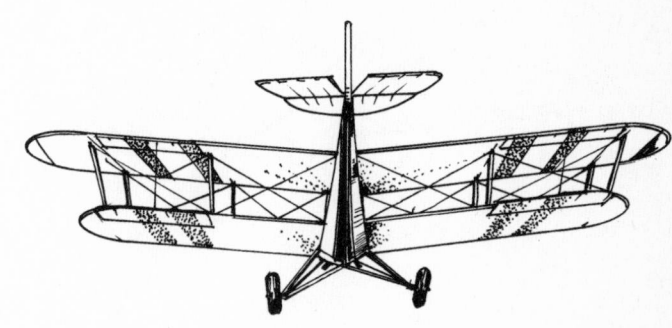

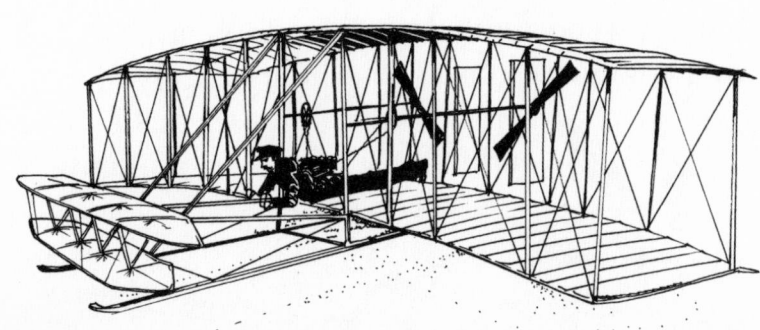

If there is only one pair of wings on an aircraft, we call it a MONOPLANE.

Single pairs of wings may be set above the fuselage. In that case it is a HIGH WING MONOPLANE.

The wings can also be placed through the centre of the fuselage. We call this design a MID WING MONOPLANE.

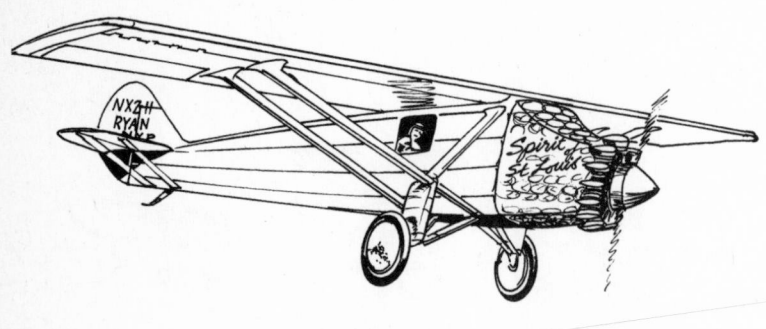

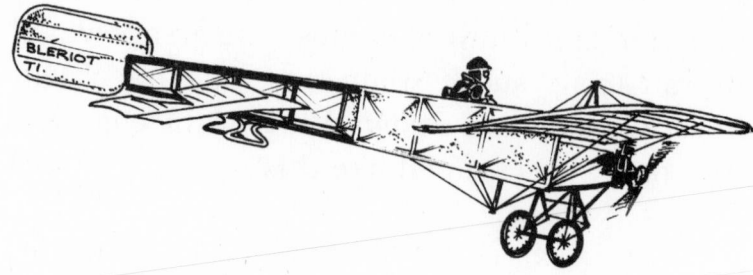

To make things a little more interesting, a wing can be joined to the fuselage with the WING ROOT (that is the part of the wing closest to the fuselage) on a perfectly horizontal line with its wing tip.

If the wings are attached to the bottom of the fuselage, we call it a LOW WING MONOPLANE.

This is a straight wing design. The wings are often attached with the wing tip higher than the wing root, giving the aircraft much more stable flying characteristics. The angle at which the wings are fitted is called the DIHEDRAL. This design can be applied to either high, mid, or low wing configurations. The dihedral helps the aircraft return to level flight more efficiently after roll maneuvers are made.

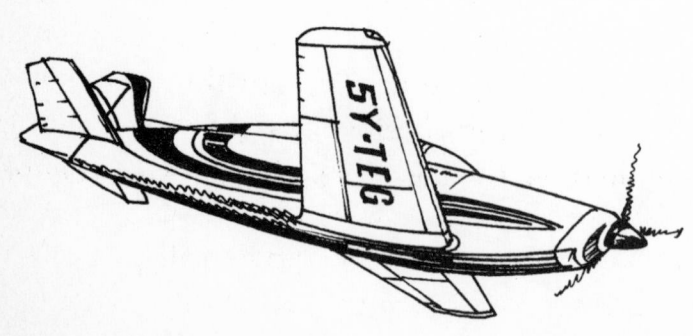

How to Control an Aircraft in Flight

Now that you know a little more about how an airplane flies, we should take a look at how to control an aircraft in flight. But first, let's take a look at the way boats turn, just to help you understand control a little better.

To turn a small boat, or indeed a large ship, you use its rudder. A turn to the right is accom-

plished by moving the rudder to the right. As you turn the rudder the flow of water around the boat is interrupted and pushes against the obstruction. This forces the stern (the back) of the boat to swing to the left and the bow (the front) of the boat to the right, which is where you want it to be. If you want the boat to turn left, you push the rudder (or tiller or wheel) to the left.

An aircraft has smaller parts attached to its wings and tail, just like the rudder on a boat. These small parts move or guide the aircraft through the air in one direction or another around its centre.

The movement of an aircraft has special aeronautical terms. When the aircraft turns left or right we call the movement YAW. When an aircraft moves up or down we use the aeronautical term PITCH. If we want to make the aircraft lift one wing or the other we use the word ROLL. All these pitch, roll and yaw movements have to be controlled from inside the cabin. A pilot uses a YOKE or STICK to control pitch and roll and uses his or her feet on RUDDER PEDALS to make the aircraft yaw.

To change direction, the yoke or stick is moved in the direction of the desired turn. When this movement is made, small panels attached to the wings called AILERONS move so that the smooth flow of air is interrupted and a force is created to either push the wings up or down. If the stick is moved to the pilot's right, the aileron on the right wing is moved up so that the air flow is pushing against the aileron, forcing the right wing down. At the same time, the aileron on the left wing is automatically moved down, which creates the opposite effect on that wing. This coordinated aileron movement creates a roll around the LONGITUDINAL axis of the aircraft. Since the wing that is higher is then traveling at a slightly faster speed than the lower wing, the plane will turn to the right. To return to straight and level flight we push the yoke to the left, causing the right aileron to move down as the left aileron moves up, straightening the wings. Pilots call this an aileron turn.

To turn the aircraft more easily, the pilot uses the rudder by pushing down one of the foot pedals at the same time as moving the stick. The rudder direction is the same as the roll movement. Pilots call this a coordinated turn. It is similar to what a motorcycle rider does to change direction. The rider leans the cycle over in the direction of the turn while turning the wheel with the handlebars at the same time.

To make the aircraft climb or dive the ELEVATORS are moved up or down, like the ailerons. But the two elevators are moved in the same direction, not opposite directions like the ailerons. To make the aircraft climb, the pilot pulls back the stick, moving the elevators up. The air flow over the tail plane is interrupted and pushes against the elevators, forcing the tail of the aircraft down and the nose up. Since the aircraft is going forward the whole time, it moves in an upward line of travel. The reverse is used to dive the aircraft. The stick is pushed forward, lowering the elevators and pitching the nose of the aircraft down. As the elevators are moved, more power is applied to climb and less to descend.

When we land an aircraft, we want to do so as slowly as possible. To do this we pull the power way back, keep the nose up a little and employ FLAPS to help increase the lift of the wings in slow flight. The flaps make the chord of the wing more curved, creating greater pressure, which leads to more lift. Flaps let a pilot descend more steeply without increasing speed.

We also FLARE the aircraft on landing. In other words, we keep the nose up so that we touch down on the main wheels. This nose-up attitude, with the flaps down, prevents us from bouncing back into the air.

Once we have all these pilot movements committed to memory, we can fly an aircraft. Let's do that.

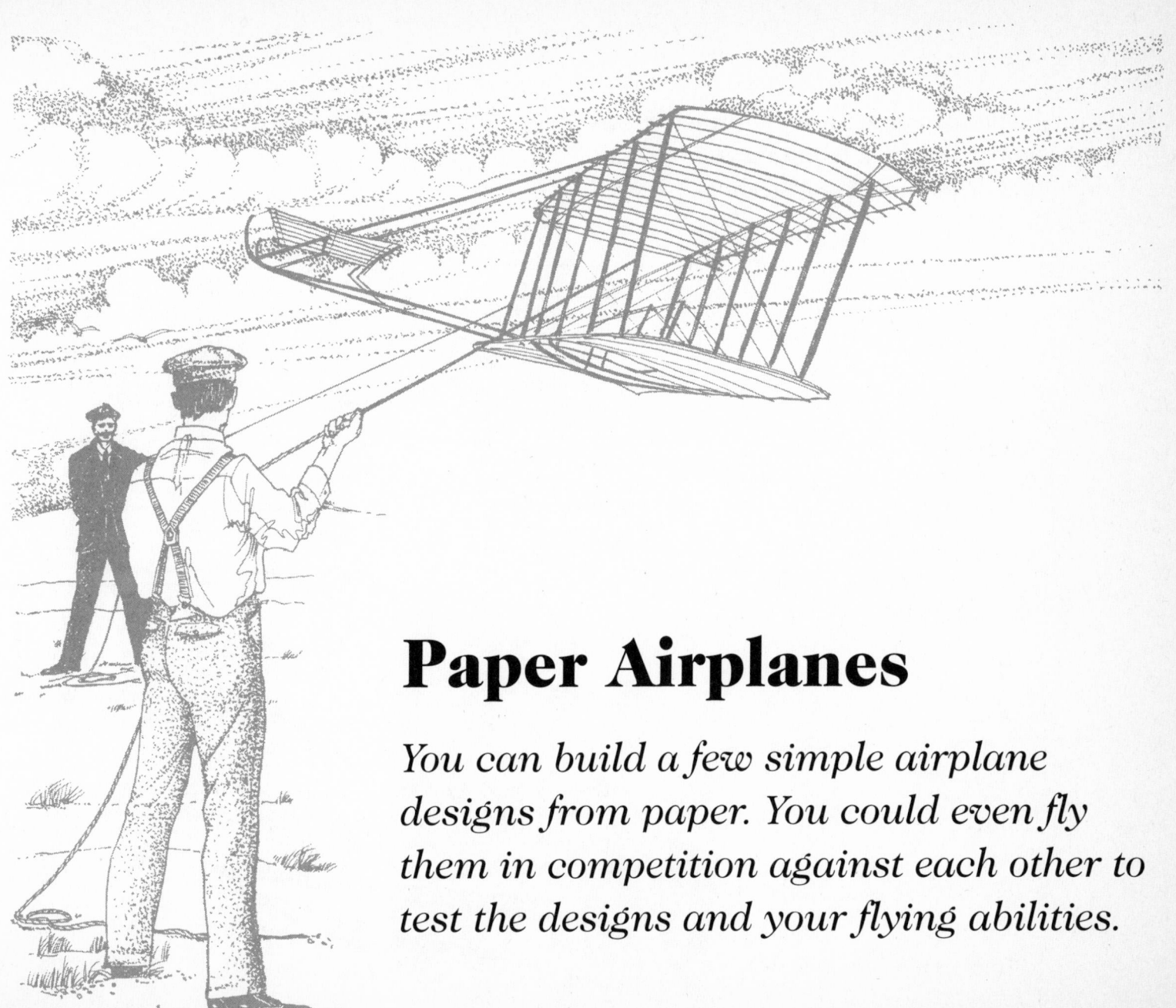

Paper Airplanes

You can build a few simple airplane designs from paper. You could even fly them in competition against each other to test the designs and your flying abilities.

World's Simplest Paper Glider

For straight flight, compete for distance flown over the competition box. Decorate your aircraft for individual or team identification. Begin with one sheet of 21.5-by-28 centimetre (8.5-by-11 inch) paper.

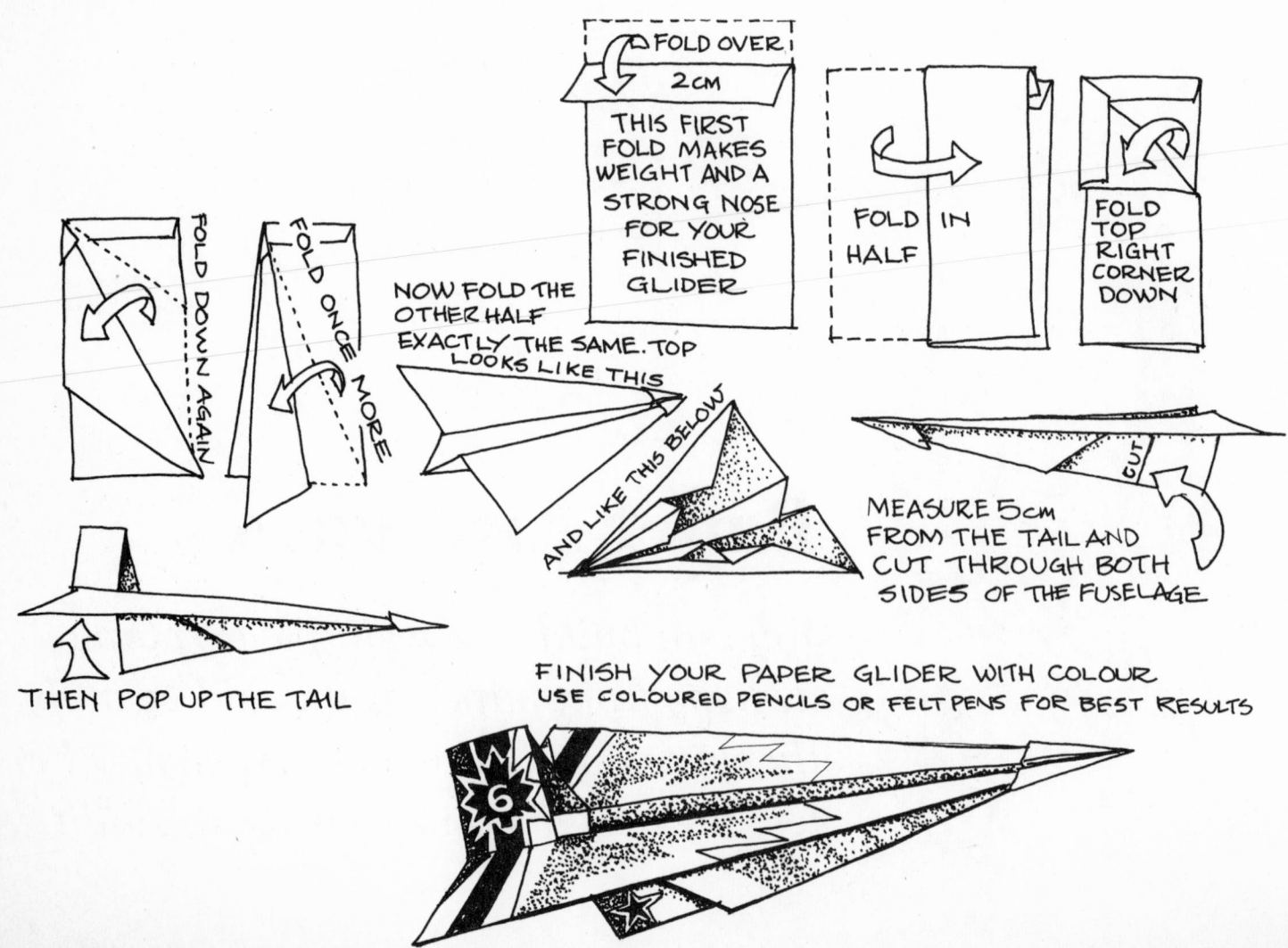

FOLD OVER
2CM
THIS FIRST FOLD MAKES WEIGHT AND A STRONG NOSE FOR YOUR FINISHED GLIDER

FOLD IN HALF

FOLD TOP RIGHT CORNER DOWN

FOLD DOWN AGAIN

FOLD ONCE MORE

NOW FOLD THE OTHER HALF EXACTLY THE SAME. TOP LOOKS LIKE THIS

AND LIKE THIS BELOW

CUT

MEASURE 5cm FROM THE TAIL AND CUT THROUGH BOTH SIDES OF THE FUSELAGE

THEN POP UP THE TAIL

FINISH YOUR PAPER GLIDER WITH COLOUR
USE COLOURED PENCILS OR FELT PENS FOR BEST RESULTS

106

Concord Glider

Another 21.5-by-28-centimetre (8.5-by-11-inch) sheet of paper, a ruler, a ball point pen, and a short piece of scotch tape is all you need. Follow the instructions carefully. This glider will fly loops and circles around the competition.

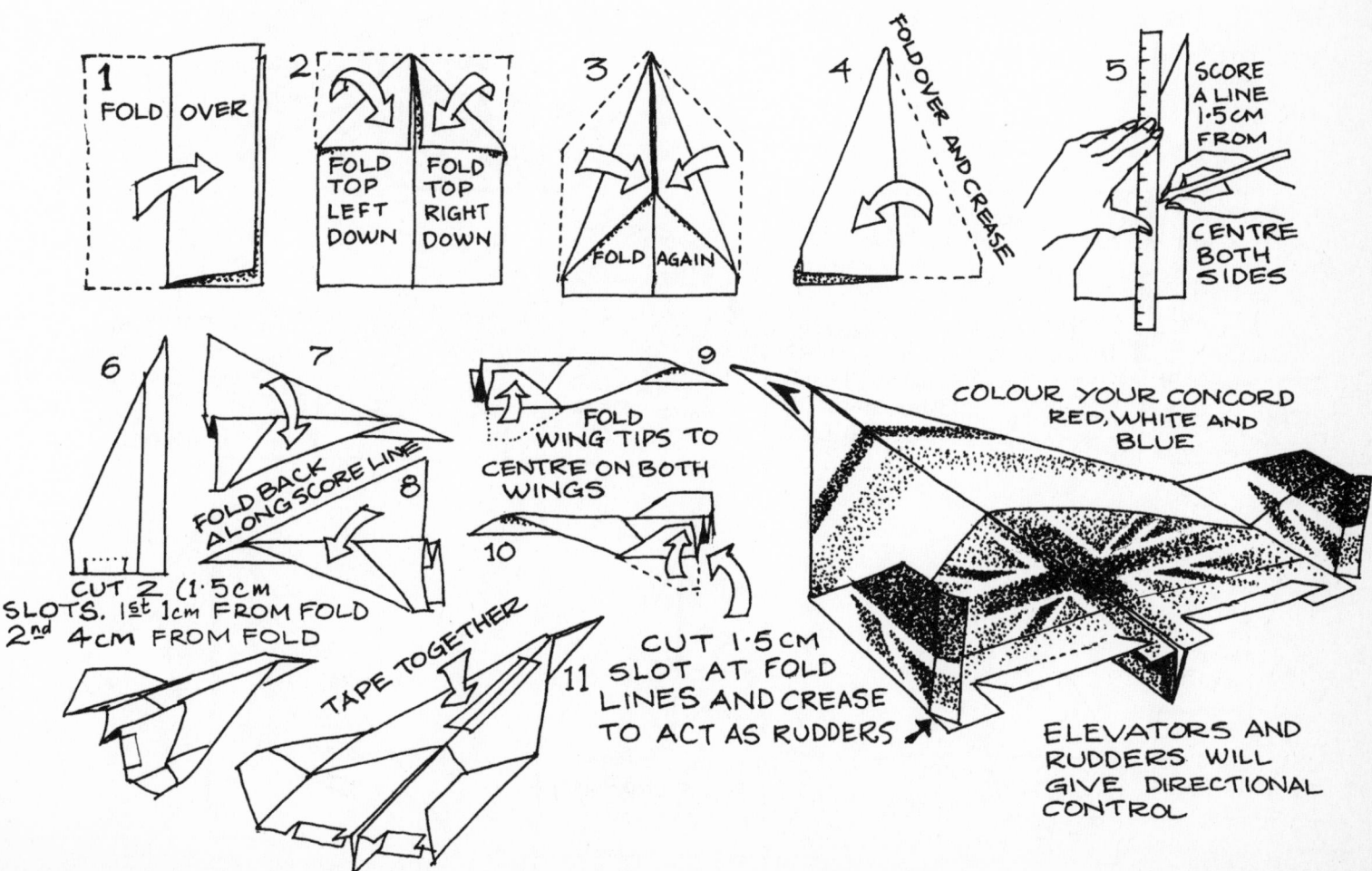

1 FOLD OVER

2 FOLD TOP LEFT DOWN · FOLD TOP RIGHT DOWN

3 FOLD AGAIN

4 FOLD OVER AND CREASE

5 SCORE A LINE 1·5CM FROM CENTRE BOTH SIDES

6

7 FOLD BACK ALONG SCORE LINE

8

CUT 2 (1·5CM SLOTS. 1st 1cm FROM FOLD 2nd 4cm FROM FOLD

9 FOLD WING TIPS TO CENTRE ON BOTH WINGS

10

TAPE TOGETHER

11 CUT 1·5CM SLOT AT FOLD LINES AND CREASE TO ACT AS RUDDERS

COLOUR YOUR CONCORD RED, WHITE AND BLUE

ELEVATORS AND RUDDERS WILL GIVE DIRECTIONAL CONTROL

World's Most Difficult Glider

Follow the instructions carefully for aerobatic competition using the box layout on page 111. You start with a 21.5-by-28-centimetre (8.5-by-11-inch) sheet of paper. Follow the instructions carefully and make sure all the folds are exact and well pressed down.

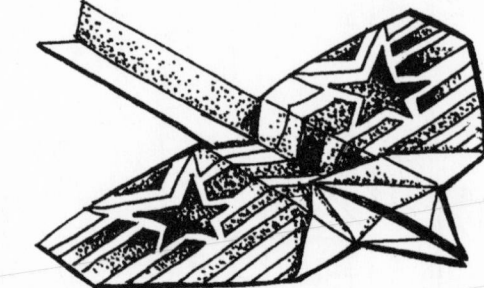

1 FOLD

TOP LEFT OVER AND CREASE

2 FOLD

TOP RIGHT OVER AND CREASE

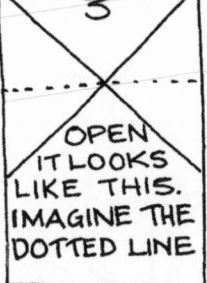
3 OPEN IT LOOKS LIKE THIS. IMAGINE THE DOTTED LINE

4 AND FOLD OVER ON THE DOTTED LINE AWAY FROM YOU

5 OPEN AGAIN AND FOLD BOTH SIDES TO THE CENTRE

6 PRESS THE TOP DOWN TO MAKE THIS SHAPE

7 FOLD BOTTOM LOOSE CORNERS UP TO THE TOP

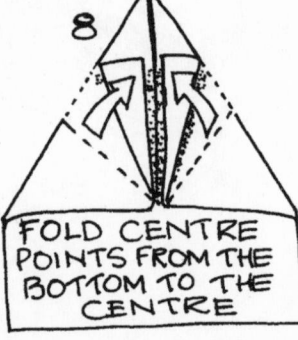
8 FOLD CENTRE POINTS FROM THE BOTTOM TO THE CENTRE

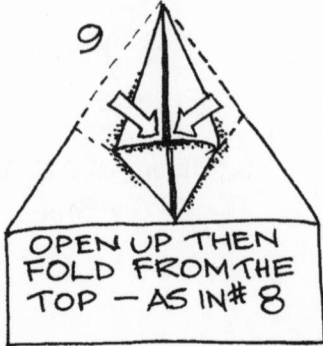
9 OPEN UP THEN FOLD FROM THE TOP — AS IN #8

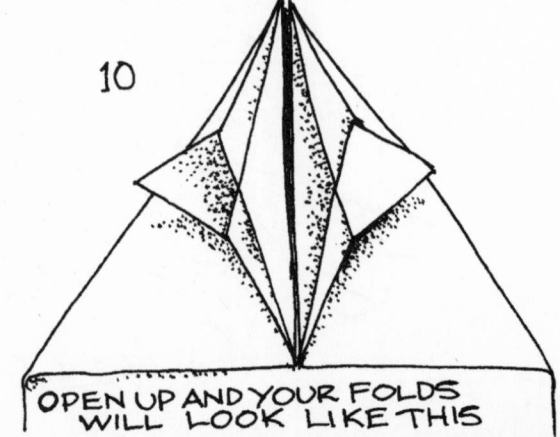
10 OPEN UP AND YOUR FOLDS WILL LOOK LIKE THIS

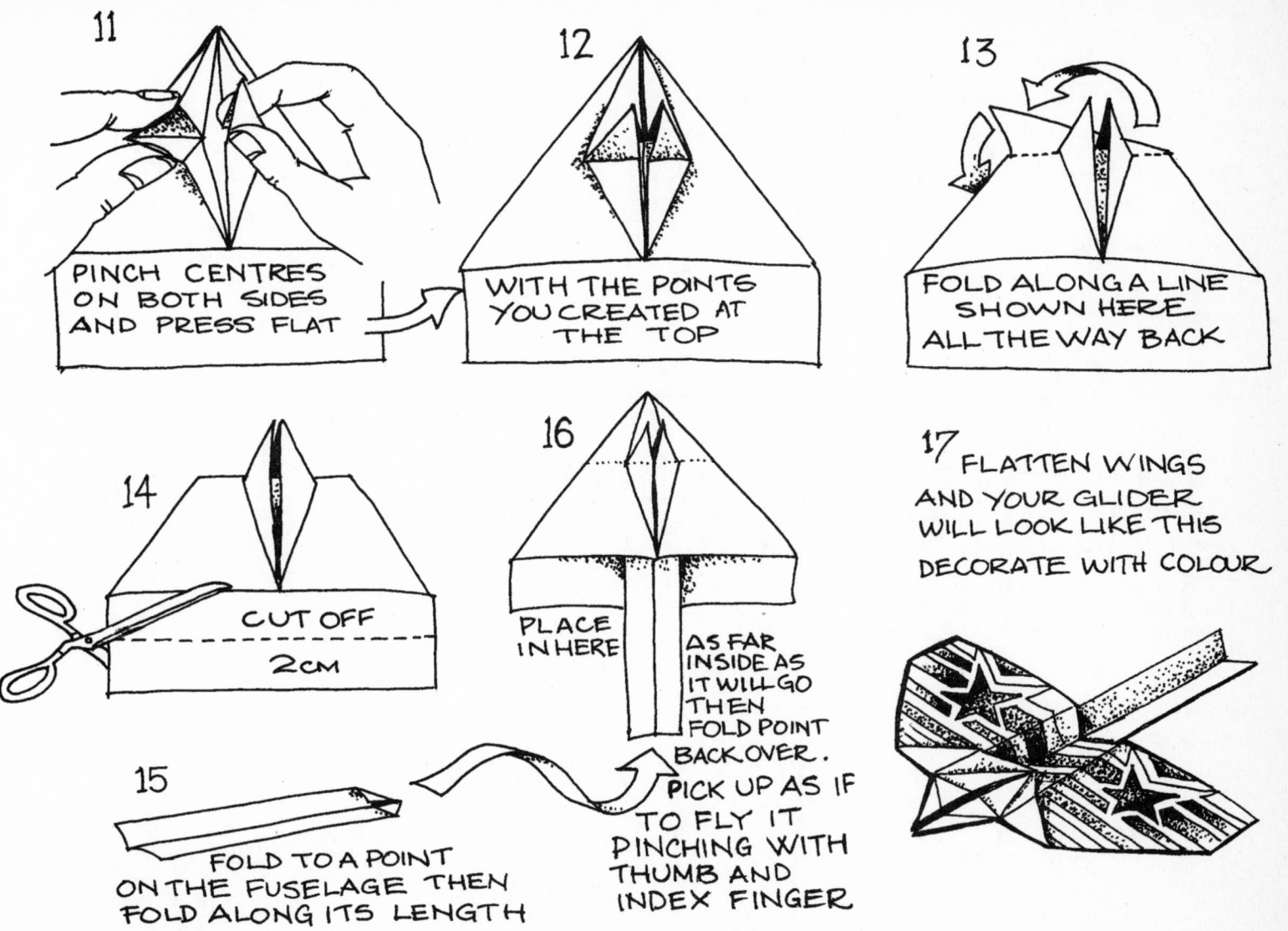

11 PINCH CENTRES ON BOTH SIDES AND PRESS FLAT

12 WITH THE POINTS YOU CREATED AT THE TOP

13 FOLD ALONG A LINE SHOWN HERE ALL THE WAY BACK

14 CUT OFF 2CM

15 FOLD TO A POINT ON THE FUSELAGE THEN FOLD ALONG ITS LENGTH

16 PLACE IN HERE AS FAR INSIDE AS IT WILL GO THEN FOLD POINT BACK OVER. PICK UP AS IF TO FLY IT PINCHING WITH THUMB AND INDEX FINGER

17 FLATTEN WINGS AND YOUR GLIDER WILL LOOK LIKE THIS DECORATE WITH COLOUR

Competition Aerobat

This is a variation of the world's most difficult-to-build glider. With this aircraft you can use your knowledge of control to fly aerobatics. You need a 21.5-by-28-centimetre (8.5-by-11-inch) sheet of paper. To start, cut off 4 centimetres (1.5 inches) from the width of your paper. Then follow the instructions carefully and press down all folds firmly.

CUT OFF 4 cm

FOLD OVER

2cm

CUT OUT

5cm

FOLD OVER

FOLD OVER

FOLD AND CREASE

PUSH IN HERE

FOR NEXT FOLDING SEQUENCES, FOLLOW INSTRUCTIONS FOR PREVIOUS GLIDER #7 THROUGH #13 UNTIL IT LOOKS LIKE THIS. FOLD OVER TAIL SECTIONS

CUT ELEVATORS 1 cm FOR CONTROL

DECORATE WITH COLOUR

Competition Box

The competition box can be chalked onto a paved area or taped onto the floor of an assembly hall or gym with masking tape. Just remember to clean it off after the fun. Either method must be measured and drawn carefully.

Competitions can be for distance, accurate landing, and aerobatics. You can compete as individuals or in teams of up to six pilots. Choose a reliable person to check and keep scores.

The score for each throw is indicated in each section of the box. Scores are added up for each pilot after three throws or for each team after one throw each. To score, the nose of the aircraft has to be inside the score box.

Launch-line two can be used for younger students or on windy days.

Decorate your gliders by individual choice or use a team-color scheme for easy identification.

COMPETITION BOX

MAX SCORE				
20	15	10	9 POINTS	8 POINTS
7 POINTS		6 POINTS		5 POINTS
4 POINTS		3 POINTS		2 POINTS
		1 POINT		

LAUNCH LINE #2

LAUNCH LINE #1

Index

A.V. Rowe Aircraft Company (Avro) 76
Addeman, Spence 76, 78
Aerial Experiment Association (AEA) 20, 22, 27, 36
Aerial League 36, 41, 42, 46, 50, 52, 59
aerobatic 99
aerodynamics 93
Africa Maru 43
aileron 56, 78, 98, 103, 104
Air Board 63, 68
Air Mail 38
airfoil 93, 94, 95
airmail 39, 42, 43
Albemarle Sound 5
Alberta Aviation Hall of Fame 83
Annies 76
Anson 76, 78, 79, 80, 82, 83
Anson Mark V 76
aspect ration 95
Associated Airways 76, 82, 83

Baddeck 20, 22, 27
Baldwin, Frederick "Casey" 20
Balgonie 25
Banff 64
Beacon Hill Park 27
Bell, Alexander Graham 20

Bernoulli, Daniel 91, 92, 94
biplane 101
blind transmission 82
Boeing Aircraft Corporation 43
Boeing, Bill 43
Boeing C3 43
Bowness Park 63
Bras d'Or Lake, Nova Scotia 22
Brown, Lieutenant H. 42

Caley, Sir George 89
Calgary 33, 39, 59, 61, 62, 64
Canadian Air Board 68
Canadian Air Force 68
Canadian Airplanes Limited 36
Canadian Department of Transport (DOT) 79, 83
Canadian Pacific Railway 59, 64
canard 101
Chanute, Octave 4
chine wings 100
Chipewyan Lake 76, 78
chord 95, 96, 104
Christina Lake 52, 53
constant chord 99
Coquihalla Pass 73
Cranbrook 53, 55

Crawford Pass 59

Creston 53

cross-feed valve 80

Currie, Jock 83

Curtiss planes 36, 38, 39, 41, 42, 46, 49, 57, 64, 68, 70

Curtiss Aircraft Company 36, 47

Curtiss, Glenn 20, 24, 36

da Vinci, Leonardo 89

Danes, Maury 78, 80, 82

Daniels, John 17, 18

Dayton, Ohio 4, 5, 9, 15, 18

De Havilland 73

Dean, Mr. 30, 32

De Havilland Dragonfly 76

De Havilland Tiger Moth 76

delta 95

delta wing 100

Department of Transport (DOT) 83

dihedral 102

drag 95

Eckley, Captain Alfred 41, 42

Edmonton 39, 76, 78, 79, 80, 82

elevator 30, 56, 98, 104

Elizabeth City 5, 7

Elk River 27

elliptical wings 100

engine torque 29

Fairey Aviation seaplane 68, 70

flaps 98, 104

flare 104

Fort McMurray 80, 82, 83

Fox, Clara 76, 82

Fox, Tom 76, 78, 79, 80, 83

Fraser Canyon 51

Gibson, William Wallace 24, 25, 26, 27, 29, 30, 32, 33

glider 4, 5, 7, 8, 9, 10, 11, 12, 14, 25, 91

Golden 46, 53, 55, 64, 66

Grand Forks 52, 53, 55

Grant, Locky 26, 27

Greenwood, Edmund 36, 38

gull wing 30

Halifax 68, 70

Hall, Captain Ernest 41, 42

Hammondsport 20, 22, 24

hang-glider 89

Harrier 25

Heath, Flight Engineer 70

Helena, Montana 39

high wing monoplane 102

Hoare, General C.G. 36, 38

Hobbs, Major Basil 68, 70

Hoy, Captain Ernest, 46, 47, 49, 50, 51, 52, 53, 55, 56, 57, 59, 61, 62, 63, 64, 66

Hubbard, Eddie 43

Hudson Bay post 76, 78, 80

Hutchinson, Dan 29, 30

Imperial Airways 76

Jenny 36, 38, 41, 42, 46, 47, 49, 50,
    52, 53, 55, 56, 57, 59, 61, 62, 63, 64, 66
Juan de Fuca Strait 27
June Bug 22

Kamloops 33, 49
Kaulbfleisch, Dr. 26
Kettle River 52
Kill Devil Hills 17
Kisikaw Wawasam 24, 33
Kitty Hawk 5, 8, 9, 10, 11, 12, 14, 15, 18, 20

Laird Looper 39
Lake Union 43
laminar 96
Lansdowne Field 30
Leckie, Colonel Robert 68, 70
Lethbridge 56, 59, 61
lift 94, 95, 99
Lighthall, George 36, 38
Lilienthal, Otto 89
log book 63, 79
longitudinal axis 103
Loon 22
low wing monoplane 102

Mathers, Corporal C. W. 36, 38
Maxim, Hiram 32
McCurdy, John A.D. 20, 22
mid wing monoplane 102

Minoru Park 47
monoplane 101
Mount Tolmie 30
Mount Tuam 41
Multi Plane 32

Norfolk 5

Ottawa 68, 70, 83
Otto Lilienthal 89
OX-5 47, 49, 50, 61, 62

Pathfinder 42
Peace River 80, 82
Peck, Captain Brian 36, 38, 39
Perry, Israel 7
pilot's log 52
pitch 30, 103
prop 14, 15, 80
propeller 12, 14, 15, 29, 30, 49, 50, 52, 55, 62

radial engines 76, 79
Red Wing 20
Revelstoke 64
Rideout, Lieutenant Robert 42
Rocky Mountains 41, 46, 56, 59, 63, 64
Rogers Pass 64
roll 30, 103, 104
Royal Canadian Air Force 46, 76
Royal Flying Corps (RFC) 36, 39, 46, 53
rudder 12, 30, 32, 56, 57, 98, 103, 104
rudder pedals 103

Salt Spring Island 41
Saunders, Ken 83
Seattle 42, 43
Selkirk Mountains 64
Silver Dart 22
skis 76, 80, 82
Sopwith Camel 46
spars 5, 7, 8, 30, 78, 79
Stettler Agriculture Exhibition 24
stick 103, 104
Stinson Flying School 39
Stinson, Katherine 39, 41
Stinson, Marjorie 39
strake wings 100
swept wings 99

tappered wings 99
Tate, William 5, 7, 8, 10, 15
Taylor, Charlie 15
Taylorcraft 78, 80, 82
theory of flight 89, 91
Thompson, George 73
thrust 94
turbulence 51, 52, 56, 59, 83
Twin Plane 30, 32
Tylee, Lieutenant Colonel 72, 73

undercarriage 32
Underwood brothers 22, 23, 24
United States 36

Vancouver, British Columbia 32, 33, 41, 43,
    46, 47, 49, 52, 59, 63, 64, 66, 68, 70, 73
Vernon 51, 52
Victoria, British Columbia   26, 27, 29,
    30, 32, 41, 42, 43, 73

well digging 12
Whidbey Island 42
White Wing 22
Wilson, Captain H.A. 68
wind tunnel 11
wing root 102
wing-loading 78
Winnipeg 68, 70
Wright Brothers 4, 5, 7, 8, 9, 10, 11,
    12, 14, 15, 17, 18, 20, 22, 24, 27, 91
Wright Flyer 17, 18, 20, 27, 101
Wright, Milton 4

yaw 30, 103
yoke 103

Measuring up: Canadian Results of the OECD PISA Study

The Performance of Canada's Youth in Mathematics, Reading, Science and Problem Solving

2003 First Findings for Canadians Aged 15

Authors

Patrick Bussière, *Human Resources and Skills Development Canada*
Fernando Cartwright, *Statistics Canada*
Tamara Knighton, *Statistics Canada*

Special Contributor

Todd Rogers, *University of Alberta*

Published by authority of the Minister responsible for Statistics Canada

December 2004

Catalogue no. 81-590-XPE — No. 2
ISBN 0-660-19397-3
ISSN 1712-5464
Catalogue no. 81-590-XIE — No. 2
ISBN 0-662-38806-2
ISSN 1712-5472

Également offert en français sous le titre : *À la hauteur : Résultats canadiens de l'étude PISA de l'OCDE — La performance des jeunes du Canada en mathématiques, en lecture, en sciences et en résolution de problèmes — Premiers résultats de 2003 pour les Canadiens de 15 ans*

Frequency: Occasional

Ottawa

Human Resources and Skills Development Canada, Council of Ministers of Education, Canada and Statistics Canada

The data interpretations presented in this report are those of the authors and do not necessarily reflect those of the granting agencies or reviewers.

National Library of Canada Canadian Cataloguing in Publication Data

Bussière , Patrick
  The performance of Canada's youth in mathematics, reading, science and problem solving :
2003 first findings for Canadians aged 15

(Measuring up : Canadian results of the OECD PISA study ; no. 2)
Issued also in French under title: La performance des jeunes du
Canada en mathématiques, en lecture, en sciences et en résolution de problèmes : premiers résultats de 2003
pour les canadiens de 15 ans.
Available also on the Internet.
ISBN 0-660-19397-3 (paper)
ISBN 0-662-38806-2 (Internet)
CS81-590-XPE
CS81-590-XIE

1. High school students – Rating of – Canada.
2. Academic achievement – Canada – Statistics.
3. High school students – Rating of – Canada – Statistics.
4. High school students – Rating of – OECD countries – Statistics.
5. Educational evaluation – Canada – Statistics.
6. Programme for International Student Assessment.
I. Bussière, Patrick. II. Cartwright, Fernando – III. Knighton, Tamara – IV. Rogers, W. Todd –
V. Statistics Canada. II. Canada. Human Resources and Skills Development Canada. –
VI. Council of Ministers of Education (Canada) – VII. Series.

LB3054.C3 B87 2004   373.126'2'0971
C2004-988006-3

Acknowledgements

We would like to thank the students, parents, teachers and principals who gave of their time to participate in the 2003 OECD PISA study and the Youth in Transition Survey. The support for this Federal-Provincial collaborative project provided by members of the PISA-YITS Steering Committee and by the coordinators in each participating Ministry or Department of Education during all steps of the study is gratefully acknowledged. The dedication of the survey development, implementation, processing and methodology teams was essential to the project's success and is appreciated.

This publication was prepared jointly by Statistics Canada, Human Resources and Skills Development Canada and the Council of Ministers of Education, Canada and was supported financially by Human Resources and Skills Development Canada.

The report has benefited from the input and comments of reviewers in provincial Ministries and Departments of Education; the Council of Ministers of Education, Canada; Human Resources and Skills Development Canada and Statistics Canada. A very special thank you is extended to Danielle Baum for her indispensable help in preparing the manuscript for publication. The contribution of editorial, communications, translation and dissemination services staff of Statistics Canada, Human Resources and Skills Development Canada and the Council of Ministers of Education, Canada was essential to the project's success and is appreciated.

Note of Appreciation

Canada owes the success of its statistical system to a long-standing partnership between Statistics Canada, the citizens of Canada, its businesses, governments and other institutions. Accurate and timely statistical information could not be produced without their continued cooperation and goodwill.

Table of contents

Acknowledgements   3

Introduction   9

The Programme for International Student Assessment   9

Why do PISA?   10

Why did Canada participate?   10

What is PISA 2003?   11

Objectives and organization of the report   12

Chapter 1

The performance of Canadian students in mathematics in an international context   13

Defining mathematics   13

Canadian students performed well in mathematics   15

Provincial results   21

Mathematics skill levels   22

Provincial variation in mathematics performance   27

How does the performance of boys and girls compare?   28

Achievement of Canadian students by language of the school system   29

Comparison of mathematics performance in PISA 2003 and PISA 2000   30

Summary   31

Chapter 2

The performance of Canadian students in reading, science and problem solving in an international context   33

Defining reading, science and problem solving   33

Canadian students performed well in reading, science and problem solving   34

Provincial results   38

How does the performance of boys and girls compare?   38

Achievement of Canadian students by language of the school system   39

Comparison of reading and science performance in PISA 2003 and 2000   40

Summary   41

Chapter 3

The relationship between student engagement, student learning, and mathematics performance   43

Engagement in mathematics   43

Mathematics learning strategies and preferences for learning   48

Summary   52

Table of contents

Chapter 4

The relationship between family characteristics, home environment, and mathematics performance 53

Parental education, occupation, and student performance 53

Socio-economic status and student performance 59

Summary 62

Conclusion 63

Appendix A: PISA sampling procedures and response rates 67

Table A1   PISA 2003 school and student response rates 68

Appendix B: Tables 69

Chapter 1

Table B1.1   Estimated average scores and confidence intervals for provinces and countries: COMBINED MATHEMATICS 70

Table B1.2   Estimated average scores and confidence intervals for provinces and countries: MATHEMATICS SPACE AND SHAPE 70

Table B1.3   Estimated average scores and confidence intervals for provinces and countries: MATHEMATICS CHANGE AND RELATIONSHIPS 71

Table B1.4   Estimated average scores and confidence intervals for provinces and countries: MATHEMATICS QUANTITY 71

Table B1.5   Estimated average scores and confidence intervals for provinces and countries: MATHEMATICS UNCERTAINTY 72

Table B1.6   Variation in combined mathematics performance, Canada and the provinces 72

Table B1.7   Percent of students at each level for provinces and countries: COMBINED MATHEMATICS 73

Table B1.8   Gender differences by country and province: COMBINED MATHEMATICS 74

Table B1.9   Gender differences by country and province: MATHEMATICS SPACE AND SHAPE 75

Table B1.10 Gender differences by country and province: MATHEMATICS CHANGE AND RELATIONSHIPS 76

Table B1.11 Gender differences by country and province: MATHEMATICS QUANTITY 77

Table B1.12 Gender differences by country and province; MATHEMATICS UNCERTAINTY 78

Chapter 2

Table B2.1   Estimated average scores and confidence intervals for provinces and countries: READING 79

Table B2.2   Estimated average scores and confidence intervals for provinces and countries: SCIENCE 79

Table B2.3   Estimated average scores and confidence intervals for provinces and countries: PROBLEM SOLVING 80

Table B2.4   Gender differences by country and province: READING 81

Table B2.5   Gender differences by country and province: SCIENCE 82

Table B2.6   Gender differences by country and province: PROBLEM SOLVING 83

Table of contents

Chapter 3

Table B3.1   Average score for indices of student
engagement in mathematics: Canada and the provinces   84

Table B3.2   Difference in mathematics performance between students
with high mathematics engagement compared to students
with low mathematics engagement, Canada and the provinces   85

Table B3.3   Student engagement regression coefficients for females relative to
males controlling for mathematics ability, Canada and the provinces   87

Table B3.4   Average scores on indices of learning strategies and preferences
for learning situations in mathematics, Canada and the provinces   88

Table B3.5   Difference in mathematics performance between students with
high levels of mathematics learning strategies and preferences
for learning compared to students with low levels, Canada and the provinces   90

Table B3.6   Average score for learning strategies and preferences for
learning: low achievers versus high achievers, Canada and the provinces   91

Chapter 4

Table B4.1   Parental educational attainment, Canada and the provinces   93

Table B4.2   Parental education and student performance in mathematics, Canada and the provinces   93

Table B4.3   Distribution of parental education for Canadian students with high and low overall
mathematics performance   94

Table B4.4   Parental educational attainment and occupation, Canada   94

Table B4.5   Parental occupation and student mathematics performance,
Canada and the provinces   95

Table B4.6   School SES and student performance in mathematics in Canada   96

Introduction

The Programme for International Student Assessment

The Programme for International Student Assessment (PISA) is a collaborative effort among member countries of the Organisation for Economic Co-operation and Development (OECD). PISA is designed to provide policy-oriented international indicators of the skills and knowledge of 15-year-old students[1] and sheds light on a range of factors that contribute to successful students, schools, and education systems. PISA measures skills that are generally recognized as key outcomes of the educational process. They are not, however, the only expected outcomes nor are they solely acquired through education. The assessment focuses on young people's ability to use their knowledge and skills to meet real life challenges. These skills are believed to be prerequisites to efficient learning in adulthood and for full participation in society.

PISA has brought significant public and educational attention to international assessment and studies by generating data to enhance the ability of policy makers to make decisions based on evidence. In Canada, PISA is carried out through a partnership consisting of Human Resources and Skills Development Canada, the Council of Ministers of Education Canada, and Statistics Canada.

PISA began in 2000 and focuses on 15-year-olds' capabilities as they near the end of compulsory education. PISA reports on reading literacy, mathematical literacy, and scientific literacy every three years and provides a more detailed look at each domain

in the years when it is the major focus. For example, mathematics was the major domain of PISA in 2003 and as such focused on both overall mathematical literacy and four mathematics sub-domains (*space and shape, change and relationships, quantity, and uncertainty*). Additionally, problem-solving skills were evaluated in PISA 2003. As minor domains in PISA 2003, only single measures of reading and science were available. On the other hand, more detailed information was available on reading and reading sub-domains in 2000 and more information will be available on science and science sub-domains in 2006.

The PISA Assessment Domains

PISA measures three domains: mathematical literacy, reading literacy, and scientific literacy. In addition, PISA 2003 measured problem-solving skills. The domains were defined as follows by international experts who agreed that the emphasis should be placed on functional knowledge and skills that allow active participation in society.

Mathematical literacy (hereafter referred to as mathematics):

An individual's capacity to identify and understand the role that mathematics plays in the world, to make well-founded judgements and to use and engage with mathematics in ways that meet the needs of that individual's life as a constructive, concerned and reflective citizen.

Reading literacy (hereafter referred to as reading):

An individual's capacity to understand, use and reflect on written texts, in order to achieve one's goals, to develop one's knowledge and potential and to participate in society.

Scientific literacy (hereafter referred to as science):

An individual's capacity to use scientific knowledge, to identify questions and to draw evidence-based conclusions in order to understand and help make decisions about the natural world and the changes made to it through human activity.

Problem-solving skills (hereafter referred to as problem solving):

An individual's capacity to use cognitive processes to confront and resolve real, cross-disciplinary situations where the solution path is not immediately obvious and where the literacy domains or curricular areas that might be applicable are not within a single domain of mathematics, science or reading. Education systems play a key role in generating the new supply of skills to meet this demand. The skills acquired by the end of compulsory schooling provide the essential foundation upon which we will develop the human capital needed to meet the economic and social challenges of the future. For more information please refer to the PISA 2003 assessment framework.

Why do PISA?

The skills and knowledge that individuals bring to their jobs, to further studies, and to our society, play an important role in determining our economic success and our overall quality of life. The importance of skills and knowledge is expected to continue to grow. The shift from manufacturing to knowledge and information intensive service industries, advances in communication and production technologies, the wide diffusion of information technologies, falling trade barriers, and the globalization of financial markets and markets for products and services have precipitated changes in the skills the present and future economy requires. These include a rising demand for a strong set of foundation skills upon which further learning builds.

Elementary and secondary education systems play a central role in laying a solid base upon which subsequent knowledge and skills can be developed. Students leaving secondary education without a strong foundation may experience difficulty accessing the postsecondary education system and the labour market and they may benefit less when learning opportunities are presented later in life. Without the tools needed to be effective learners throughout their lives, these individuals, with limited skills, risk economic and social marginalization.

Governments in industrialized countries have devoted large portions of their budgets to provide high quality universal elementary and secondary schooling.

Despite these investments, there is concern among these governments about the relative effectiveness of their education systems. To address these issues, member governments of the Organisation for Economic Co-operation and Development (OECD) developed a common tool to improve their understanding of what makes young people—and education systems as a whole—successful. This tool is the Programme for International Student Assessment (PISA).

Information gathered through PISA enables a thorough comparative analysis of the skill level of students near the end of their compulsory education. PISA also permits exploration of the ways that skills vary across different social and economic groups and the factors that influence the level and distribution of skills within and among countries.

Why did Canada participate?

Canada's participation in the PISA study stems from many of the same concerns as have been expressed by other participating countries. Canada invests significant public resources in the provision of elementary and secondary education. Canadians are concerned about the quality of education provided to their youth by elementary and secondary schools. How can expenditures be directed to achieve higher levels of skills upon which lifelong learning is founded, and to potentially reduce social inequality in life outcomes?

Canada's economy is also evolving rapidly. For the past two decades, the growth rate of knowledge-intensive occupations has been twice that of other occupations.[22]

Even employees in traditional occupations are expected to upgrade their skills to meet the rising demands of new organisational structures and production technologies. Elementary and secondary education systems play a key role in generating the new supply of skills to meet this demand. The skills acquired by the end of compulsory schooling provide individuals with the essential foundation necessary to further develop human capital.

Questions about educational effectiveness can be partly answered with data on the average performance of Canada's youth. However, two other questions can only be answered by examining the distribution of skills: Who are the students at the lowest levels? Do certain groups or regions appear to be at greater risk? These are important questions because, among other things, skill acquisition during compulsory schooling influences access to postsecondary education, eventual success in the labour market, and the effectiveness of continuous, lifelong learning.

What is PISA 2003?

Forty-one countries participated in PISA 2003, including all 30 OECD countries[3]. Between 5,000 and 10,000 students aged 15 from at least 150 schools were typically tested in each country. In Canada, approximately 28,000 15-year-olds from about 1,000 schools participated across the ten provinces[4]. The large Canadian sample was required to produce reliable estimates representative of each province, and for both French and English language school systems in Nova Scotia, New Brunswick, Quebec, Ontario, and Manitoba.

The 2003 PISA assessment was administered in schools, during regular school hours in April and May 2003. This assessment was a paper-and-pencil test lasting a total of two hours. Students also completed a 20-minute student background questionnaire providing information about themselves and their home and a 10-minute questionnaire on information technology and communications, while school principals were asked to complete a 20-minute questionnaire about their schools. As part of PISA, national options could also be implemented. Canada chose to add a 20-minute student questionnaire from the Youth in Transition Survey in order to collect more information on 15-year-olds' school experiences, work activities and relationships with others. Additionally, a 30-minute interview was conducted with parents.

Box 1		

Overview of PISA 2003

	International	Canada
Participating countries/provinces	• 41 countries	• 10 provinces
Population	• Youth aged 15	• Same; youth born in 1987
Number of participating students	• Between 5,000 and 10,000 per country with some exceptions for a total of close to 272,000 students	• Approximately 28,000 students
Domains	• Major: mathematics • Minor: reading, science and problem solving	• Same

Amount of testing time devoted to domains	• 390 minutes of testing material organized into different combinations of test booklets 120 minutes in length
	  • 210 minutes devoted to mathematics
	  • 60 minutes each devoted to reading, science and problem solving
		• Same

Languages in which the test was administered	• 32 languages	• English and French
International assessment	• Two hours of direct skills assessment through mathematics, reading and science, and problem-solving • Twenty minute contextual questionnaire administered to youth • A school questionnaire administered to school principals	• Same
International options	• Ten-minute optional questionnaire on information technology and communications administered to students • Ten-minute optional questionnaire on educational career administered to students	• Ten-minute optional questionnaire on information technology administered to students administered to students
National options	• Grade-based assessment • Other options were undertaken in a limited number of countries	• Twenty-minute questionnaire on school experiences, work activities and relationships with others administered to students • Thirty-minute interview with parents to collect detailed information on youths' school experiences, parental education and occupation, labour market participation and household income

Objectives and organization of the report

This report provides the first pan-Canadian results of the 2003 PISA assessment of mathematics, reading, science, and problem solving. The information is presented at the national and provincial levels in order to complement the information presented in "Learning for Tomorrow's World – First Results from PISA 2003"[5]. Wherever possible, an attempt has been made to put results into context through comparisons to student peers, internationally and within Canada.

Chapter 1 provides information on the relative performance of Canadian 15-year-old students on the 2003 PISA assessment in mathematics. It looks at the average level of performance on the overall mathematics scale as well as the four mathematics sub-domains, the distribution of achievement scores and proficiency levels in mathematics, gender differences, the differences between English-language and French-language school systems, and comparisons with PISA 2000. Chapter 2 presents information on the mean performance of Canadian students in reading, science and problem solving. Chapters 3 and 4 use PISA 2003 data to explore two themes related to mathematics performance. In Chapter 3, the relationship between student engagement in mathematics, student learning and mathematics performance is explored. Chapter 4 examines the impact of student socio-economic background on mathematics performance. Finally, the major findings and opportunities for further study are discussed in the conclusion.

Notes

1. OECD (1999), *Measuring Student Knowledge and Skills: A New Framework for Assessment*, Paris.

2. Lavoie, Marie and Richard, Roy (June 1998). *Employment in the Knowledge-Based Economy: A Growth Accounting Exercise for Canada*, Ottawa: HRDC Applied Research Branch Research Papers Series R-98-8E.

3. OECD countries include Australia, Austria, Belgium, Canada, Czech Republic, Denmark, Finland, France, Germany, Greece, Hungary, Iceland, Ireland, Italy, Japan, Korea, Luxembourg, Mexico, Netherlands, New Zealand, Norway, Poland, Portugal, Slovak Republic, Spain, Sweden, Switzerland, Turkey, United Kingdom, United States. Partner countries include Brazil, Hong Kong-China, Indonesia, Latvia, Liechtenstein, Macao-China, Russian Federation, Serbia and Montenegro (Ser.), Thailand, Tunisia, Uruguay. Although the United Kingdom participated in PISA 2003, technical problems with its sample prevent its results from being discussed here.

4. No data were collected in the three territories and on Indian Reserves.

5 . OECD (2004), *Learning for Tomorrow's World – First results from PISA 2003*, Paris.

Chapter 1

The performance of Canadian students in mathematics in an international context

This chapter compares the Canadian results of the PISA 2003 assessment in terms of average scores and proficiency levels. First, the performance of Canadian 15-year-old students is compared to the performance of 15-year-old students from countries that participated in PISA 2003. Second, the results of students' performance in the ten Canadian provinces are analyzed. This information is followed by a comparison between the performance of boys and the performance of girls in Canada and the provinces. Fourth, the performance of students enrolled in English-language and French-language school systems are compared for the five provinces in which the two groups were sampled separately. Finally, the results of PISA 2003 are compared with those of PISA 2000.

Defining mathematics

Mathematics performance as measured by PISA involves more than the ability to perform arithmetic computations. The assessment items also emphasized mathematical knowledge put to functional use in a variety of situations and contexts. This emphasis is reflected in the PISA definition of mathematics:

> An individual's capacity to identify and understand the role that mathematics plays in the world, to make well-founded judgements and to use and engage with mathematics in ways that meet the needs of that individual's life as a constructive, concerned and reflective citizen.

Mathematics results are presented not only in terms of students' overall mathematics performance but also for four mathematics sub-domains. These sub-domains are defined in terms of four content areas that cover the range of mathematics 15-year-old students need as a foundation for life. The OECD defined the four content areas for mathematics as follows:

- *Space and shape* relates to spatial and geometric phenomena and relationships, drawing on the discipline of geometry. It requires looking for similarities and differences when analysing the components of shapes, recognising shapes in different representations and different dimensions as well as understanding the properties of objects and their relative positions.
- *Change and relationships* involves mathematical manifestations of change as well as functional relationships and dependency among variables. It relates most closely to algebra. Mathematical relationships often take the shape of equations or inequalities, but relationships of a more general nature (*e.g.*, equivalence, divisibility, inclusion) are relevant as well. Relationships are given a variety of different representations, including symbolic, algebraic, graphical, tabular, and geometrical representations. Since different representations may serve different purposes and have different properties, translation between representations is often of key importance in dealing with situations and tasks.
- *Quantity* involves numeric phenomena as well as quantitative relationships and patterns. It relates to the understanding of relative size, the recognition of numerical patterns, and the use of numbers to

represent quantities and quantifiable attributes of real-world objects (counts and measures). Furthermore, *quantity* deals with the processing and understanding of numbers that are represented in various ways. An important aspect of dealing with quantity is also *quantitative reasoning*, which involves number sense, representing numbers, understanding the meaning of operations, mental arithmetic, and estimating. The most common curricular branch of mathematics with which it is associated is arithmetic.

- *Uncertainty* involves probabilistic and statistical phenomena and relationships that become increasingly relevant in the information society. These phenomena are the subject of mathematical study in statistics and probability.

The mathematics scores are expressed on a scale with an average of 500 points for the OECD countries[6] and about two-thirds of the students scoring between 400 and 600 (i.e. a standard deviation of 100).

While PISA is not a test of curriculum, the points on the mathematics scale can be interpreted in the context of the school environment. For example, 26 of the 30 OECD countries that participated in PISA 2003 had a sizable number of 15-year-olds in the sample who were enrolled in at least two different, but consecutive grades. For these 26 countries, the OECD analyses revealed that one additional school year corresponds to an increase of 41 score points on the PISA combined mathematics scale[7]. For Canada, the OECD analyses revealed that one additional school year corresponds to an increase of 53 score points on the combined mathematics scale.

One way to summarize student performance and to compare the relative standing of countries is by examining their average test scores. However, simply ranking countries based on their average scores can be misleading because there is a margin of error associated with each score. This margin of error should be taken into account in order to identify whether differences in average scores exist. See text box 'A note on statistical comparisons'.

A note on statistical comparisons

The averages were computed from the scores of random *samples* of students from each country and not from the *population* of students in each country. Consequently it cannot be said with certainty that a *sample* average has the same value as a *population* average that would have been obtained had all 15-year-old students been assessed. Additionally, a degree of error is associated with the scores describing student skills as these scores are estimated based on student responses to test items. We use a statistic, called the *standard error*, to express the degree of uncertainty associated with sampling error and measurement error. The standard error can be used to construct a *confidence interval*, which provides a means of making inferences about the population means and proportions in a manner that reflects the uncertainty associated with sample estimates. A 95% confidence interval is used in this report and represents a range of plus or minus about two standard errors around the sample average. Using this confidence interval it can be inferred that the population mean or proportion would lie within the confidence interval in 95 out of 100 replications of the measurement, using different samples randomly drawn from the same population.

When comparing scores among countries, provinces, or population subgroups the degree of error in each average should be considered in order to determine if averages are different from each other. Standard errors and confidence intervals may be used as the basis for performing these comparative statistical tests. Such tests can identify, with a known probability, whether there are actual differences in the populations being compared.

For example, when an observed difference is *significant at the 0.05 level*, it implies that the probability is less than 0.05 that the observed difference could have occurred because of sampling and measurement error. When comparing countries and provinces, extensive use is made of this type of test to reduce the likelihood that differences due to sampling and measurement errors will be interpreted as real.

Only statistically significant differences at the 0.05 level are noted in this report, unless otherwise stated. This means that the 95% confidence intervals for the averages being compared do not overlap. Due to rounding error, some non-overlapping confidence intervals share an upper or lower limit. All statistical differences are based on un-rounded data.

Canadian students performed well in mathematics

Overall, Canadian students performed well in mathematics, as illustrated in Figures 1.1 to 1.5. Listed in Table 1.1 are the countries that performed significantly better than Canada or equally as well as Canada on the combined mathematics scale as well as the four mathematics sub-domains. The average scores of students in the remaining countries that took part in PISA 2003 were statistically below that of Canada. Among 41 countries, only two countries performed better than Canada on the combined mathematics scale.

Canadian students also performed well in the mathematics sub-domains (Figure 1.2 to Figure 1.5; Table 1.1). Only one country performed significantly better than Canada in the *uncertainty* sub-domain, while students from two countries performed significantly better than Canadian students in the *quantity*, and *change and relationships* sub-domains. Eight countries performed significantly better than Canadian students in the *space and shape* sub-domain.

Further examination of the performance of Canadian students in the four mathematics sub-domains provides insight into the relative strengths and weaknesses of Canadian students. By comparing Canada's relative performance across the four sub-domains, the results show that the strengths of Canada's 15-year-old students are in the areas of *change and relationships*, *quantity* and *uncertainty*, while their relative weakness is in the area of *space and shape*.

Table 1.1		
Countries performing better than or about the same as Canada		
	Countries performing significantly better* than Canada	Countries performing as well* as Canada
Mathematics – combined scale	Hong Kong-China, Finland	Korea, Netherlands, Liechtenstein, Japan, Belgium, Macao-China, Switzerland
Mathematics – *space and shape*	Hong Kong-China, Japan, Korea, Switzerland, Finland, Liechtenstein, Belgium, Macao-China	Czech Republic, Netherlands, New Zealand, Australia, Austria, Denmark
Mathematics – *change and relationships*	Netherlands, Korea	Finland, Hong Kong-China, Liechtenstein, Japan, Belgium
Mathematics – *quantity*	Finland, Hong Kong-China	Korea, Liechtenstein, Macao-China, Switzerland, Belgium, Netherlands, Czech Republic, Japan
Mathematics – *uncertainty*	Hong Kong-China	Netherlands, Finland, Korea

* Differences in scores are statistically significant only when confidence intervals do not overlap. Countries performing about the same as Canada have a confidence interval that overlaps that of Canada's.

Figure 1.1

Estimated average scores and confidence intervals for provinces and countries: COMBINED MATHEMATICS

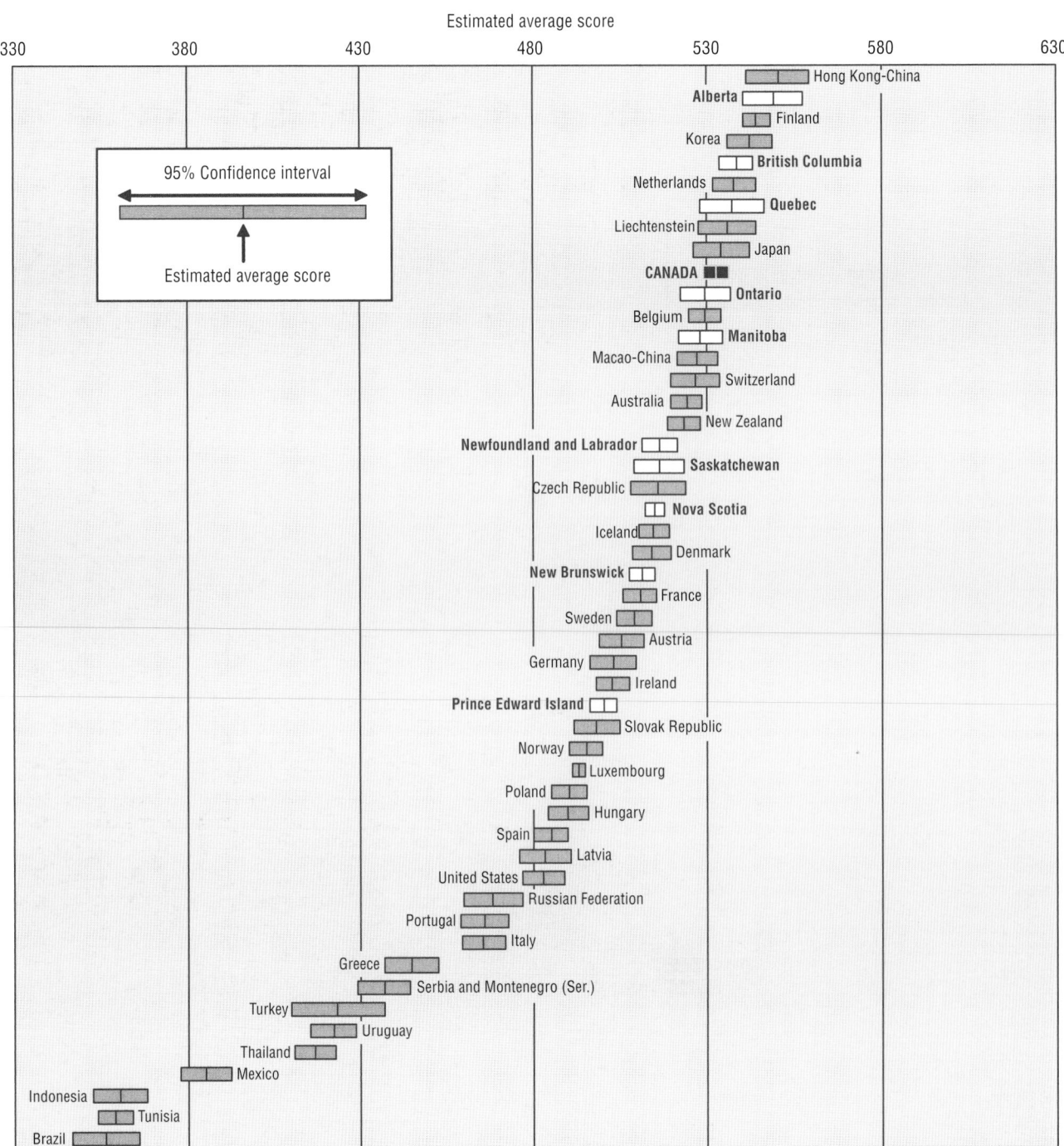

Note: The OECD average is 500 with a standard error of 0.6.

Figure 1.2

Estimated average scores and confidence intervals for provinces and countries:
MATHEMATICS *space and shape*

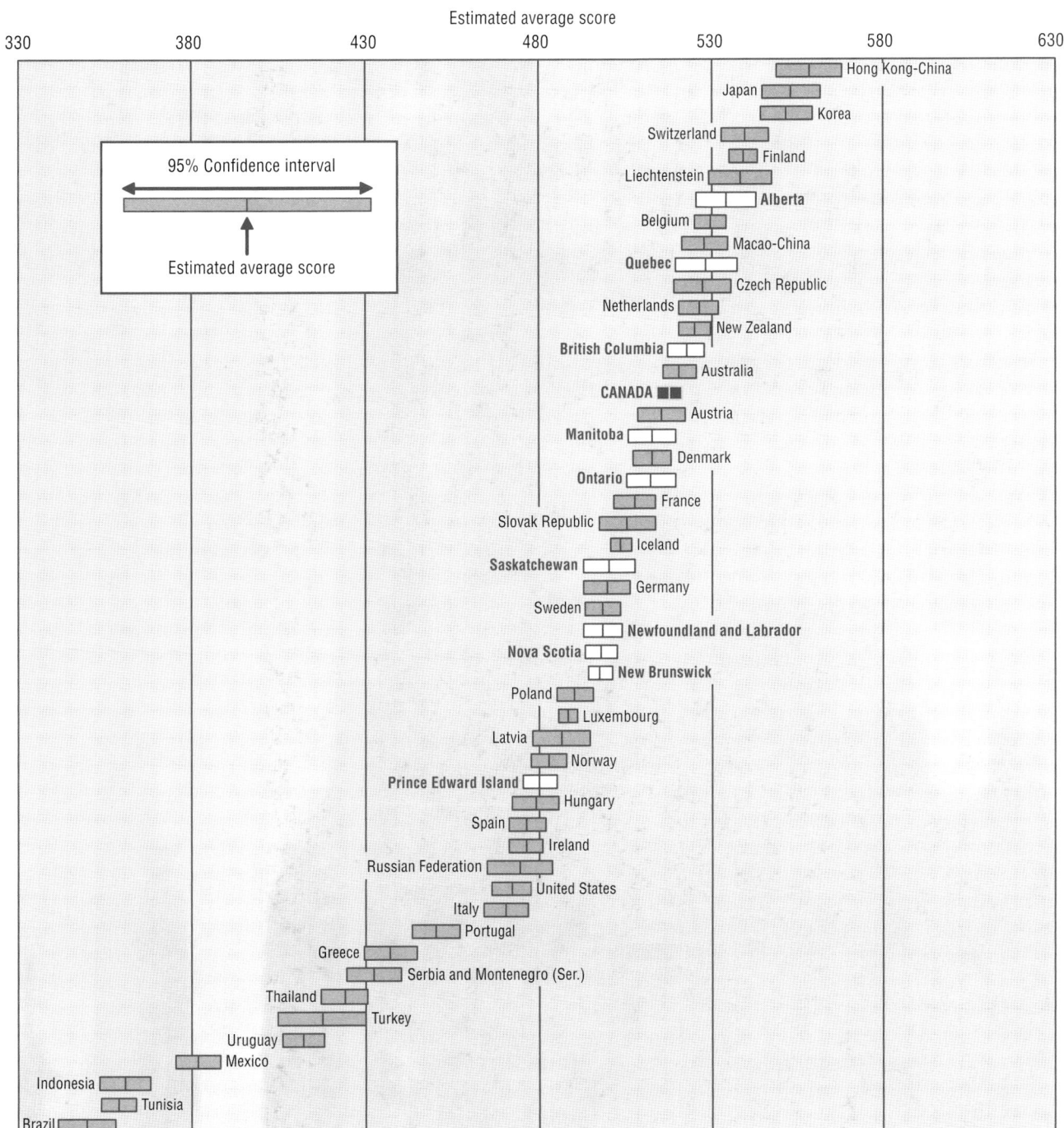

Note: The OECD average is 496 with a standard error of 0.7.

Figure 1.3

Estimated average scores and confidence intervals for provinces and countries: MATHEMATICS *change and relationships*

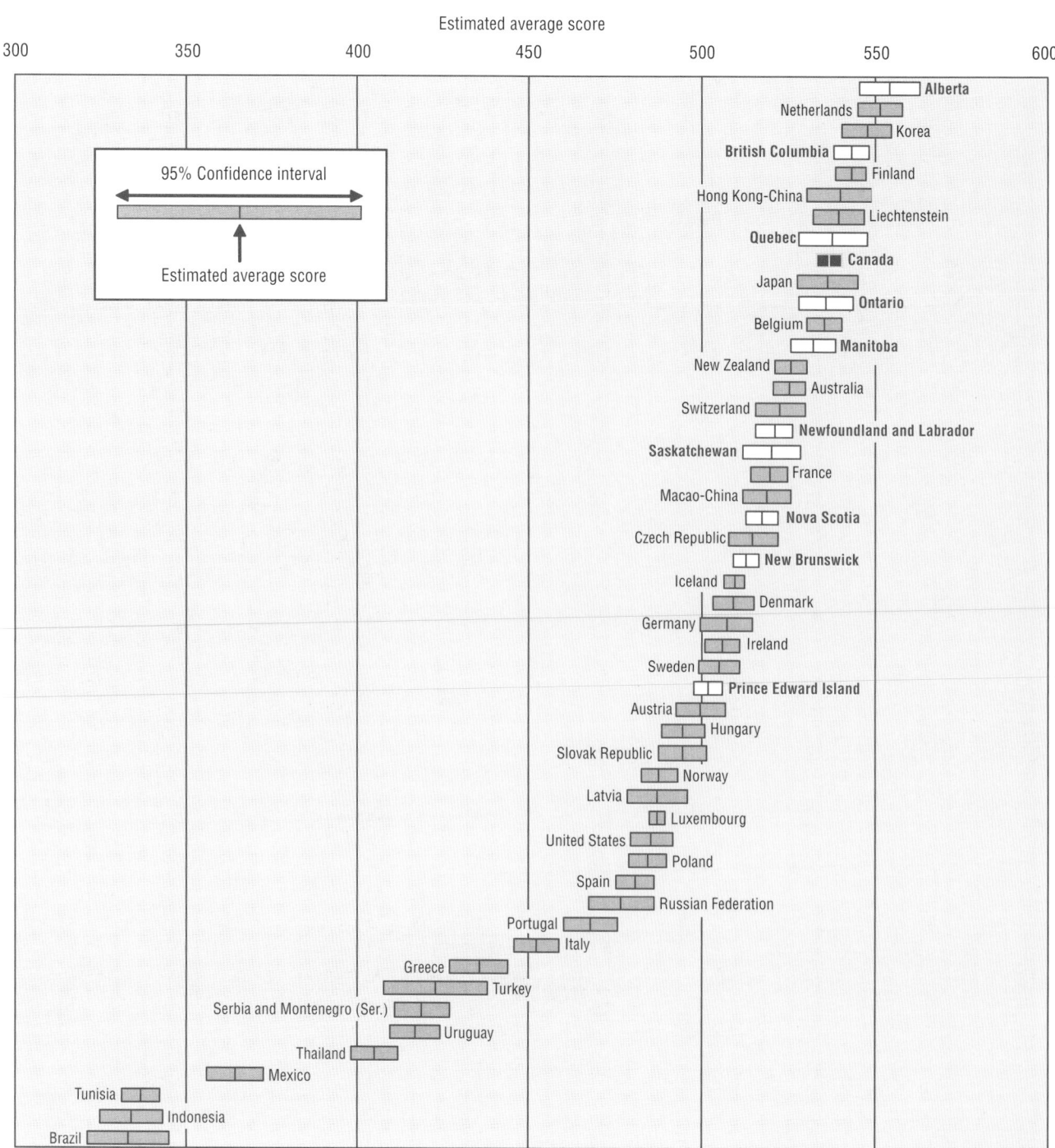

Estimated average score

Note: The OECD average is 499 with a standard error of 0.7.

Figure 1.4

Estimated average scores and confidence intervals for provinces and countries:
MATHEMATICS *quantity*

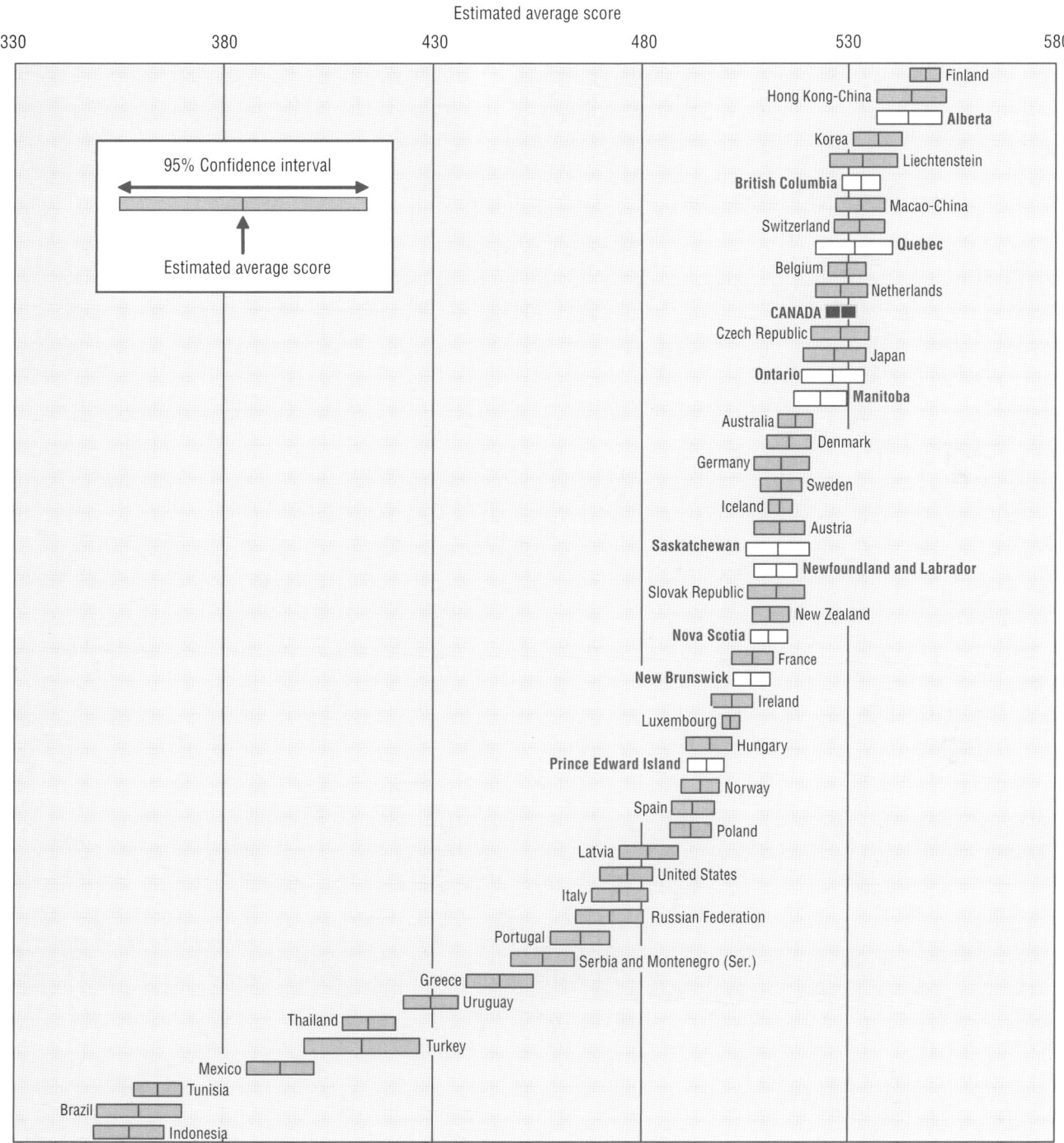

Note: The OECD average is 501 with a standard error of 0.6.

Figure 1.5

Estimated average scores and confidence intervals for provinces and countries:
MATHEMATICS *uncertainty*

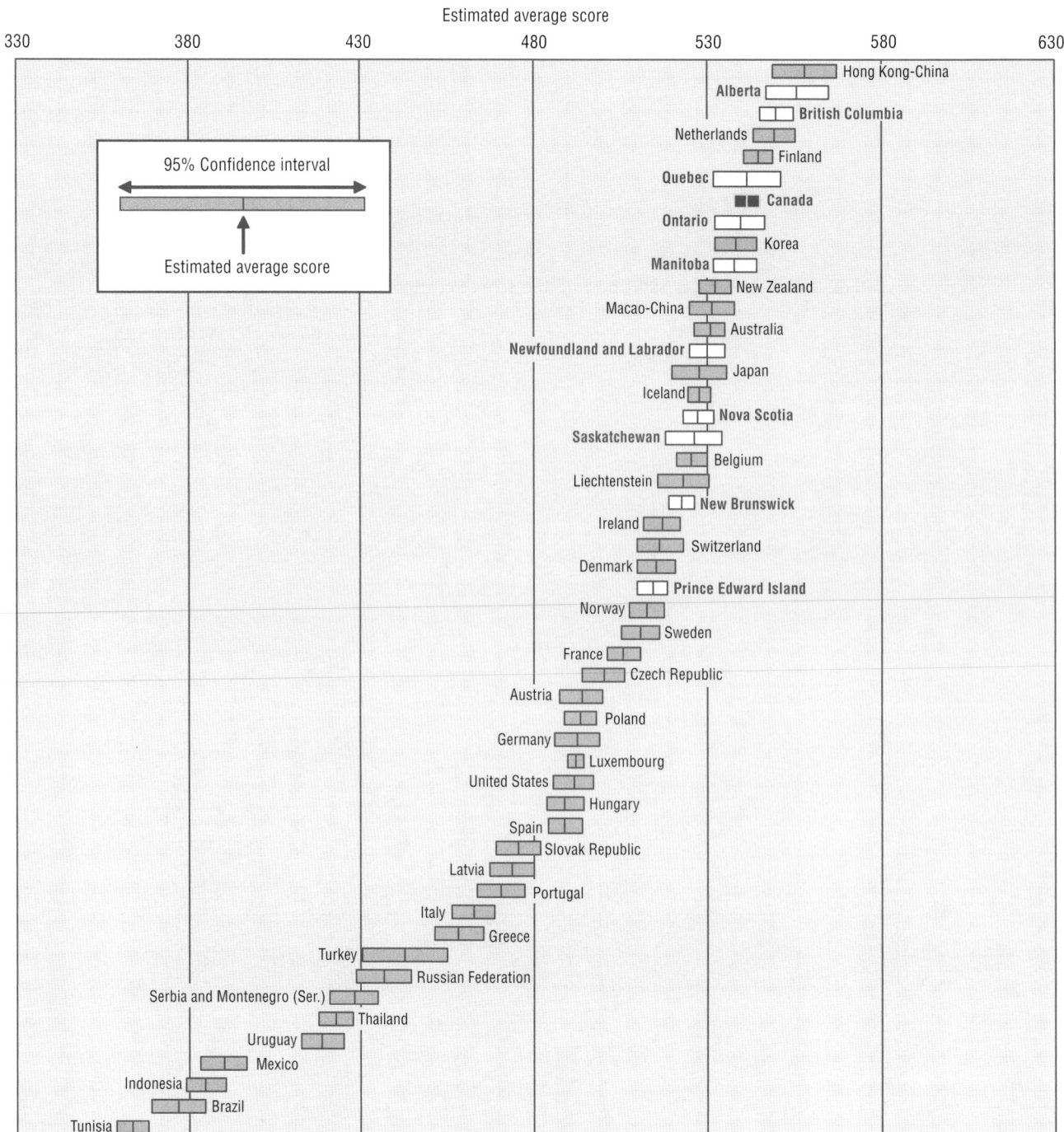

Note: The OECD average is 502 with a standard error of 0.6.

Provincial results

Most provinces performed well in mathematics (Figures 1.1 to 1.5). All provinces performed at or above the OECD mean in the combined mathematics scale and mathematics sub-scale with one exception: Prince Edward Island performed below the OECD mean in the *space and shape* sub-domain. Several provinces performed as well as the top-ranked countries. For example, on the combined mathematics scale the performance of students in Alberta, Quebec and British Columbia compared favourably with the performance of students in Hong Kong-China.

A note on interpreting provincial differences

Although PISA measures skills beyond the school curriculum, most mathematics skills are learned in school. Therefore, students in higher grades may have an advantage in mathematics simply because they have been exposed to more advanced topics. The figure below illustrates the differences in performance between 15-year-old Canadian students in grades 9, 10 and 11 who had not repeated any grades. As expected, the performance of students increased with increasing grade level, although there is substantial overlap among the grades.

Most students born in 1987 were in grade 10 in 2003. However, provincial educational policies on age of enrolment and grade repetition result in differences among the proportions of 15-year-olds enrolled in higher or lower grades. Quebec, for example, has a higher proportion of students from the 1987 cohort in grade 9 than other provinces. Interpretation of provincial differences in performance should consider that this report describes the performance of all 15-year-olds as is the intent of PISA and not the performance of 15-year-olds by grade.

Distribution of overall mathematics score by grade level, Canadian 15-year-olds

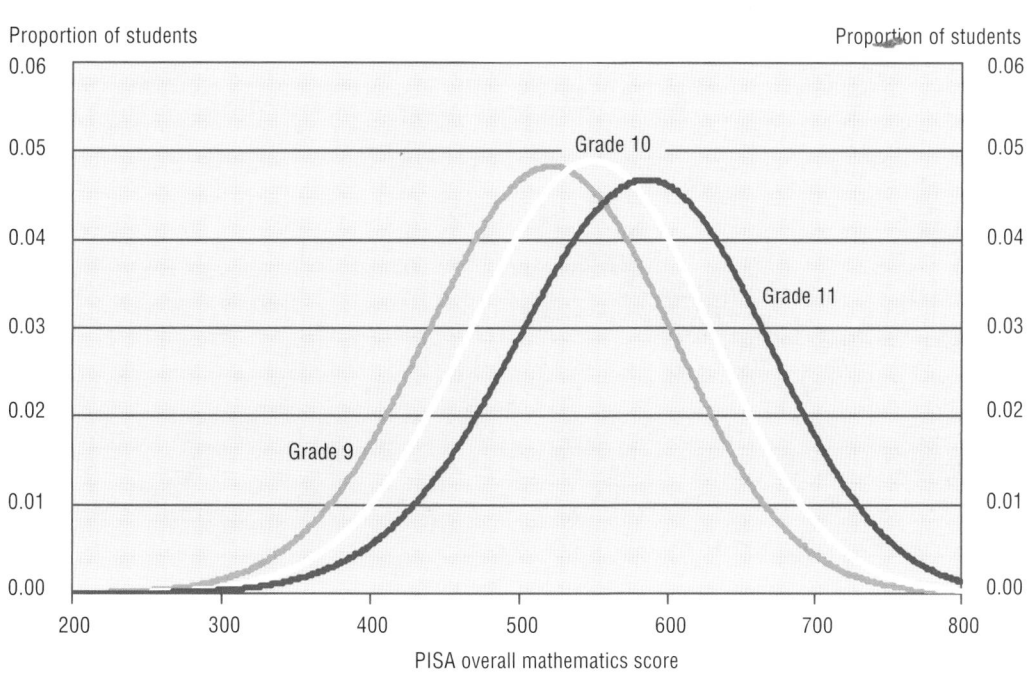

Provinces generally fall into one of three groups when compared to the Canadian averages (Table 1.2). The average performance of students in Alberta was significantly above the Canadian average for combined mathematics and the four mathematics sub-domains. Students in British Columbia, Manitoba, Quebec, and Ontario performed about the same as the Canadian average with one exception: students in British Columbia performed above the Canadian average in *uncertainty*.

Students in Newfoundland and Labrador, Saskatchewan, Nova Scotia, New Brunswick and Prince Edward Island performed significantly lower than the Canadian average across all mathematics scales.

	Table 1.2		

Provincial results in mathematics in relation to the Canadian average

	Provinces performing significantly better* than the Canadian average	Provinces performing as well* as the Canadian average	Provinces performing significantly lower* than the Canadian average
Mathematics – combined scale	Alberta	Quebec, Ontario, Manitoba, British Columbia	Newfoundland and Labrador, Prince Edward Island, Nova Scotia, New Brunswick, Saskatchewan
Mathematics – *space and shape*	Alberta	Quebec, Ontario, Manitoba, British Columbia	Newfoundland and Labrador, Prince Edward Island, Nova Scotia, New Brunswick, Saskatchewan
Mathematics – *change and* relationships	Alberta	Quebec, Ontario, Manitoba, British Columbia	Newfoundland and Labrador, Prince Edward Island, Nova Scotia, New Brunswick, Saskatchewan
Mathematics – *quantity*	Alberta	Quebec, Ontario, Manitoba, British Columbia	Newfoundland and Labrador, Prince Edward Island, Nova Scotia, New Brunswick, Saskatchewan
Mathematics –*uncertainty*	Alberta, British Columbia	Quebec, Ontario, Manitoba	Newfoundland and Labrador, Prince Edward Island, Nova Scotia, New Brunswick, Saskatchewan

* Differences in scores are statistically significant only when confidence intervals do not overlap. Provinces performing about the same as Canada have a confidence interval that overlaps with that of Canada's. Provinces within each cell are ordered from east to west.

Mathematics skill levels

The average scores reported in the previous section provide a useful but limited way of comparing performance of different groups of students. Another way to look at performance is to examine the proportions of students who can accomplish tasks at various proficiency or skill levels. This kind of analysis allows a further breakdown of average scores and an examination of groups of students who show similar abilities. In PISA, mathematics skill is a continuum – that is, mathematics skill is not something a student has or does not have, but rather every 15-year-old shows a certain level of mathematics skill. The mathematics skill or proficiency levels used in PISA 2003 are described in the text box 'Mathematics Proficiency levels'.

Figure 1.6 (based on data from Table B1.7) shows the distribution of students by skill level by country, and includes the Canadian provinces. Results for countries and provinces are presented in descending order according to the proportion of the 15-year-olds who performed at level 2 or higher.

Mathematics proficiency levels

Mathematics achievement was divided into six proficiency levels representing a group of tasks of increasing difficulty, with Level 6 as the highest and Level 1 as the lowest. Students performing below Level 1 (mathematics score below 359) are not able to show routinely the most basic type of knowledge and skills that PISA seeks to measure. Such students have serious difficulties in using mathematical literacy as a tool to advance their knowledge and skills in other areas. Placement at this level does not mean that these students have no mathematics skills. Most of these students are able to correctly complete some of the PISA items. Their pattern of responses to the assessment is such that they would be expected to solve less than half of the tasks from a test composed of only Level 1 items.

In PISA, students were assigned to a proficiency level based on their probability of answering correctly the majority of items in that range of difficulty. A student at a given level could be assumed to be able to correctly answer questions at all lower levels. To help in interpretation, these levels were linked to specific score ranges on the original scale. Below is a description of the abilities associated with each proficiency level. (Source: Organisation for Economic Cooperation and Development, Programme for International Student Assessment, PISA, 2003).

Level 6 (score above 668)

At Level 6 students can conceptualise, generalise, and utilise information based on their investigations, and modelling of complex problem situations. They can link different information sources and representations and flexibly translate among them. Students at this level are capable of advanced mathematical thinking and reasoning. These students can apply this insight and understanding along with a mastery of symbolic and formal mathematical operations and relationships to develop new approaches and strategies for attacking novel situations. Students at this level can formulate and precisely communicate their actions and reflections regarding their findings, interpretations, arguments, and the appropriateness of these to the original situations.

Level 5 (score from 607 to 668)

At Level 5 students can develop and work with models for complex situations, identifying constraints and specifying assumptions. They can select, compare, and evaluate appropriate problem solving strategies for dealing with complex problems related to these models. Students at this level can work strategically using broad, well-developed thinking and reasoning skills, appropriate linked representations, symbolic and formal characterisations, and insight pertaining to these situations. They can reflect on their actions and formulate and communicate their interpretations and reasoning.

Level 4 (score from 545 to 606)

At Level 4 students can work effectively with explicit models for complex concrete situations that may involve constraints or call for making assumptions. They can select and integrate different representations, including symbolic ones, linking them directly to aspects of real-world situations. Students at this level can utilise well-developed skills and reason flexibly, with some insight, in these contexts. They can construct and communicate explanations and arguments based on their interpretations, arguments, and actions.

Level 3 (score from 483 to 544)

At Level 3 students can execute clearly described procedures, including those that require sequential decisions. They can select and apply simple problem-solving strategies. Students at this level can interpret and use representations based on different information sources and reason directly from them. They can develop short communications reporting their interpretations, results, and reasoning.

Level 2 (score from 421 to 482)

At Level 2 students can interpret and recognise situations in contexts that require no more than direct inference. They can extract relevant information from a single source and make use of a single representational mode. Students at this level can employ basic algorithms, formulae, procedures, or conventions. They are capable of direct reasoning and of making literal interpretations of the results.

Level 1 (score from 359 to 420)

At Level 1 students can answer questions involving familiar contexts where all relevant information is present and the questions are clearly defined. They are able to identify information and to carry out routine procedures according to direct instructions in explicit situations. They can perform actions that are obvious and follow immediately from the given stimuli.

Figure 1.6

Percentage of students at each level of proficiency on the combined mathematics scale

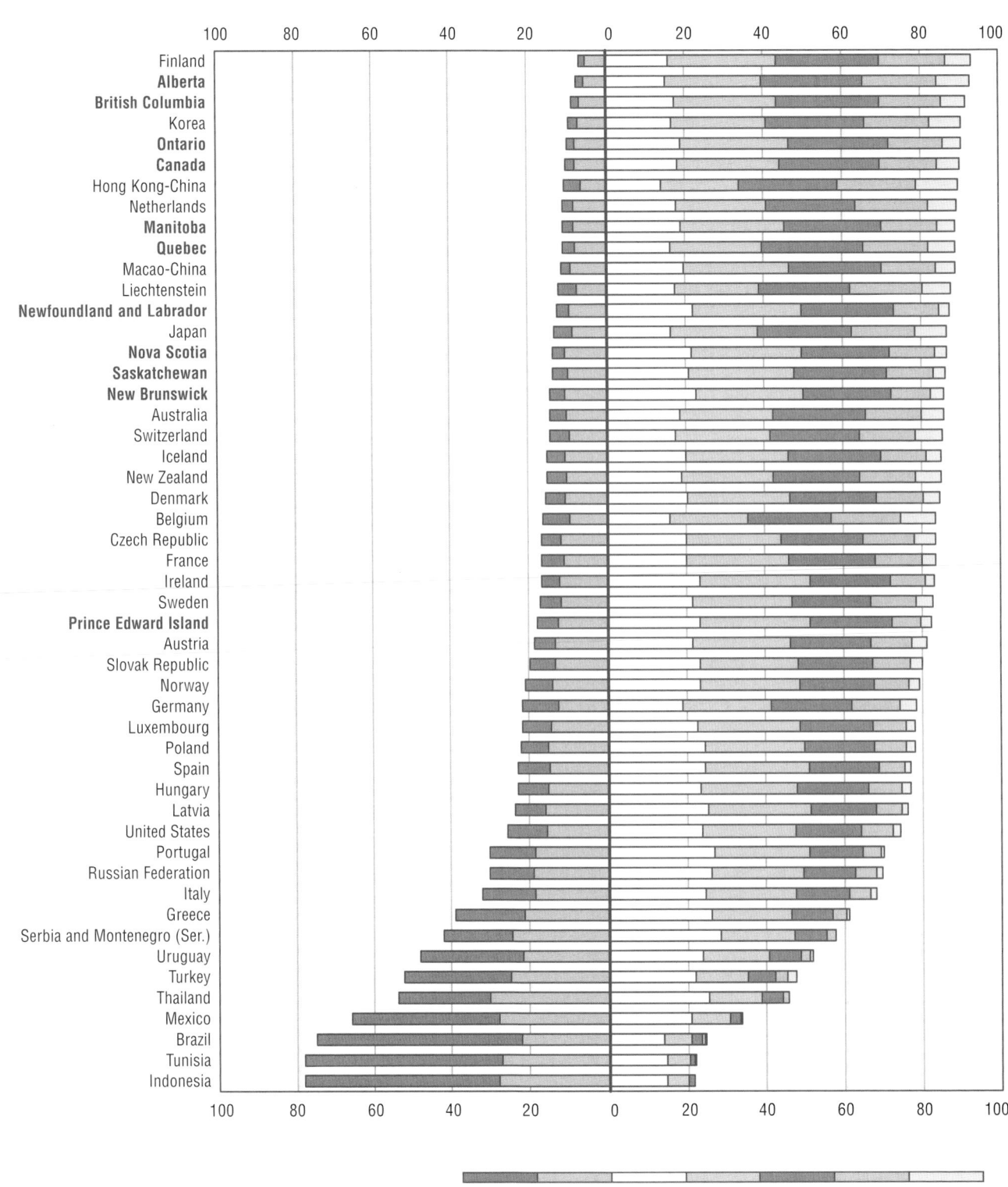

< level 1   Level 1   Level 2   Level 3   Level 4   Level 5   Level 6

Using these proficiency levels, students with very high and very low levels of proficiency can be identified. Listed in Table 1.3 are the percentages of students who performed at Level 1 or below and the percentages of students who performed at Level 5 or above for each country and the ten provinces.

The lower group includes students who would have great difficulty continuing studies in mathematics and in daily life activities involving the application of mathematics skills. In contrast, the students in the upper group are likely to be well qualified to do so.

Compared to the OECD average, a significantly smaller proportion of Canadian students performed at Level 1 or below in mathematics. The Canadian proportion at Level 1 or below was approximately half the proportion of the OECD average (10% versus 21% respectively). Only Finland had a significantly smaller proportion of students at Level 1 or below than Canada.

In contrast, a significantly higher proportion of Canadian students performed at Level 5 or above in mathematics. The OECD average was approximately 15%, five percentage points lower than the average for Canada. Four countries (Hong Kong-China, Belgium, Liechtenstein and the Netherlands) had significantly greater percentages of students with higher skills than Canada.

Turning to the provinces, the percentages of students who performed at Level 1 or below on the combined mathematics scale were, with the exception of New Brunswick and Prince Edward Island, similar to the percentage for Canada. The percentages of students in New Brunswick performing at Level 1 or below (14%) were significantly higher than the Canadian percentage performing at Level 1 or below but lower than the percentage observed for the OECD average. The percentages of students in Prince Edward Island performing at Level 1 or below (18%) were significantly higher than the Canadian percentage performing at Level 1 or below and statistically the same as the percentage observed for the OECD average.

The proportion of students in Alberta at Level 5 or above (27%) was significantly greater than the Canadian percentage (20%). The proportion of students in Quebec, British Columbia, Manitoba, and Ontario who performed at Levels 5 or higher were comparable to the proportion for Canada.

Lower percentages of students in Newfoundland and Labrador, Prince Edward Island, Nova Scotia, New Brunswick and Saskatchewan performed at Level 5 or above compared to the Canadian percentage (Table 1.3). However, with the exception of Prince Edward Island, the provincial percentages were statistically the same as the OECD average.

Table 1.3

Percentage of students with high level skills in mathematics and low level skills in mathematics, by country and province

Percentage of students with low level skills (Level 1 or below)		Percentage of students with high level skills (Level 5 or above)	
Country and province	%	Country and province	%
Finland	7	Hong Kong-China	31
Alberta	7	Alberta	27
British Columbia	9	Belgium	26
Korea	10	Liechtenstein	26
Ontario	10	Netherlands	26
Canada	10	Korea	25
Hong Kong-China	10	Japan	24
Manitoba	11	Quebec	24
Quebec	11	Finland	23
Netherlands	11	British Columbia	22
Macao-China	11	Switzerland	21
Liechtenstein	12	New Zealand	21
Newfoundland and Labrador	13	Canada	20
Japan	13	Australia	20
Nova Scotia	14	Manitoba	19
Saskatchewan	14	Macao-China	19
Australia	14	Czech Republic	18
New Brunswick	14	Ontario	18
Switzerland	15	Germany	16
Iceland	15	Denmark	16
New Zealand	15	Sweden	16
Denmark	15	OECD average	15
Belgium	16	Iceland	15
Czech Republic	17	France	15
France	17	Saskatchewan	15
Ireland	17	Nova Scotia	14
Sweden	17	Austria	14
Prince Edward Island	18	Newfoundland and Labrador	14
Austria	19	New Brunswick	14
Slovak Republic	20	Slovak Republic	13
OECD average	21	Norway	11
Norway	21	Ireland	11
Germany	22	Luxembourg	11
Luxembourg	22	Hungary	11
Poland	22	Prince Edward Island	10
Spain	23	United States	10
Hungary	23	Poland	10
Latvia	24	Latvia	8
United States	26	Spain	8
Portugal	30	Russian Federation	7
Russian Federation	30	Italy	7
Italy	32	Turkey	5
Greece	39	Portugal	5
Serbia and Montenegro (Ser.)	42	Greece	4
Uruguay	48	Uruguay	3
Turkey	52	Serbia and Montenegro (Ser.)	2
Thailand	54	Thailand	2
Mexico	66	Brazil	1
Brazil	75	Mexico	0
Tunisia	78	Indonesia	0
Indonesia	78	Tunisia	0

Percentage significantly higher than the Canadian percentage   Percentage not significantly different from the Canadian percentage   Percentage significantly lower than the Canadian percentage

Provincial variation in mathematics performance

The performance of Canada and the provinces that participated in PISA 2003 was first described in terms of the average performance. This is a measure of central tendency around which the majority of students score. However, as just seen with the proficiency levels, there is variability among the students, and the amount of variability differed by province. The amount of variability can be assessed more directly by examining the variance of the scores. The concept of variance is described in more detail in text box 'A note on variation'. What is important to note here is that the greater the variance, the more variable the performance of the students. When the variance has a small value, there is small variation in performance and the scores of the students are similar. Conversely, when the variance has a large value, there is more variation in performance and the scores of the students differ more widely.

A note on variation

When looking at a group of students on a characteristic such as mathematics performance, it is obvious that not all students have the same test score. In fact, very few people have the same scores. Furthermore, the differences among scores are greater in some populations than in other populations. One statistic used to summarize and describe the differences between members of a population is called *variance.*

The statistical estimate of variance describes the average squared difference between each person's score and the average score. A small estimate of variance indicates that members of the population tend to be similar, while a large estimate of variance indicates that members of populations tend to be different from each other. Sometimes the term *standard deviation* is also used to describe difference between people in a population. The standard deviation is the square root of the variance.

Figure 1.7 shows how much variance there was in student performance in each province relative to the variance in performance for Canada as a whole. The provinces can be divided into three groups based on whether they have more, the same, or less variation in student performance than Canada as a whole.

The first group contains just Quebec, which had the greatest variance among the students' combined mathematics score. The second group contains the provinces with variance similar in value to the variance for Canada: Manitoba, Alberta, Saskatchewan, New Brunswick and Prince Edward Island. The third group contains the provinces in which the variance of the students' scores was less than the variance for Canada: British Columbia, Nova Scotia, Ontario, and Newfoundland and Labrador.

There was not a clear relationship between the rank of provinces based on average performance on the combined mathematics and in the variance of the scores. For example, the performance of students in Alberta and Quebec was above average. However, while the variance among the student scores in Quebec was above the variance for Canada, the variance among student scores in Alberta was the same as the variance for Canada. While British Columbia also had above average performance in mathematics, the variance among the scores was below the variance for Canada.

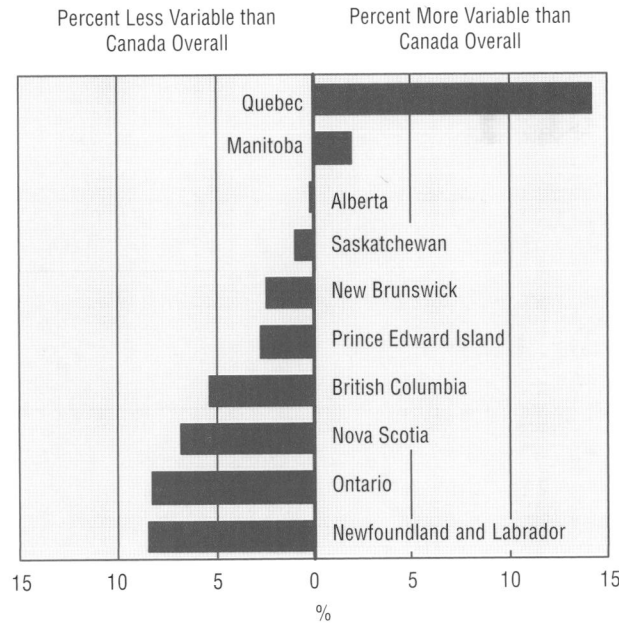

Figure 1.7

Variance in mathematics performance: combined mathematics scale

How does the performance of boys and girls compare?

Parents and policy makers are interested in comparing the performance of boys and girls in mathematics. This issue has been examined in the previous PISA assessment. For example, in PISA 2000 Canada was one of only three countries (France and Germany) where gender differences in mathematics performance were significant[8].

In PISA 2003, boys performed significantly better than girls on the combined mathematics scale in 27 participating countries, including Canada[9]. However, the magnitude of these gender differences was generally small. In Canada, boys outperformed girls by an average of eleven points, which is the same as the OECD average of eleven points (which represents about one-sixth of a proficiency level). No gender differences were observed in 12 countries and in one country (Iceland) girls performed significantly better than boys (Appendix Table B1.8).

As shown in Table 1.4, gender differences were observed in seven of the ten provinces on the combined mathematics scale. Boys performed significantly better than girls in Newfoundland and Labrador, Nova Scotia, New Brunswick, Ontario, Manitoba, Alberta and British Columbia. No significant gender differences were observed in Prince Edward Island, Quebec, or Saskatchewan.

For Canada overall, as well as for many OECD countries, gender differences in mathematics performance were also observed across the four mathematics sub-domains to varying degrees. Gender differences were most pronounced on the *space and shape* scale and least pronounced on the *quantity* scale (Appendix Tables B1.9-B1.12). Canada was one among eleven countries (Denmark, Greece, Ireland, Korea, Luxemburg, New Zealand, Portugal, the Slovak Republic, Macao-China and Tunisia) where gender differences were significant across all four mathematics content areas. However, these gender differences tended to be much smaller than those observed in the area of reading in PISA 2000.

As shown in Table 1.4, gender differences were also observed to varying degrees among the provinces across the four sub-domains. No gender differences were observed among the provinces on *quantity*. On the other hand, boys performed significantly higher than girls across seven provinces in *change and relationships* and across eight provinces in *space and shape* and *uncertainty*.

Table 1.4		
Summary of gender differences for Canada and the provinces		
	Boys performed significantly better* than girls	**No significant differences existed between boys and girls**
Mathematics – combined scale	Canada Newfoundland and Labrador, Nova Scotia, New Brunswick, Ontario, Manitoba, Alberta, British Columbia	Prince Edward Island, Quebec, Saskatchewan
Mathematics – *space and shape*	Canada, Newfoundland and Labrador, Nova Scotia, New Brunswick, Quebec, Ontario, Manitoba, Alberta, British Columbia	Prince, Edward Island, Saskatchewan
Mathematics – *change and relationships*	Canada Newfoundland and Labrador, Nova Scotia, New Brunswick, Ontario, Manitoba, Alberta, British Columbia	Prince Edward Island, Quebec, Saskatchewan
Mathematics – *quantity*	Canada	Newfoundland and Labrador, Prince Edward Island, Nova Scotia, New Brunswick, Quebec, Ontario, Manitoba, Saskatchewan, Alberta, British Columbia
Mathematics – *uncertainty*	Canada Newfoundland and Labrador, Nova Scotia, New Brunswick, Quebec, Ontario, Manitoba, Alberta, British Columbia	Prince Edward Island, Saskatchewan

* Difference is significant when the gender difference gap is significantly different from zero. Provinces within each cell are ordered from east to west.

Achievement of Canadian students by language of the school system

This section examines the mathematics performance of students in the French-language and English-language school systems for the five Canadian provinces in which these populations were separately sampled. The focus is on the performance of the minority group (students in French-language school systems in Nova Scotia, New Brunswick, Ontario, and Manitoba, and on students in the English-language school system in Quebec) relative to the majority group.

Results from PISA 2000 found that, for mathematics, only Ontario had significant differences between the two school systems, with results favouring the English-language school system. The PISA 2003

data confirm this finding (Table 1.5). Students in the English-language school system in Ontario outperformed students in the French-language school system by 26 points on the combined scale. No significant differences in combined mathematics performance were observed between the two school systems in Nova Scotia, New Brunswick, Quebec, and Manitoba.

With respect to mathematics performance in the four mathematics sub-domains, significant differences favouring the English-language school system were observed in Ontario across all mathematics sub-domains. Significant differences favouring the English-language school system were also observed in the *change and relationships* sub-domain in Nova Scotia and New Brunswick and in the *uncertainty* sub-domain in New Brunswick.

Table 1.5

Estimated average mathematics scores by province and language of the school system

	English-language school system		French-language school system	
	Estimated average score	95% confidence interval	Estimated average score	95% confidence interval
Mathematics – combined				
Nova Scotia	515	511-519	500	486-514
New Brunswick	514	511-517	505	499-511
Quebec	541	531-551	536	526-546
Ontario	**531**	524-538	**505**	496-514
Manitoba	528	522-534	522	511-533
Mathematics – *space and shape*				
Nova Scotia	498	493-503	485	468-502
New Brunswick	498	494-502	495	489-501
Quebec	526	516-536	528	519-537
Ontario	**513**	506-520	**491**	481-501
Manitoba	513	506-520	509	495-523
Mathematics – *change and relationships*				
Nova Scotia	**518**	513-523	**497**	482-512
New Brunswick	**516**	513-519	**505**	499-511
Quebec	543	532-554	536	526-546
Ontario	**537**	529-545	**505**	496-514
Manitoba	532	526-538	522	510-534
Mathematics – *quantity*				
Nova Scotia	511	506-516	495	479-511
New Brunswick	509	505-513	500	494-506
Quebec	535	524-546	530	520-540
Ontario	**527**	519-535	**500**	491-509
Manitoba	523	517-529	516	504-528
Mathematics – *uncertainty*				
Nova Scotia	528	524-532	514	500-528
New Brunswick	**527**	524-530	**514**	508-520
Quebec	547	537-557	541	531-551
Ontario	**541**	534-548	**512**	504-520
Manitoba	538	532-544	531	520-542

Note: Statistically significant differences are in bold.

Comparison of mathematics performance in PISA 2003 and PISA 2000

The availability of a third set of PISA assessment results in 2006 will allow for a reasonably reliable estimate of trends in performance over time. Nevertheless, it is still possible to compare PISA 2000 and 2003 results to assess whether performance among 15-year-olds has changed since 2000[10]. However differences should be interpreted with caution for several reasons. While the measurement approach used in PISA is consistent across cycles, small refinements were made. Consequently, small changes in results should be interpreted with care.

Given the differences between the PISA 2000 and 2003 assessment in mathematics in the content areas covered in each assessment, it is not appropriate to compare the overall mathematics scores of 2000 and 2003. However, it is possible to compare change in the two sub-domains – *space and shape*, and *change and relationships* – that were included in both assessments.

For Canada, as for the majority of the 25 OECD countries for which it is possible to make the comparison, there was no significant change in the performance on the *space and shape* sub-domain[11].

In contrast, for Canada as well as across OECD countries on average, performance on the *change and relationships* sub-domain improved[12] and represented the largest overall change observed across all areas of the PISA assessment including reading and science. For the OECD countries with comparable data, the average score increased from 488 points in 2000 to 499 points in 2003. For Canada the average score increased from 520 points to 537 points.

Across the provinces, there was also no significant change in the performance in *the space and shape* sub-domain (Table 1.6). Performance in the *change and relationships* sub-domain improved in Newfoundland and Labrador, New Brunswick, Ontario, Alberta, and British Columbia while performance was not significantly different in Prince Edward Island, Nova Scotia, Quebec, Manitoba, and Saskatchewan.

Table 1.6

Comparison of average performance in mathematics PISA 2003 and PISA 2000

	PISA 2000		PISA 2003	
	Estimated average score	95% confidence interval	Estimated average score	95% confidence interval
Mathematics – *space and shape*				
Newfoundland and Labrador	489	482-496	498	485-511
Prince Edward Island	500	492-508	480	467-493
Nova Scotia	498	491-505	498	485-510
New Brunswick	497	490-504	498	485-510
Quebec	536	531-541	528	514-543
Ontario	504	498-510	512	499-526
Manitoba	517	507-527	513	499-526
Saskatchewan	507	500-514	500	486-514
Alberta	523	516-530	534	520-549
British Columbia	519	513-525	523	510-535
Canada	515	512-518	518	505-530
Mathematics – *change and relationships*				
Newfoundland and Labrador	**497**	491-503	**521**	510-531
Prince Edward Island	506	499-513	502	492-512
Nova Scotia	505	500-510	517	507-528
New Brunswick	**497**	492-502	**513**	503-524
Quebec	529	524-534	538	524-551
Ontario	**513**	508-518	**536**	524-548
Manitoba	523	515-531	532	521-544
Saskatchewan	517	511-523	520	508-532
Alberta	**533**	527-539	**554**	542-567
British Columbia	**525**	519-531	**543**	532-554
Canada	**520**	517-523	**537**	526-547

Note: The 2003 confidence interval includes a linking error associated with the uncertainty that results from making comparisons with PISA 2000 (see endnote 10). Statistically significant differences are in bold.

Summary

In an increasingly technical world, mathematics is key to many areas of activity both inside and outside of school. Canada's performance in PISA 2003 suggests that, on the whole, Canadian 15-year-olds will have the skills and knowledge to participate in today's knowledge-based economy and will have a strong foundation upon which to continue with learning throughout life. However, while Canada's performance in PISA overall was good, the existence of disparities among provinces, and disparities among some students within some provinces warrants further analysis.

While the comparative approach taken in this chapter does not lend itself to developing explanations for these disparities, the PISA dataset along with other data available will allow an in-depth exploration of how resources, schools and classroom conditions, as well as individual and family circumstances, affect variation in achievement.

Factors that influence mathematics performance are complex and varied and these detailed relationships should be the focus of future research using the PISA data. However, two themes related to mathematics performance will be explored in Chapter 3 and 4 of this report.

Notes

6. The OECD average for the combined mathematics score was established with the data weighted so that each OECD country contributed equally. As the anchoring of the scale was done for the combination of the four sub-domain scales, the average mean and standard deviation for the sub-domain scales differ from 500 and 100 score points.

7. OECD (2004), *Learning for Tomorrow's World – First results from PISA 2003*, Paris.

8. It should be noted, however, that only two mathematics content areas were included in the 2000 assessment. The fact that gender differences were not observable does not mean that they do not exist in other countries but rather that the PISA 2000 design may not have been sensitive enough to detect them reliably.

9. OECD (2004), *Learning for Tomorrow's World – First results from PISA 2003*, Paris.

10. Please refer to Annex A8 of the OECD (2004) *Learning for Tomorrow's World – First results from PISA 2003* for an explanation of the methods used to establish the link between the PISA 2000 and 2003 assessment.

11. OECD (2004), *Learning for Tomorrow's World – First results from PISA 2003*, Paris.

12. OECD (2004), *Learning for Tomorrow's World – First results from PISA 2003*, Paris.

© SchoolNet, Industry Canada

© SchoolNet, Industry Canada

Chapter 2

The performance of Canadian students in reading, science and problem solving in an international context

This chapter presents the overall results of the PISA 2003 assessments in the minor domains of reading, science and problem solving. Assessment in these minor domains was not as detailed as the mathematics assessment, which was the major focus of PISA 2003. Consequently, this chapter focuses on providing an update on overall performance in these three domains. First, the average performance of Canadian 15-year-old students is compared to the performance of 15-year-old students from countries that participated in PISA 2003. Second, students' performance in the ten Canadian provinces are presented and discussed. Third, this is followed by a comparison between the performance of boys and girls in Canada and the provinces. Fourth, the performance of students enrolled in English-language and French-language school systems are compared for the five provinces in which the two groups were separately sampled. Lastly, the results of PISA 2003 are compared with those of PISA 2000 for reading and science. A similar comparison is not possible for problem solving since this area was assessed for the first time in 2003.

Defining reading, science and problem solving

Both reading and science were minor domains in PISA 2003. On the other hand, reading was the major domain of PISA 2000 while science will be the major domain in

PISA 2006. Additionally, problem solving, a new minor assessment domain in PISA 2003, was introduced to complement the assessment of the more academic domains. Reading, science and problem solving were defined as follows by international experts who agreed that the emphasis should be placed on functional knowledge and skills that allow active participation in society.

Reading literacy (hereafter referred to as reading):

> An individual's capacity to understand, use and reflect on written texts in order to achieve one's goals, to develop one's knowledge and potential, and to participate in society;

Scientific literacy (hereafter referred to as science):

> An individual's capacity to use scientific knowledge, to identify questions, and to draw evidence-based conclusions in order to understand and help make decisions about the natural world and the changes made to it through human activity;

Problem-solving skills (hereafter referred to as problem solving):

> An individual's capacity to use cognitive processes to confront and resolve real, cross-disciplinary situations where the solution path is not immediately obvious and where the literacy domains or curricular

areas that might be applicable are not within a single domain of mathematics, science, or reading.

For PISA, the scores for reading[13], science, and problem solving are expressed on a scale with an average or mean of 500 points and a standard deviation of 100. Approximately two-thirds of the students scored between 400 and 600 (i.e. within one standard deviation of the average) for the OECD countries.

Canadian students performed well in reading, science and problem solving

One way to summarize student performance, and to compare the relative standing of countries is by examining their average test scores. However, simply ranking

countries based on their average scores can be misleading because there is a margin of error associated with each score. As discussed in Chapter 1, when interpreting average performances, only those differences between countries that are statistically significant should be taken into account. Table 2.1 shows the countries that performed significantly better than or the same as Canada in reading, science and problem solving. The averages of the students in all of the remaining countries were significantly below those of Canada. Overall, Canadian students performed well. Among the 41 countries that participated in PISA 2003, only Finland performed better than Canada in reading, and four countries performed better than Canada in science and problem solving.

Table 2.1

Countries performing better than, or the same as Canada

	Countries performing significantly better* than Canada	Countries performing the same* as Canada
Reading	Finland	Korea, Australia, Liechtenstein, New Zealand
Science	Finland, Japan, Hong Kong-China, Korea	Liechtenstein, Australia, Macao-China, Netherlands, Czech Republic, New Zealand, Switzerland, France
Problem Solving	Korea, Hong Kong-China, Finland, Japan	New Zealand, Macao-China, Australia, Liechtenstein, Belgium, Switzerland, Netherlands

* Differences in scores are statistically significant only when confidence intervals do not overlap. Countries performing about the same as Canada have a confidence interval that overlaps that of Canada.

Results of PISA 2003 in reading confirm the findings that were observed in 2000 when reading was the major emphasis (Figure 2.1). Canadian 15-year-olds continue to perform very well in reading: the overall achievement of Canadian students was significantly above the OECD average and only students in Finland outperformed Canadian students.

The performance of Canadian 15-year-olds in science and problem solving was also significantly above the OECD average (Figures 2.2 and 2.3). However, relative to Canada's position in mathematics and reading, Canadian students did not perform as strongly in these two domains. Four countries performed significantly better than Canada in both science and problem solving. Eight countries performed as well as Canada in science and seven countries performed as well as Canada in problem solving.

Figure 2.1

Estimated average scores and confidence intervals for provinces and countries: READING

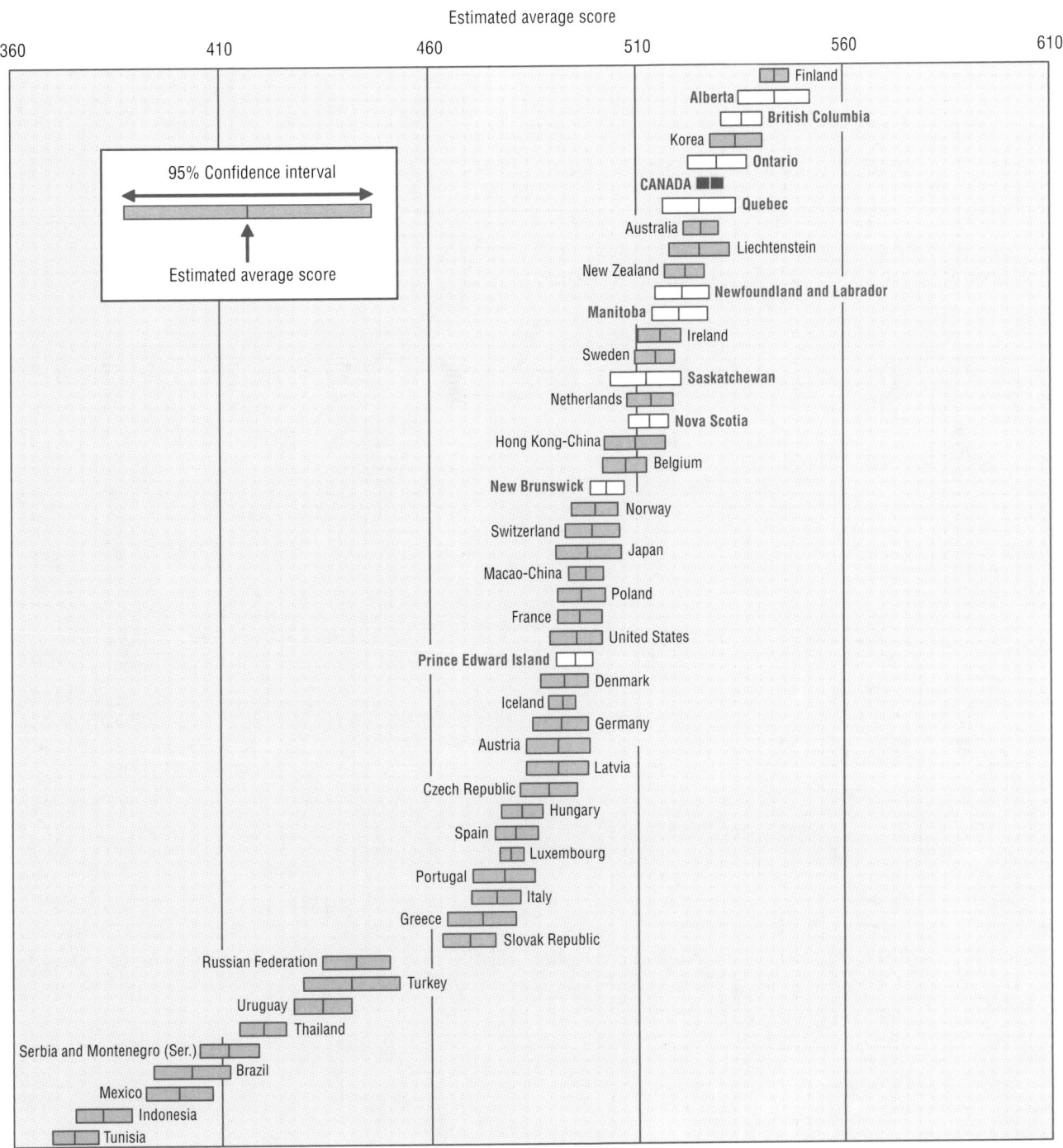

Note: The reading results for 2003 are based on the reading literacy proficiency scale that was developed for PISA 2000 which had a mean of 500 for the 27 countries that participated in PISA 2000. However, because three additional OECD countries are included in the PISA 2003 reading test, the overall OECD mean for PISA 2003 is 494 with a standard error of 0.6.

Figure 2.2

Estimated average scores and confidence intervals for provinces and countries: SCIENCE

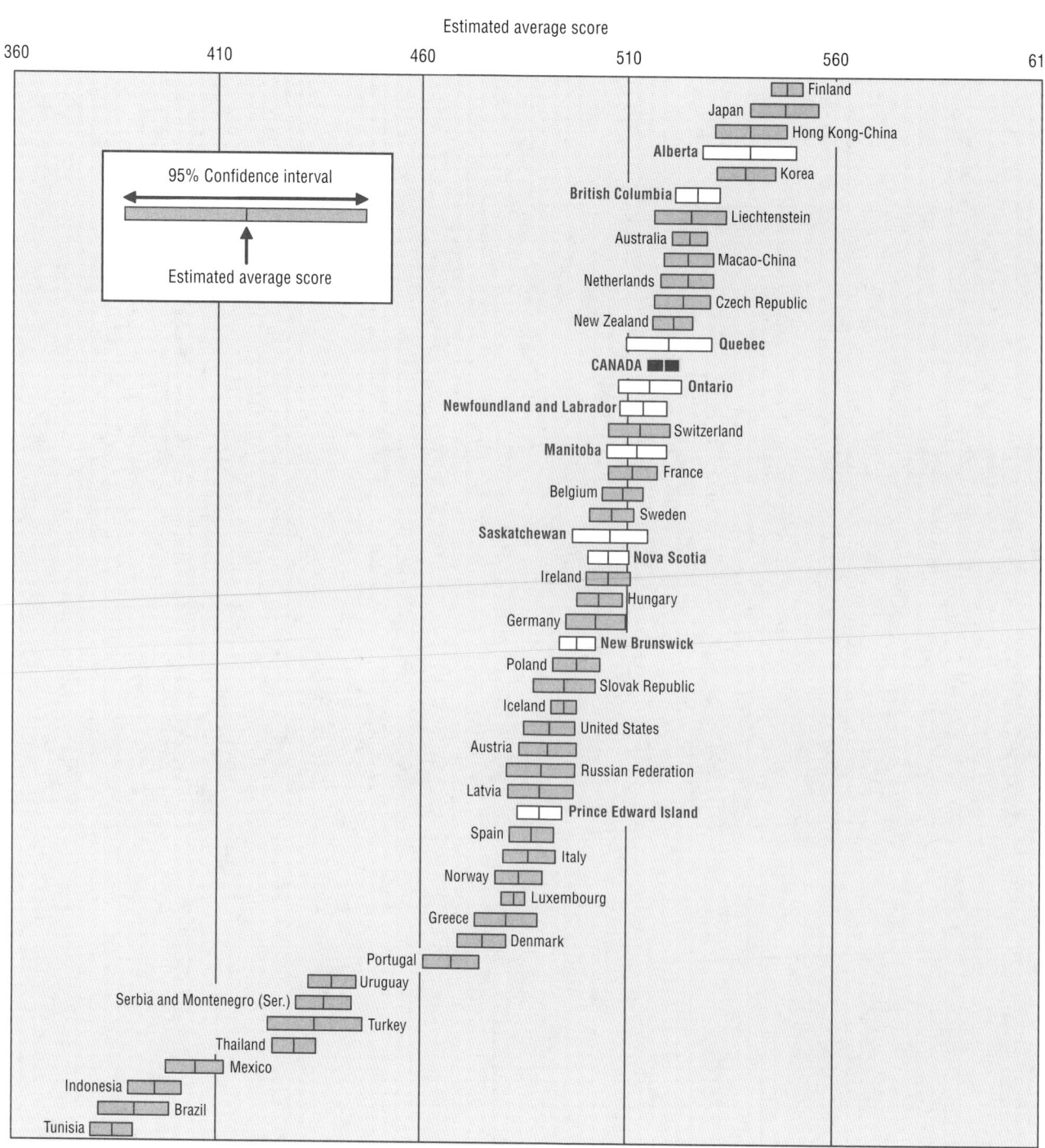

Note: The OECD mean is 500 with a standard error of 0.6.

Figure 2.3

Estimated average scores and confidence intervals for provinces and countries: PROBLEM SOLVING

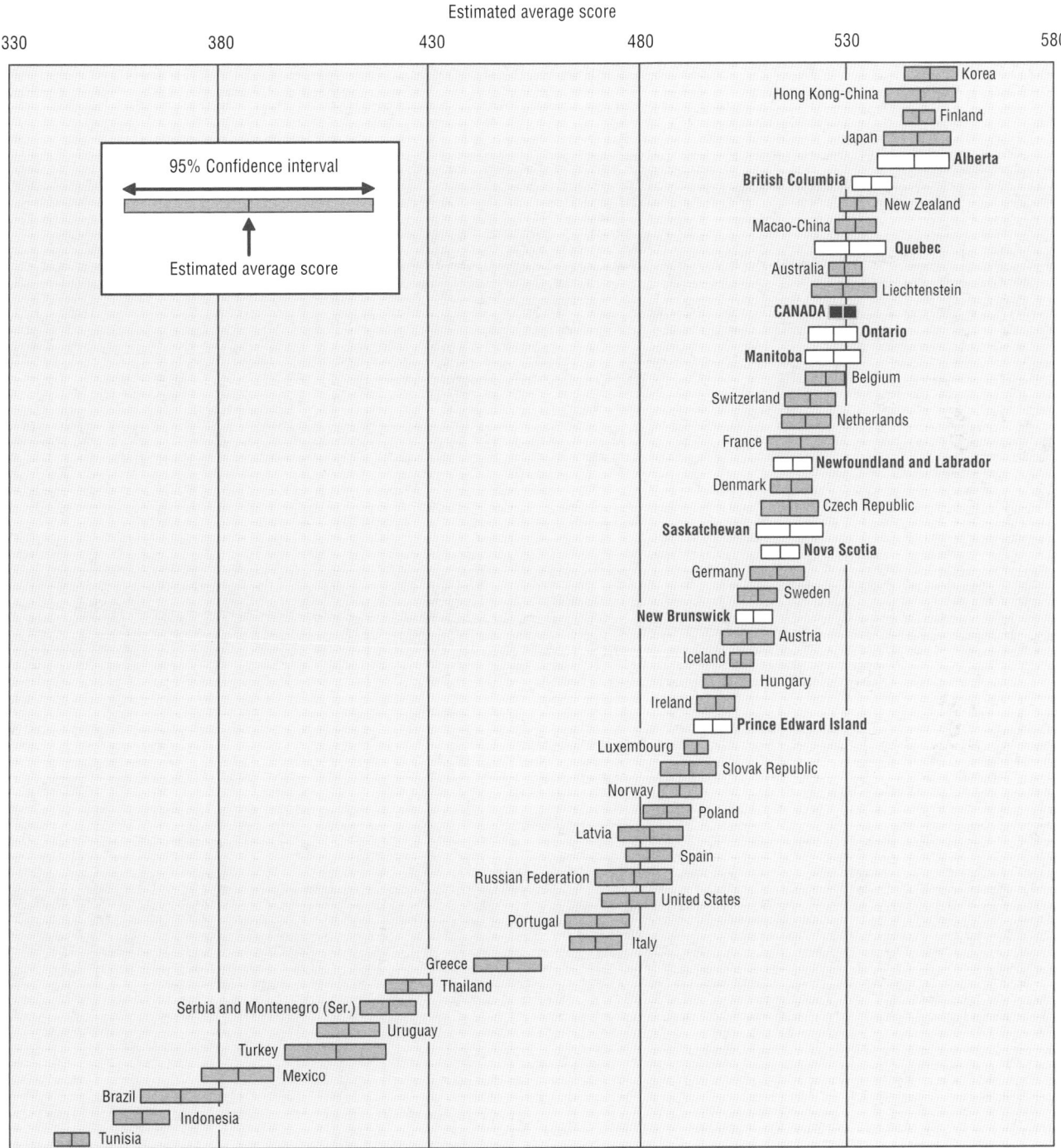

Note: The OECD mean is 500 with a standard error of 0.6.

Provincial results

Across the three minor domains of PISA 2003 the performance of students in all provinces was, with a few exceptions, above the OECD average. Students in New Brunswick, Nova Scotia and Saskatchewan performed at the OECD average in science while students in Prince Edward Island performed at the OECD average in reading and problem solving and below the OECD average in science.

As shown in Table 2.2, students in Alberta performed above the Canadian average in all the minor domains while students in Quebec, Ontario, Manitoba and British Columbia performed at the Canadian average in all the minor domains. Students in Newfoundland and Labrador performed at the Canadian average in reading and science, but below the average in problem solving. Students in Prince Edward Island, New Brunswick, Nova Scotia and Saskatchewan performed below the Canadian average in all minor domains.

Table 2.2

Provincial results in reading, science and problem solving in relation to the Canadian average

	Provinces performing significantly better* than the Canadian average	Provinces performing the same* as the Canadian average	Provinces performing significantly lower* than the Canadian average
Reading	Alberta	Newfoundland and Labrador, Quebec, Ontario, Manitoba, British Columbia	Prince Edward Island, Nova Scotia, New Brunswick, Saskatchewan
Science	Alberta	Newfoundland and Labrador, Quebec, Ontario, Manitoba, British Columbia	Prince Edward Island, Nova Scotia, New Brunswick, Saskatchewan
Problem Solving	Alberta	Quebec, Ontario, Manitoba, British Columbia	Newfoundland and Labrador, Prince Edward Island, Nova Scotia, New Brunswick, Saskatchewan

* Differences in scores are statistically significant only when confidence intervals do not overlap. Provinces performing about the same as Canada as a whole have a confidence interval that overlaps that of Canada. Provinces within each cell are ordered east to west.

How does the performance of boys and girls compare?

Table 2.3 summarizes the gender differences for PISA 2003 in reading, science, and problem solving. As was the case in PISA 2000, in PISA 2003 girls performed significantly better than boys on the reading test in all but one country[14] and in all provinces (Appendix tables B2.4-B2.6). The gap between girls and boys in reading was much larger than the gap between boys and girls in mathematics. In Canada, while boys outperformed girls by eleven points in mathematics, girls outperformed boys by 32 points in reading.

In PISA 2000, no significant gender differences were observed between boys and girls in any country or any province on the science test. In PISA 2003, in Canada as well as eleven other countries, boys performed significantly better than girls on the science test[15]. However, as with mathematics, the gap was small at six points in Canada and six points at the OECD average. At the provincial level, boys outperformed girls in Manitoba, Nova Scotia, and Ontario[16].

For problem solving, girls outperformed boys in six countries. No significant gender differences were observed in Canada. At the provincial level, girls outperformed boys in Prince Edward Island and Saskatchewan[17].

Table 2.3

Summary of gender differences for Canada and the provinces

	Girls performed significantly higher* than boys	Boys performed significantly higher* than girls	No significant differences between boys and girls
Reading	Canada, All provinces		
Science		Canada, Nova Scotia, Ontario, Manitoba	Newfoundland and Labrador, Prince Edward Island, New Brunswick, Quebec, Saskatchewan, Alberta, British Columbia
Problem Solving	Prince Edward Island, Saskatchewan		Canada, Newfoundland and Labrador, Nova Scotia, New Brunswick, Quebec, Ontario, Manitoba, Alberta, British Columbia

* Difference is significant when the gender difference gap is significantly different from zero. Provinces within each cell are ordered from east to west.

Achievement of Canadian students by language of the school system

This section examines the performance of students in the English-language and French-language school systems for the five Canadian provinces that sampled these population groups separately. The focus is on the performance of the minority group (students in French-language school systems in Nova Scotia, New Brunswick, Ontario and Manitoba and students in the English-language school system in Quebec) relative to the majority.

A comparison of PISA results within each of these five provinces is given in Table 2.4. As was the case in PISA 2000, students enrolled in the French-language school systems in Nova Scotia, New Brunswick, Ontario and Manitoba performed significantly lower in both reading and science than did students in the English-language system in the same provinces. In Quebec, student performance in reading, and science did not differ between the English-language and French-language school systems.

For problem solving, there were significant differences favouring the English-language system in Nova Scotia, New Brunswick, and Ontario, while no significant differences were observed in Quebec and Manitoba.

Table 2.4

Estimated average reading, science and problem solving scores by province and language of the school system

	English-language school system		French-language school system	
	Estimated average score	95% confidence interval	Estimated average score	95% confidence interval
Reading				
Nova Scotia	**514**	509-519	**467**	453-481
New Brunswick	**510**	506-514	**485**	479-491
Quebec	530	520-540	524	515-533
Ontario	**531**	524-538	**495**	485-505
Manitoba	**521**	514-528	**494**	482-506
Science				
Nova Scotia	**506**	501-511	**465**	450-480
New Brunswick	**505**	501-509	**480**	473-487
Quebec	523	511-535	518	507-529
Ontario	**517**	509-525	**479**	469-489
Manitoba	**513**	506-520	**490**	477-503
Problem Solving				
Nova Scotia	**514**	509-519	**493**	479-507
New Brunswick	**511**	507-515	**497**	491-503
Quebec	538	528-548	529	520-538
Ontario	**528**	521-535	**504**	495-513
Manitoba	527	521-533	516	504-528

Note: Statistically significant differences are in bold. Differences in scores are statistically significant only when confidence intervals do not overlap

Comparison of reading and science performance in PISA 2003 and 2000

It is possible to compare PISA 2000 and 2003 results for reading and science to assess whether performance among 15-year-olds has changed since 2000[18]. However, as mentioned in Chapter 1, small differences should be interpreted with caution.

In Canada, as well as for sixteen other countries, the mean reading performance of 15-year-olds did not change measurably from 2000 to 2003. Reading performance increased in five countries and decreased for ten countries for which there is comparable data[19]. While reading performance did not change for Canada overall and for eight provinces, reading performance among 15-year-olds decreased in Prince Edward Island and Saskatchewan (Table 2.5).

In Canada, as well as in four other countries (Austria, Norway, Mexico, Korea), students had lower science performance in PISA 2003 compared to PISA 2000. Science performance of 15-year-olds increased significantly in thirteen countries while performance remained unchanged in the remaining fourteen countries for which comparative data are available[20]. Lower performance in science was observed in Prince Edward Island, Quebec, and Saskatchewan. No significant changes in science performance were observed in the other provinces (Table 2.5).

Table 2.5

Comparison of estimated average performance in reading and science PISA 2003 and PISA 2000

	PISA 2000		PISA 2003	
	Estimated average score	95% confidence interval	Estimated average score	95% confidence interval
Reading				
Newfoundland and Labrador	517	512-522	521	511-531
Prince Edward Island	**517**	512-522	**495**	486-503
Nova Scotia	521	516-526	513	504-521
New Brunswick	501	497-505	503	494-511
Quebec	536	530-542	525	514-536
Ontario	533	527-539	530	520-540
Manitoba	529	522-536	520	511-530
Saskatchewan	**529**	524-534	**512**	501-523
Alberta	550	544-556	543	532-554
British Columbia	538	532-544	535	526-544
Canada	534	531-537	528	520-536
Science				
Newfoundland and Labrador	516	509-523	514	506-522
Prince Edward Island	**508**	503-513	**489**	481-497
Nova Scotia	516	510-522	505	498-513
New Brunswick	497	492-502	498	491-505
Quebec	**541**	534-548	**520**	508-532
Ontario	522	515-529	515	506-525
Manitoba	527	520-534	512	503-522
Saskatchewan	**522**	516-528	**506**	495-516
Alberta	546	539-553	539	527-552
British Columbia	533	527-539	527	519-535
Canada	**529**	526-532	**519**	512-526

Note: The 2003 confidence interval includes a linking error associated with the uncertainty that results from making comparisons with PISA 2000 (see endnote 18). Statistically significant differences are in bold. Due to rounding error, non-overlapping confidence intervals in Science for Saskatchewan and Canada share an upper or lower limit.

Summary

Because reading, science and problem solving were considered to be minor domains in PISA 2003, a smaller proportion of students were assessed in those domains compared to the mathematics assessment, which was the major focus of the 2003 assessment. Additionally, a smaller number of items were included in each of these assessments than were included in the mathematics assessment. Consequently, this chapter focuses on providing an update on overall performance in each of these domains.

PISA 2003 results confirmed the PISA 2000 findings with respect to the performance of Canadian students in reading. Canadian 15-year-olds continue to perform very well in reading, being outperformed by students in only Finland among a total of 41 countries. Canada also performed well in science and problem solving, with four countries outperforming Canadian students in each of these two domains.

Although performing well overall in all skill domains, the existence of disparities among provinces across the domains warrants further analysis. Canada's relative performance in science also warrants further investigation. Compared to Canada's relative position in mathematics and reading, Canadian students fare less well in science. Additionally, Canada was only one of five countries that had lower science performance in 2003 than in 2000. The next PISA assessment in 2006, focusing on science, will provide a more definitive profile of Canada's performance in this domain.

Notes

13. The reading results for 2003 are based on the reading scale that was developed for PISA 2000 which had a mean average of 500 and a standard deviation of 100 for the 27 OECD countries that participated in PISA 2000. However, because three additional OECD countries are included in the PISA 2003 reading test, the overall OECD average for reading for PISA 2003 is 494.

14. OECD (2004), *Learning for Tomorrow's World – First results from PISA 2003*, Paris.

15. OECD (2004), *Learning for Tomorrow's World – First results from PISA 2003*, Paris.

16. The fact that gender differences were not observable does not mean that they do not exist in other countries but rather that the PISA 2000 design was not sensitive enough to detect them reliably.

17. See footnote above.

18. Please refer to Annex A8 of the OECD (2004) *Learning for Tomorrow's World – First results from PISA 2003* for an explanation of the methods used to establish the link between the PISA 2000 and 2003 assessment.

19. OECD (2004), *Learning for Tomorrow's World – First results from PISA 2003*, Paris.

20. OECD (2004), *Learning for Tomorrow's World – First results from PISA 2003*, Paris.

Chapter 3

The relationship between student engagement, student learning, and mathematics performance

The level of student engagement in mathematics is important for acquiring skills and knowledge in mathematics. Students who are engaged in the learning process will tend to learn more and be more receptive to the pursuit of knowledge. Furthermore, student engagement in mathematics has an impact upon course selection, educational pathways, and career choices. Likewise, the learning strategies that students employ may also have an impact on both their ability to succeed in school and in their ability to pursue lifelong learning. For example, students who leave school with the ability to set their own learning objectives are well equipped to continue the learning process throughout their lives. Consequently, students' engagement with learning and the learning strategies they employ constitute an important outcome of education.

In this chapter, the relationships between student engagement, learning strategies, preferences for learning, and mathematics achievement are explored. To begin, student engagement as measured by motivation to learn, confidence in learning, and anxiety associated with learning mathematics is described for both Canadian students in comparison with OECD students as a whole and for students across the provinces in relationship to the Canadian average. Next, the impact of these engagement measures on mathematics performance is described. This is followed by an examination of gender differences in mathematics engagement.

The second part of this chapter examines the various learning strategies used and the type of learning situations preferred by Canadian students in relation to other OECD students and students across the provinces compared to the Canadian average. Next, the relationship between learning strategies and preferences for learning situations and mathematics achievement is explored. Lastly, a comparison is made between high and low achievers in mathematics vis-à-vis their learning strategies and preferences for learning situations.

Engagement in mathematics

PISA collected information on a variety of dimensions of student engagement to explore the extent to which students believe that they can succeed in mathematics, why they want to learn mathematics, and what they feel about learning mathematics. Student engagement in mathematics refers to students' motivation to learn mathematics, their confidence in their ability to succeed in mathematics, and their emotional feelings about mathematics. Based on student responses to a series of questions, PISA constructed five indices related to these variables:

Motivation

Interest and enjoyment in mathematics measures an individual's interest and enjoyment in mathematics.

Instrumental motivation to learn mathematics reflects an individual's belief that mathematics will be useful for future employment or education. Students were asked to what extent they are encouraged to learn by external rewards such as good job prospects. Instrumental motivation is also referred to as *belief in the usefulness of mathematics.*

Confidence

Mathematics self-efficacy measures students' feelings of confidence about being able to solve specific mathematical problems. Mathematics self-efficacy is also referred to as *mathematics confidence.*

Mathematics self-concept measures an individual's perception of their ability to learn mathematics. Mathematics self-concept is also referred to as *perceived ability in mathematics.*

Anxiety

Mathematics anxiety is concerned with feelings of helplessness and emotional stress when dealing with mathematics.

Each index was constructed so that the average score across the OECD countries is 0 and two-thirds of the scores are between -1.0 and 1.0 (i.e. a standard deviation of 1).

When comparisons are made between Canada and the provinces, provincial averages are considered different from the Canadian average if their confidence intervals do not overlap with the confidence interval for Canada. All confidence intervals for Canada and the provinces are presented in the appendix tables.

Comparing Canada with the OECD and provinces with Canada

In this chapter, scores for Canada are compared with the OECD average. The OECD average can be used to see how a country compares on a given indicator with a typical OECD country. The OECD average does not take into account the absolute size of the student population in each country, i.e., each country contributes equally to the average.

Significant differences are calculated by constructing a 95% confidence interval around the average (for more information on confidence intervals, please refer to chapter 1 – A note on statistical comparisons). In comparing Canada with the OECD average for a given indicator, scores not significantly different from zero indicate *average* levels of the attribute measured by a given index. Scores significantly above 0 represent *above-average* levels and scores significantly below 0 represent *below-average* levels of the attribute measured by a given characteristic. For example, a positive value for Canada on the index of instrumental motivation to learn mathematics, with a corresponding 95% confidence interval whose lower bound is above zero (i.e. average=0.23, 95% confidence interval=0.20-0.26), means that the average score for Canadian 15-year-olds on this index is *above-average* compared to the OECD average of zero.

Canadian students believe strongly in the usefulness of mathematics to their future education and employment

Motivation to learn is a driving force behind learning and Canadian 15-year-old students appear to be well motivated to learn mathematics. While Canadian students were just as interested in mathematics and enjoyed it as much as students in OECD countries as a whole, they believed more strongly in its usefulness to their future employment and education.

Motivation to learn can be activated through an interest in and enjoyment of mathematics. Compared to the OECD average, Canadian 15-year-old students reported similar levels of interest in and enjoyment of mathematics. While there was variation in the provincial averages, the average scores of all provinces were not different from the Canadian average with the exception of British Columbia where students reported levels of interest and enjoyment in mathematics that were below the Canadian average (Table 3.1).

Motivation to learn mathematics may also be driven by the belief that mathematics will be useful to one's future job or further studies. Compared to the OECD average, Canadian 15-year-olds held an above-average belief that mathematics would be useful for their future employment and education (Appendix Table B3.1). The averages for all provinces were also above the OECD average. However, there were differences across the provinces. Students in Nova Scotia and Quebec possessed the strongest belief, above the Canadian average. The average scores for students in Newfoundland and Labrador, Prince Edward Island, Manitoba, Alberta, and Saskatchewan were not significantly different from the Canadian average. Lastly, the average scores for students in New Brunswick, Ontario, and British Columbia were below the Canadian average, suggesting that they were not as positive about the usefulness of mathematics to their future jobs and education.

Canadian students were more confident that they could succeed in mathematics than students in all OECD countries combined

The views that students form about their own competence in mathematics may impact on the goals they set as well as on their achievement. Compared to the OECD average, Canadian students were more confident that they could succeed in mathematics.

Canadian students reported above-average levels of mathematics confidence and above-average levels in their perceived ability in mathematics. There were,

however, differences among the provinces (Appendix Table B3.1). Compared to the Canadian average, students in Quebec and Alberta reported higher levels of mathematics confidence; students in Newfoundland and Labrador and British Columbia did not differ significantly from the Canadian average while students in the remaining provinces reported lower levels of mathematics confidence compared to the Canadian average (Table 3.1). Compared to the Canadian average, students in Alberta and Quebec reported above-average levels in their perceived ability in mathematics while students in Ontario, Manitoba, and British Columbia reported below-average levels (Table 3.1).

Table 3.1

Provincial scores on indices of student engagement in mathematics relative to the Canadian average

	Provinces performing significantly higher* than the Canadian average	Provinces performing the same* as the Canadian average	Provinces performing significantly lower* than the Canadian average
Interest and enjoyment in mathematics		Newfoundland and Labrador, Prince Edward Island, Nova Scotia, New Brunswick, Quebec, Ontario, Manitoba, Saskatchewan, Alberta	British Columbia
Belief in the usefulness of mathematics	Nova Scotia, Quebec	Newfoundland and Labrador, Prince Edward Island, Manitoba, Saskatchewan, Alberta	New Brunswick, Ontario, British Columbia
Mathematics confidence	Quebec, Alberta	Newfoundland and Labrador, British Columbia	Prince Edward Island, Nova Scotia, New Brunswick, Ontario, Manitoba, Saskatchewan
Perceived ability in mathematics	Quebec, Alberta	Newfoundland and Labrador, Prince Edward Island, Nova Scotia, New Brunswick, Saskatchewan	Manitoba, Ontario, British Columbia
Mathematics anxiety	Ontario	New Brunswick, Quebec, Manitoba, Saskatchewan, Alberta, British Columbia	Newfoundland and Labrador, Prince Edward Island, Nova Scotia

* Differences in scores are statistically significant only when confidence intervals do not overlap. Provinces performing about the same as Canada as a whole have a confidence interval that overlaps that of Canada. Provinces within each cell are ordered from east to west.

Canadian students are slightly less anxious in dealing with mathematics than students in all OECD countries combined

Emotional stress in learning mathematics may lead to avoidance of mathematics and impede learning. Compared to the OECD average, fifteen-year-old students in Canada reported slightly lower levels of anxiety in dealing with mathematics (see Appendix Table B3.1). Students in Newfoundland and Labrador, Prince Edward Island, and Nova Scotia reported levels of mathematics anxiety below the Canadian average. Students in Ontario reported levels of anxiety above the Canadian average. The level of anxiety reported by students in other provinces was not significantly different from the Canadian average (Table 3.1).

Canadian students with high levels of engagement in mathematics have higher mathematics performance

There is a complex and often circular relationship between student engagement in mathematics and actual performance. For example, the more students succeed in mathematics the more likely they are to believe they can succeed. The more students believe they can succeed the more engaged they will become with learning mathematics. The relationship between mathematics achievement and the various measures of engagement in mathematics is strong. Canadian students reporting high levels (one standard deviation above the average) of

mathematics confidence scored 133 points higher on the combined mathematics scale than did students reporting low levels (one standard deviation below the average, Figure 3.1). This represents a difference of two mathematics proficiency levels in mathematics.

The average combined mathematics score of students with high levels of perceived ability in mathematics was 111 points higher than the average combined mathematics score of students with low levels of perceived ability in mathematics. Similarly, the difference in the average combined mathematics score between students with high and low interest and enjoyment in mathematics and students with high and low levels of belief in the usefulness of mathematics were 70 and 62 points respectively (Figure 3.1). Mathematics anxiety had a strong negative relationship with mathematics performance: the average performance of students with high levels of mathematics anxiety was 71 points lower than the average performance of students with low levels of mathematics anxiety.

The patterns of the effects of student motivation (belief in the usefulness of mathematics and interest and enjoyment in mathematics), mathematics confidence, and mathematics anxiety on mathematics performance across the provinces mirror those for Canada. In all provinces, students with high levels of student motivation and mathematics confidence and low levels of mathematics anxiety outperformed students with low levels of student motivation and mathematics confidence and high levels of mathematics anxiety (Appendix Table B3.2).

Figure 3.1

Combined mathematics score for students with high mathematics engagement compared to students with low mathematics engagement

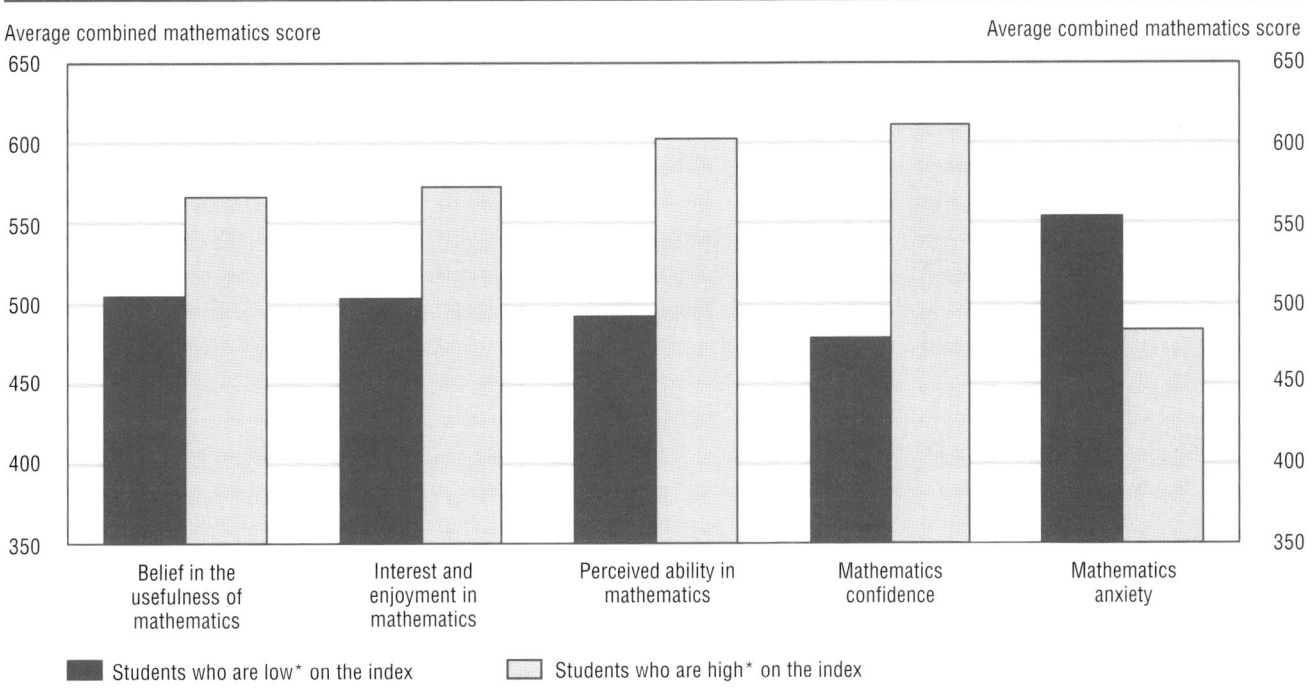

Average combined mathematics score

* Students low on a given index are defined as those falling one standard deviation below the average, students high on a given index are defined as those falling one standard deviation above the average.

Canadian girls and boys are not equally engaged in mathematics

Students' mathematics confidence, their perceived abilities in mathematics, and their beliefs in the value of mathematics for future work and education may have an important impact on their course selections, educational pathways and career choices. Differences exist between the mathematics engagement of Canadian boys and girls (Table 3.2). For example, after controlling for mathematics performance, girls reported lower levels of confidence in their ability to solve specific mathematical problems, lower levels of their perceived ability to learn mathematics and higher levels of anxiety in dealing with mathematics. Girls were also less likely to believe that mathematics will be useful for their future employment and education and were more likely to report lower levels of interest and enjoyment in mathematics.

The same pattern was observed across provinces with the following exceptions: in Newfoundland and Labrador boys and girls with the same level of ability did not differ in their level of interest and enjoyment in mathematics; girls in Prince Edward Island, Nova Scotia, Manitoba, and Saskatchewan had higher levels of interest and enjoyment in mathematics than males; and in Newfoundland and Labrador, both boys and girls with the same level of ability reported similar levels of belief in the usefulness of mathematics (Table 3.2, Appendix Table B3.3).

Table 3.2

Summary of gender difference in engagement in mathematics controlling for mathematics performance, Canada and the provinces

	Interest and enjoyment in mathematics	Belief in usefulness of mathematics	Perceived ability in mathematics	Mathematics confidence	Mathematics Anxiety
Canada	♂	♂	♂	♂	♀
Newfoundland and Labrador	○	○	♂	♂	♀
Prince Edward Island	♀	♂	♂	♂	♀
Nova Scotia	♀	♂	♂	♂	♀
New Brunswick	♂	♂	♂	♂	♀
Quebec	♂	♂	♂	♂	♀
Ontario	♂	♂	♂	♂	♀
Manitoba	♀	♂	♂	♂	♀
Saskatchewan	♀	♂	♂	♂	♀
Alberta	♂	♂	♂	♂	♀
British Columbia	♂	♂	♂	♂	♀

Note: ♂ = boys scored significantly higher on the index
♀ = girls scored significantly higher on the index
○ = no significant difference

Mathematics learning strategies and preferences for learning

Students develop and employ different cognitive strategies to learn mathematics. Additionally, some students learn better in a competitive learning environment while others learn better in a cooperative environment. Through a series of questions on the PISA student questionnaire, PISA measured the following learning strategies in mathematics and preferences for learning situations.

Learning strategies in mathematics

Memorization/rehearsal is a learning strategy that involves the use of memorization and rehearsing techniques and includes learning key themes and doing repeated learning of materials.

Elaboration is a learning strategy that involves elaborating mathematics concepts beyond the topic at hand such as making connections to related areas and thinking about alternative solutions, etc.

Control is a learning strategy that involves planning, regulating, and monitoring of learning in mathematics.

Preferences for learning situations

Preferences for cooperative learning situations reflect the preference for cooperative learning such as learning in groups.

Preferences for competitive learning situations reflect the preference on striving to be better than others.

Canadian students are more likely to use memorization, elaboration, and control strategies

Compared to the OECD average, Canadian students reported higher levels of using memorization and rehearsing techniques (learning answers and problems off by heart, repeating learning materials, and remembering every step in a mathematics procedure) for learning mathematics (Appendix Table B3.4). There were, however, differences among the provinces (Table 3.3). Compared to the Canadian average, students in Newfoundland and Labrador, and Alberta reported higher levels of memorization and rehearsal strategies, students in Prince Edward Island reported lower levels while students in the other provinces did not differ from the Canadian average (Appendix Table B3.4). However, this does not mean that memorization alone defines or characterizes Canadian and provincial approaches to mathematics.

Compared to the OECD average, Canadian students also reported slightly higher levels of elaborating mathematics concepts beyond the topic at hand such as making connections to related areas and thinking about alternative solutions. At the provincial level, only students in British Columbia differed from the Canadian average by reporting lower levels of elaboration strategies (Appendix Table B3.4).

PISA also explored the extent to which students take control over their learning of mathematics by involving themselves in the planning, regulating and monitoring of their learning in mathematics. However, it should be noted that there might be notable differences in how students from different countries perceive control strategies. For example, the degree to which students report that they are involved in their learning may depend on differences in the culturally-driven expectations of the learning process among different countries.

Compared to the OECD average, Canadian students were more likely to make use of these types of control strategies. There was a great deal of provincial variation in the level of control strategies reported by students (Table 3.3). Compared to the Canadian average, students in Prince Edward Island, Nova Scotia, New Brunswick, Ontario, Manitoba, Saskatchewan, Alberta, and British Columbia reported below-average use of control strategies. Students in Newfoundland and Labrador and Quebec reported levels above the Canadian average (Appendix Table B3.4).

Canadian students are more likely to prefer both cooperative and competitive learning situations

Learning behaviour can also be influenced by students' preferences for different kinds of learning situations. Compared to the OECD average, Canadian students as a whole were more likely to express preferences for both cooperative learning such as learning in groups and competitive learning such as striving to be better than others. It should be noted that preferences for cooperative and competitive learning are not mutually exclusive of each other. Provincial averages did not differ from the Canadian average with the following exceptions: students in Newfoundland and Labrador and New Brunswick reported higher levels of preferences for cooperative learning situations; students in Alberta reported higher levels of preferences for competitive learning situations; students in Quebec reported lower levels of preferences for cooperative learning; and students in Prince Edward Island and Manitoba reported lower levels of preferences for competitive learning situations (Appendix Table B3.4).

Table 3.3

Provincial average scores on indices of learning strategies and preferences for learning relative to the Canadian average

	Provinces performing significantly higher* than the Canadian average	Provinces performing the same* as the Canadian average	Provinces performing significantly lower* than the Canadian average
Memorization/rehearsal	Newfoundland and Labrador, Alberta	Nova Scotia, New Brunswick, Quebec, Ontario, Manitoba, Saskatchewan, British Columbia	Prince Edward Island
Elaboration strategies		Newfoundland and Labrador, Prince Edward Island, Nova Scotia, New Brunswick, Quebec, Ontario, Manitoba, Saskatchewan, Alberta	British Columbia
Control strategies	Newfoundland and Labrador, Quebec		Prince Edward Island, Nova Scotia, New Brunswick, Ontario, Manitoba, Saskatchewan, Alberta, British Columbia
Preferences for cooperative learning	Newfoundland and Labrador, New Brunswick	Prince Edward Island, Nova Scotia, Ontario, Manitoba, Saskatchewan, Alberta, British Columbia	Quebec
Preferences for competitive learning	Alberta	Newfoundland and Labrador, Nova Scotia, New Brunswick, Quebec, Ontario, Saskatchewan, British Columbia	Prince Edward Island, Manitoba

* Differences in scores are statistically significant only when confidence intervals do not overlap. Provinces performing about the same as Canada as a whole have a confidence interval that overlaps that of Canada. Provinces within each cell are ordered from east to west.

Student learning strategies and preferred learning situations are related to mathematics performance

How do learning strategies relate to mathematics performance? Do various learning strategies directly impact performance or do students with different abilities have preferences for different learning strategies? It is difficult to determine whether various learning strategies directly impact performance or whether students with different abilities prefer different learning strategies or are in learning situations where different strategies are encouraged. For example, while it may be that students perform well because of the strategies they use for learning, it may also be the case that teachers tailor learning for individual students by encouraging high-performing students and low-performing students to use different learning strategies.

Overall, learning strategies were related to mathematics performance but the difference was not as pronounced as those observed for student engagement (Figure 3.2). Students who exhibited high levels of control strategies (one standard deviation above the average) scored 49 points higher than did students who exhibited low levels (one standard deviation below the average). The use of memorization and rehearsal strategies, as well as elaboration strategies, was also positively related to mathematics achievement. For each of these indices, students who exhibited high levels scored 34 and 43 points higher respectively than students who exhibited low levels.

While preferences for competitive learning situations were positively related to mathematics achievement, preferences for cooperative learning were not significantly related to achievement. Students with high levels of preference for competitive learning situations scored 52 points higher than did students with low levels of preference.

Figure 3.2

Combined mathematics score for students with high levels of various learning strategies and preferences for learning compared to students with low levels

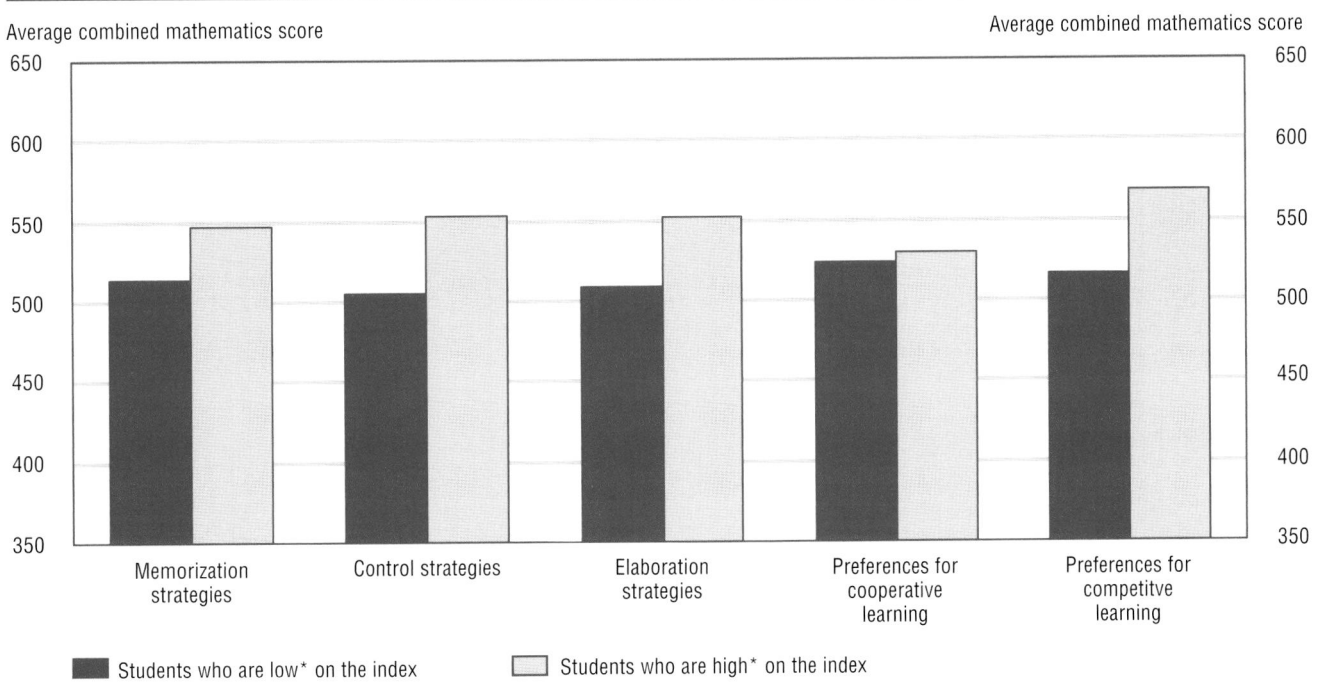

Average combined mathematics score

Average combined mathematics score

* Students low on a given index are defined as those falling one standard deviation below the mean. Students high on a given index are defined as those falling one standard deviation above the mean.

High performers exhibit different learning strategies and preferences for learning situations than low achievers.

Table 3.4 shows the average score on the various indices of learning strategies and preferences for learning situations for high and low performers on the combined mathematics scale[21]. This table shows that high and low performers in mathematics prefer a different set of learning strategies. Overall, high performers tended to report higher levels of elaboration and control strategies than low performers. High performers also reported higher preferences for competitive learning environments whereas low performers reported higher preferences for cooperative learning. The same patterns were observed in all provinces with the exception of Quebec. In Quebec, high performers reported lower levels of both memorization strategies and elaboration strategies than low performers (Appendix Table B3.5).

Table 3.4

Average score for learning strategies and preferences for learning: low versus high performers on the combined mathematics scale, Canada

	Low performers on the combined mathematics scale		High performers on the combined mathematics scale	
	Index average	Standard error	Index average	Standard error
Memorization/rehearsal strategies	0.00	(0.04)	0.24	(0.02)
Control strategies	-0.25	(0.04)	0.24	(0.03)
Elaboration strategies	0.09	(0.03)	0.23	(0.02)
Preferences for cooperative learning	0.19	(0.04)	-0.02	(0.02)
Preferences for competitive learning	0.09	(0.03)	0.44	(0.03)

Note: Low performers are defined as those who score below 420 points on the combined mathematics scale which corresponds to a proficiency level of one or less. High performers are defined as those who score above 606 points on the combined mathematics scale, which corresponds to a proficiency level of five or higher.

Summary

The results from this chapter show that student engagement in mathematics is related to mathematics achievement. Both provincially and Canada-wide, students with high levels of mathematics confidence performed the equivalent of two proficiency levels higher (133 points) on the combined mathematics scale than did students with low levels. Students with high levels of mathematics anxiety performed the equivalent of one proficiency level lower (71 points) in mathematics than did students with low levels. Motivation to learn mathematics as measured by interest and enjoyment in mathematics and belief in the usefulness of mathematics was also positively related to achievement. It is difficult to disentangle the associations observed between mathematics engagement and performance. For example, are high motivation and confidence and reduced anxiety the causes of strong performance or by-products of doing well in mathematics? Nevertheless, the strong link between student engagement in mathematics and mathematics performance suggest that high motivation and self-confidence and low mathematics anxiety are important outcomes in themselves.

Of particular interest is the finding that even when controlling for ability, girls consistently show much lower interest and enjoyment in mathematics, lower self-related beliefs and higher levels of mathematics anxiety than boys. This gender inequity may contribute to gender differences in the educational and occupational career choices.

Learning strategies and preferences for learning were not as strongly related to mathematics performance as was student engagement. However, the results revealed that high and low performers in mathematics had different learning strategies and preferences for learning. While high performers in mathematics were more likely to prefer memorization/rehearsal, elaboration and control strategies and competitive learning environments, low performers were more likely to prefer cooperative learning environments.

Notes

21   Low performers are defined as those who score below 420 points on the combined mathematics scale which corresponds to a proficiency level of one or less. High performers are defined as those who score above 606 points on the combined mathematics scale which corresponds to a proficiency level of five or higher.

Chapter 4

The relationship between family characteristics, home environment, and mathematics performance

Parental education, occupation, and student performance

As shown in Chapter 1, the mathematics performance of students differed considerably across countries and across provinces. The previous chapter discussed how these differences may be related to attitudes and perceptions of students. This chapter examines two important family characteristics – parental education and occupation – and how they relate to overall mathematics performance.

Parents play an important role in how students learn. Aside from being actively involved in their childrens' education, parents also provide a home environment that can impact learning. Parents serve as a model for learning, determine the educational resources available in the home, and hold particular attitudes and values towards education. Although it is difficult to examine the home environment of each student, the educational attainment and occupation of parents reflect the values and resources with which parents create this environment.

Parental education and occupation are two major components of the *socio-economic status* (SES) of a student. The association between student SES and test performance describes the relative advantage or disadvantage that can be explained by family circumstances. Just as each student can be described by his or her home environment, so can a school be described by the family background of its students (school socio-economic background).

This chapter begins with an examination of the relationships of parental education and occupation to overall mathematics performance. The next section looks to see if the relationship between socio-economic background and mathematics performance differs across provinces. The chapter ends with a discussion of how schools and school systems may moderate the effects of individual socio-economic background.

High parental education is associated with higher mathematics performance

In PISA 2003, students were asked to indicate the highest level of education attained by each of their parents/guardians. The categories were: No education, Elementary school, Junior high or middle school, High school, College, and University. In Canada, very few parents were reported to have less than high school education. Therefore, the lowest four categories were grouped together as High school or less. The highest level of parental education for a family is considered. For example, for a student whose father had a college diploma and whose mother had a university degree, the level of parental education would be university. Figure 4.1 shows the proportion of students in each province with each level of parental education.

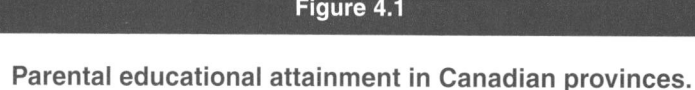

Figure 4.1

Parental educational attainment in Canadian provinces.

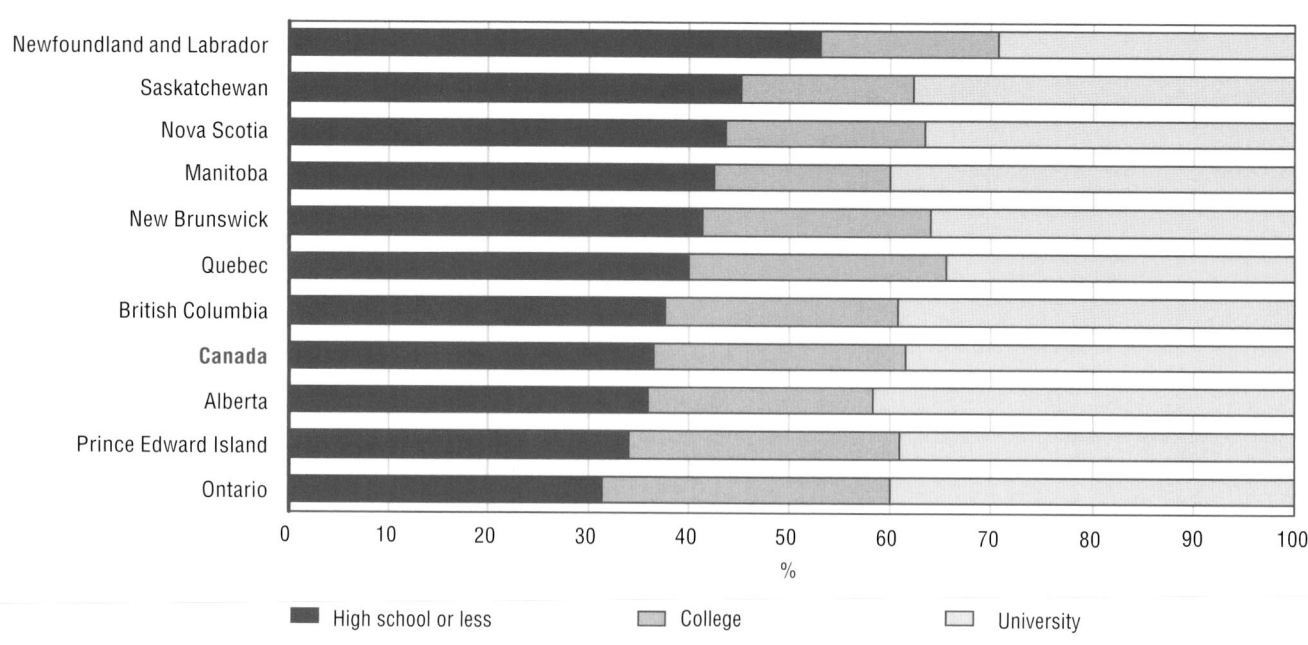

The results displayed in Figure 4.1 illustrate the education levels of the adults that 15-year-olds in each province and Canada overall are most likely to encounter in their everyday lives (their own parents and the parents of their peers). The proportions at each level of education can be described as the educational context of 15-year-olds in each province. The value of education may be reinforced when students are surrounded by adults who demonstrate its worth by investing the necessary time and money (e.g., direct costs such as tuition fees, cost of books, room and board, and indirect costs such as lost wages during the time of study) to pursue higher education. This context was different across provinces. In Newfoundland and Labrador, over half of the students had parents whose highest educational attainment was high school or less. In contrast, four of every ten students had at least one parent with a university education in Alberta, Ontario, and Manitoba.

Students whose parents had a higher level of education tended to perform better in mathematics than students whose parents had a lower level of education. For Canada as a whole, the average score of students whose parents had high school or less was 515, while the average performance of the students whose parents had college level and university education were, respectively, 531 and 553. The difference in average performance between students whose parents had university education versus high school or less was around two-thirds of a proficiency level. These results suggest a positive relationship between the educational level of the parents and the performance of their children in mathematics. This relationship is displayed in Figure 4.2. Each bar shows the performance of typical students within each level of parental education in each province. The length of each bar represents the range of mathematics scores between the 25th percentile and the 75th percentile in each group. Therefore, each bar represents 50% of students, while 25% scored below the bottom limit of the bar and 25% scored above the top limit.

Figure 4.2

Parental education and student performance in mathematics in Canadian provinces

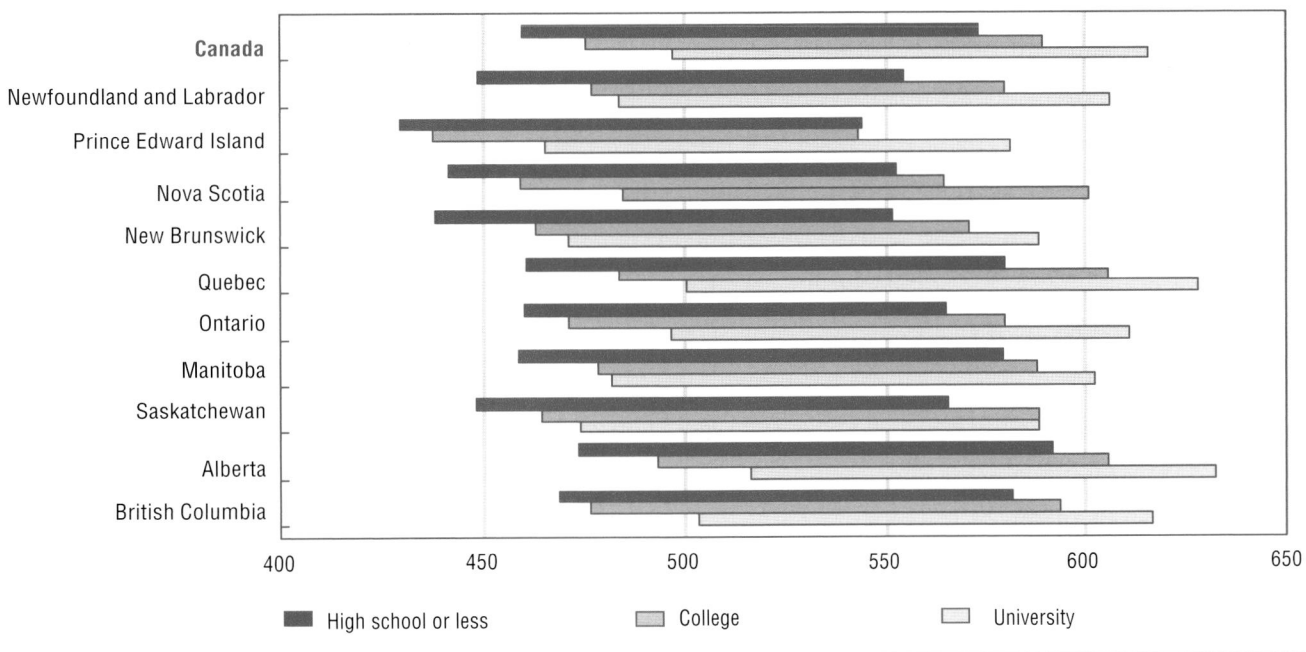

Figure 4.2 reveals that, while higher parental education tended to be associated with higher mathematics performance, there was substantial overlap of performance between the different levels of parental education. Many students whose parents had high school education or less outperformed students whose parents had university education. Given the wide range of student performance within each group, it is clear that the success of many students appears to be dependent on factors other than their parents' level of education. For example, as shown in Figure 4.3, although most of the students whose performance was in the top 15% of students had at least one parent with a university education, one in four of these highest performing students had parents with only high school or less. Further, one in four of the students whose performance was in the bottom 15% also had at least one parent with a university degree.

Figure 4.3

Parental education of high and low performing students in Canada

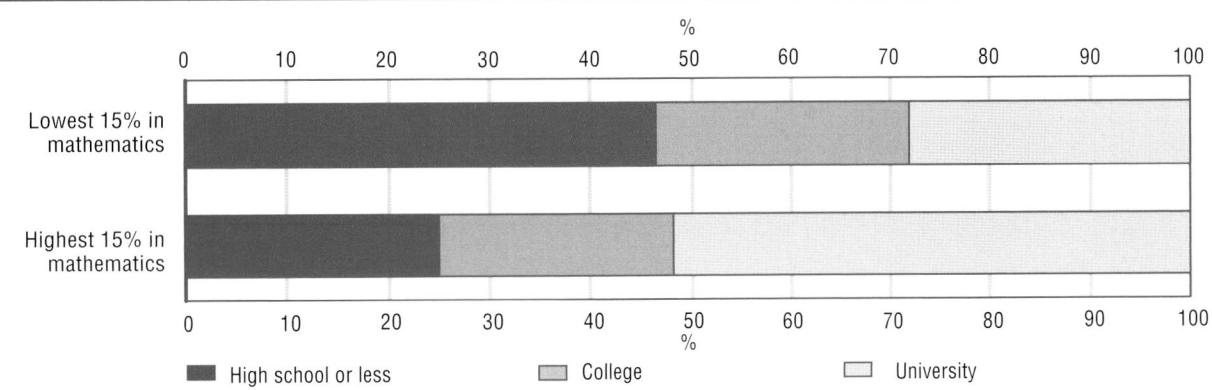

Parental occupation is related to the skills used by parents

In PISA 2003, students were asked to report the occupations held by both their mother and father. These occupations have been grouped into six categories according to the types of skills that are associated with each occupation (see text box 'Describing Parental Occupation with the International Standard Classification of Occupation (ISCO)'). Some examples of the occupations that characterise each category are provided as follows:

- **Higher service:** lawyers, scientists, executive officers of large corporations and divisional managers
- **Lower service:** laboratory technicians, midwives, computer programmers, insurance salespersons, real estate brokers, managers of small businesses
- **Routine clerical/sales:** administrative assistants, client information clerks, cashiers, sales assistants
- **Skilled manual:** carpenters, welders, jewellery makers, upholsterers, engine machinists
- **Semi-unskilled manual:** manufacturing machine operators, taxi drivers, building cleaners
- **Farmers/ farm managers:** supervisory farm workers, self-employed farmers

Describing Parental Occupation with the International Standard Classification of Occupation (ISCO)

PISA 2003 asked students if their parents were working, and if so, what type of work they did. The responses were then assigned to specific categories in a classification system called the International Standard Classification of Occupation (ISCO). ISCO uses a four-digit code to describe different occupations, where each digit represents a particular group of occupations within a broader group. The first digit in ISCO distinguishes ten major groups:

1000 *Legislators, Senior Officials and Managers*

2000 *Professionals*

3000 *Technicians and Associate Professionals*

4000 *Clerks*

5000 *Service Workers and Shop and Market Sales Workers*

6000 *Skilled Agricultural and Fishery Workers*

7000 *Craft and Related Trades Workers*

8000 *Plant and Machine Operators and Assemblers*

9000 *Elementary Occupations*

0000 *Armed Forces Personnel*

Within these groups, there are 28 sub-major groups, 116 minor groups and 390 unit groups. Each of the groups and units are defined by the specific skills associated with the occupations rather than industry or income. This framework allows ISCO to describe the activities of each person's occupation. The level of description may be very specific, depending on the number of ISCO digits used. For example, the specific occupation *Computer systems designers, analysts and programmers* has a four-digit ISCO code of 2131; it falls within the three-digit minor group of *Computing professionals* (2130) and also within the sub-major group of occupations *Physical, mathematical and engineering science professionals* (2100).

Using the detailed information provided by ISCO, several methods have been developed to translate the ISCO categories into categories that can be used to further group or order individuals according to the social status, prestige, or skill level associated with their occupations. This chapter uses two of the methods described in Ganzeboom and Treiman (1996)[1]. The first, referred to as the EGP classification, first identifies workers according to whether their occupations are manual or non-manual. Within these two broad groups, workers can have varying skill levels or be self-employed or not. Only six of the 11 EGP categories (1, 2, 3, 8, 9, 11) are used in this report. These groups accounted for the parental occupations of 97% of Canadian 15-year-olds. The second method, referred to as the International Socio-economic Index (ISEI), adapts the ISCO framework to describe the status associated with each occupation. Social status has been defined as the degree to which each occupation converts education into earnings. For example, occupations which tend to reward higher-educated individuals are associated with higher status. Conversely, occupations where earnings are not strongly related to education have lower status. For students with more than one working parent, highest occupational status was used to assign a single parental occupation. This measure has been used with other indicators to create the overall index of *socio-economic status* associated with each student's home environment.

1.   Ganzeboom, H.B.G. & D.J. Treiman. 1996. "Internationally comparable measures of occupational status for the 1988 International Standard Classification of Occupations." *Social Science Research.* 25:201-239

Parental occupation is an indicator of the education-related skills used by parents. The relationship between parental education and occupation is illustrated in Figure 4.4. As the level of parental education attainment increased, parents of 15-year-olds were more likely to participate in service occupations with both high and low skill requirements, and were less likely to participate in routine or manual occupations. Conversely, individuals with lower education were more likely to be manual worker and self-employed farmers, both skilled and unskilled. This relationship between education and occupation is not surprising, because many service and professional occupations also have specific education or certification requirements.

Figure 4.4

Parental educational attainment and occupation

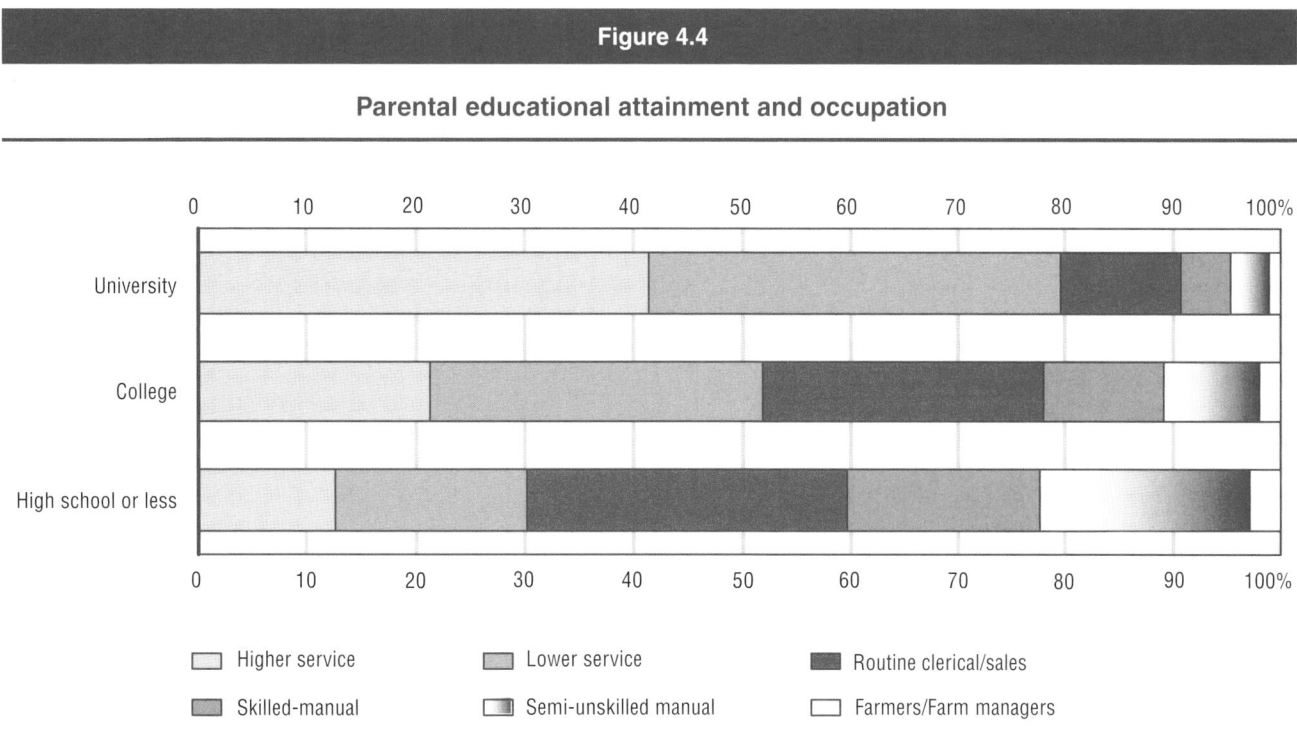

Parental occupation may influence student performance in many ways. For example, occupation-related income may determine access to learning opportunities and resources thus impacting learning outcomes. The role of education and the types of skills associated with different occupations and modeled by parents may motivate students to develop their own skills in particular ways. Parental occupation may also influence how students perceive the value of mathematics learning, their beliefs about the usefulness of mathematics, and the learning environment at home.

The relationship between student mathematics performance and parental occupational category is shown in Figure 4.5. Each bar represents the range of mathematics scores between the 25th and 75th percentiles. If occupation is considered as an indicator of parental skill use, it appears that students whose parents worked in occupations with greater skill requirements also performed better in mathematics. However, the large overlap between groups also indicates that there are still large differences within each occupational category. Some of these differences may be explained by the specific skills parents use in their occupations.

Figure 4.5

Parental occupation and student mathematics performance in Canada

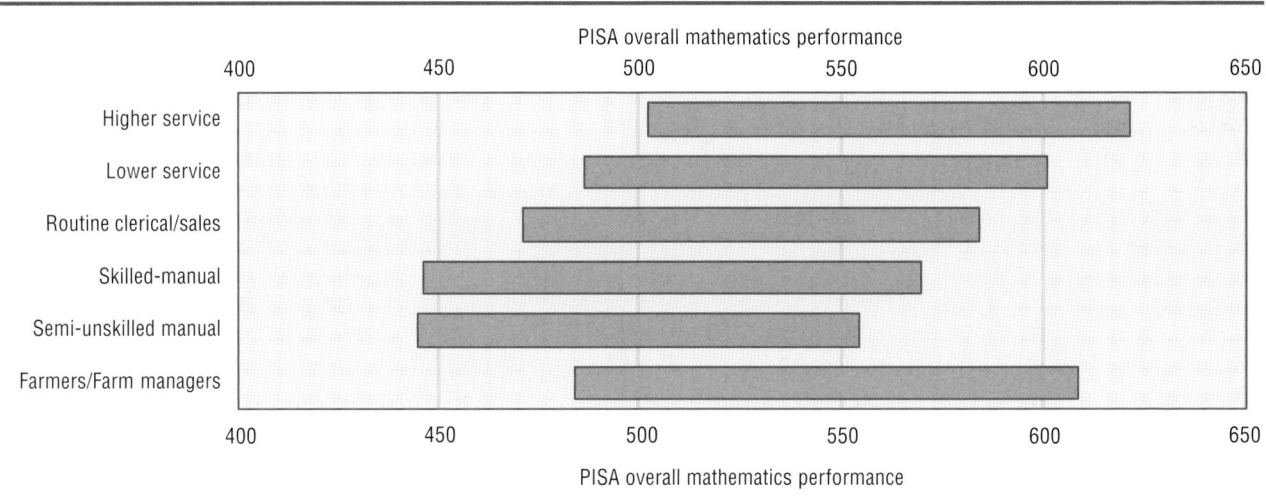

To illustrate this point, the average mathematics performance of students with selected parental occupations defined using the International Standard Classification of Occupation (ISCO) is displayed in Table 4.1. The ISCO sub-major group 2100 (Physical, mathematical & engineering science professionals) is the only occupational group characterised specifically by the use of advanced mathematics. The other four occupational groups selected for this comparison are professional or managerial occupations typically associated with at least a college education and higher-than-average income. Even among these relatively advantaged students, those whose parents had occupations that specifically require mathematics skill (group 2100) tended to perform higher than other students.

Table 4.1

Mathematics performance of students with parents in high-skill service occupations

ISCO group	Description of typical occupations	Average	Standard error
2100	Physical, mathematical and engineering science professionals	598	(8.23)
2300	Teaching professionals	581	(5.10)
2200	Technicians and associated professionals	561	(2.93)
1000	Legislators, senior officials, executives and managers	549	(3.60)
3000	Life science and health professionals	547	(5.06)

Although parental income may result in greater opportunities and resources, it appears to play a secondary role to the skill use associated with parental occupation. For example, occupations in the ISCO major group 1000 (legislators, senior officials, executives and managers) are associated with higher income than most other occupations[22]. However, students with parents in this group performed almost one proficiency level lower than those with parents whose occupations were directly related to mathematics use.

Looking at occupation highlights the importance of home environment in developing the skills of students. Like parental education, parental occupation is an indicator of the influences present in the home of each student. Although many other factors contribute to a child's home environment, examination of these variables reinforces the idea that parental role modeling may be an important influence on a student's learning. To better understand the role of the home environment for mathematics performance, the section below examines a summary measure of the resources, possessions, and values in each student's home called *socio-economic status* (SES) and its relationship with student performance.

Socio-economic status and student performance

Socio-economic status (SES) is a term used to summarise a variety of factors, including parental education and occupation, which influence student performance. In PISA 2003, SES is measured by an index that includes information describing family structure, parental education and occupation, parental labour market participation, and whether a student's family has specific educational and cultural possessions at home. This index is standardized to have an average of 0 and standard deviation of 1 across all OECD countries.

The averages of SES for Canada and the provinces are reported in Table 4.2. The average student in Canada had a relative socio-economic advantage compared to 15-year-olds in all OECD countries combined. There were substantial differences in the distributions of SES between provinces. As shown in Table 4.2, the provinces can be divided into three groups in terms of SES. Alberta, British Columbia, and Ontario comprise one group, characterised by average SES higher than the Canadian average. The second group includes the wide range of average SES in Manitoba, Saskatchewan, Nova Scotia, Prince Edward Island, and Quebec that was slightly lower than Canada overall. The last group contains New Brunswick and Newfoundland and Labrador with average SES much lower than Canada. Although students in all provinces tend to be more advantaged than 15-year-olds in all OECD countries combined, the differences across provinces suggest that all students in Canada may not have access to the same resources or opportunities.

Table 4.2

Socio-economic status in Canadian provinces

	Index average	Standard error	Standard deviation
Canada	**0.45**	**(0.02)**	**0.82**
Alberta	0.58	(0.05)	0.81
British Columbia	0.52	(0.03)	0.80
Ontario	0.52	(0.03)	0.74
Manitoba	0.37	(0.03)	0.82
Saskatchewan	0.35	(0.03)	0.80
Nova Scotia	0.34	(0.02)	0.83
Prince Edward Island	0.31	(0.02)	0.84
Quebec	0.30	(0.03)	0.83
New Brunswick	0.25	(0.01)	0.85
Newfoundland and Labrador	0.25	(0.02)	0.89

Socio-economic gradients show that some provincial differences in performance can be explained by differences in socio-economic conditions

Students with higher SES tended to perform better in mathematics than students with lower SES, but there were also large differences in performance among students with similar SES. This relationship is illustrated in Figure 4.6. The pattern of dots, or the *scatter plot*, is illustrated using the socio-economic backgrounds and mathematics scores of 500 randomly selected Canadian students. The relationship between SES and performance in mathematics for students in Canada is represented by the solid line passing through the centre of this scatter plot. This line predicts the mathematics performance of students based on their level of SES. The endpoints of the line are the 25th and 75th percentiles of SES. Therefore, the line represents the relationship and distribution of SES and mathematics performance of a typical range of students. The dashed line illustrates the relationship for students in all OECD countries combined.

These lines are referred to as *socio-economic gradients*, because they summarise the impact of socio-economic status on student performance. The OECD gradient is longer because Canadian students are much more similar to each other in terms of SES than are other students in the OECD. The slope of the OECD gradient is greater than that of the Canadian gradient because the differences in performance of students with different levels of SES are greater in the OECD than in Canada. The strength of the relationship between SES and performance, given in parentheses, is measured on a scale from 0 to 1. The value of 0.10 for Canada indicates that 10% of the variance in student performance in Canada can be explained by SES. If SES were a perfect predictor of performance in Canada, the strength of the gradient would be 1 and all points would lie on the gradient. However, at every level of SES in Canada, there is still substantial variability in student performance. In the OECD, 22% of the differences in performance of students in OECD countries are explained by SES, indicating a much stronger gradient. The shorter line, shallower slope and lower strength of the Canadian gradient indicate that students in Canada tend to have a more equitable distribution of resources and that differences in the level of these resources do not matter as much to performance in Canada as in OECD countries overall.

figure 4.6

Socio-economic gradients for Canada and the OECD

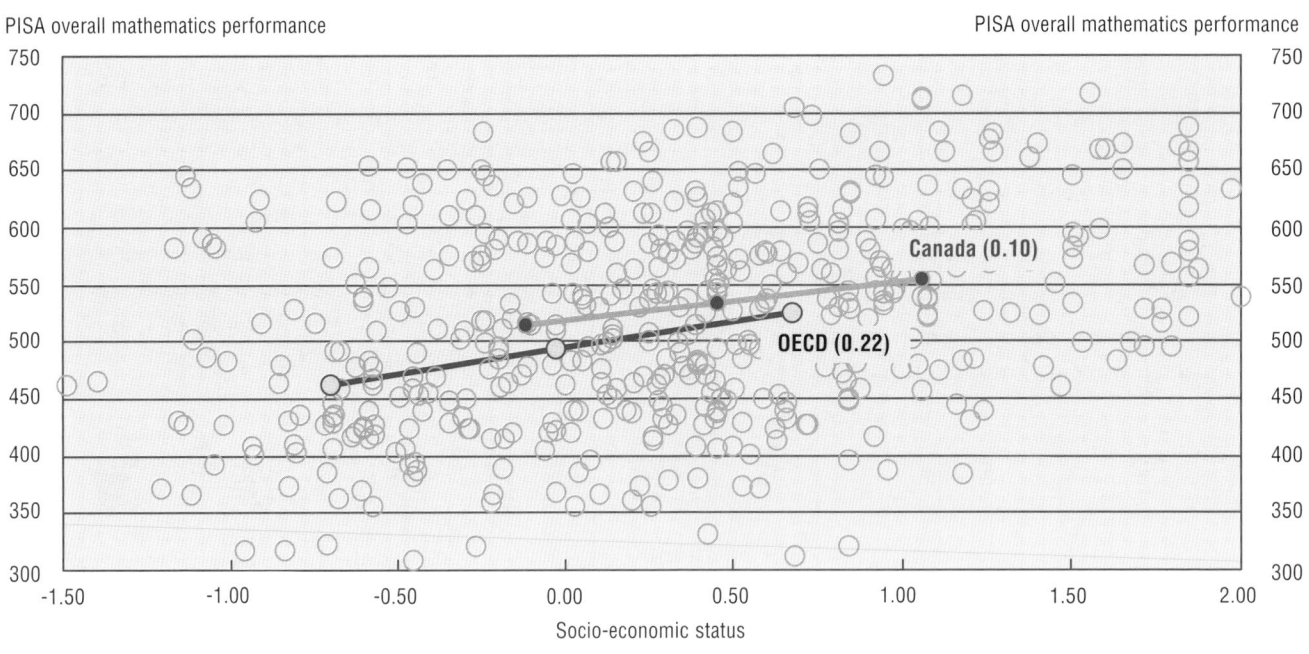

PISA overall mathematics performance

PISA overall mathematics performance

Socio-economic status

Gradients may be used to examine the extent to which groups of students perform differently from other groups due to differences in SES. At all comparable levels between the 25th and 75th percentiles, the Canadian gradient is higher than the OECD gradient, suggesting that most students in Canada performed better, on average, than students in OECD countries regardless of SES. However, the two gradients are not parallel. At higher levels of SES, the OECD countries gradient becomes closer to the Canadian gradient and, if it were to be extended further, would intersect Canada's gradient around the SES value of 1.00. The closeness of the gradients at high levels of SES suggests that high SES students perform similarly, regardless of whether they attend school in Canada or on average OECD countries. Thus, some of the difference in average performance between the OECD countries and Canada can be explained by a) the greater relative disadvantage of low-SES students in the OECD, and b) the lower SES of students in OECD countries overall.

Across most Canadian provinces, the gradients are similar in length, slope and strength to the gradient for all Canadian students (Figure 4.7). This similarity suggests that, in all provinces, the disparity in performance between students of different SES is of similar magnitude. In most provinces, around 10% of

the differences in student performance can be explained by differences in SES. The exception is Manitoba, where the relationship is less pronounced, and Newfoundland and Labrador, where the relationship is more pronounced.

The relative positions of the gradients illustrate how provincial differences in SES relate to differences in performance. Alberta's higher levels of SES are associated with higher average performance, but its gradient does not overlap or intersect any others, suggesting that students in Alberta would still perform better on average than students in other provinces with comparable levels of SES. The closeness of the Quebec gradient to Alberta's suggests that performance in Quebec would be more comparable if Quebec students had similar SES as their peers in Alberta. Although British Columbia had a higher average performance than Quebec, the gradient in British Columbia is lower than that in Quebec at all levels of SES. This comparison suggests that the high performance of students in British Columbia is related to their higher-than-average SES. The gradients of Newfoundland and Labrador, Ontario, Saskatchewan, Nova Scotia and New Brunswick intersect, despite having similar slopes, indicating that much of the difference between these provinces in average performance may be explained by differences in their distributions of SES.

The low position of the gradient in Prince Edward Island indicates that students in Prince Edward Island tend to perform lower than students in other provinces regardless of their level of SES.

The socio-economic composition of schools can help or hinder student learning by compounding the effect of individual SES

Both theory and empirical evidence suggest that students' knowledge and behaviour, including academic outcomes, are influenced by the characteristics of the schools they attend. Schools can be characterized by the socio-economic composition of their student population. Schools may have higher or lower average SES, depending on whether their students are predominantly from low or high SES families. Schools may also differ in how they mix students from different backgrounds. Schools are more segregated if most of the students tend to have the same level of SES or more inclusive if students come from a variety of backgrounds. To some extent, the socio-economic background of the school population may reflect the socio-economic conditions of the community where the school is located and thus be a community characteristic as well as a school characteristic. In other jurisdictions, however, it may also be the result of administrative decisions affecting student intake, either through the definition of school catchment areas or the degree to which students and families are able to choose schools and school programs.

Figure 4.7

Socio-economic gradients for Canadian provinces

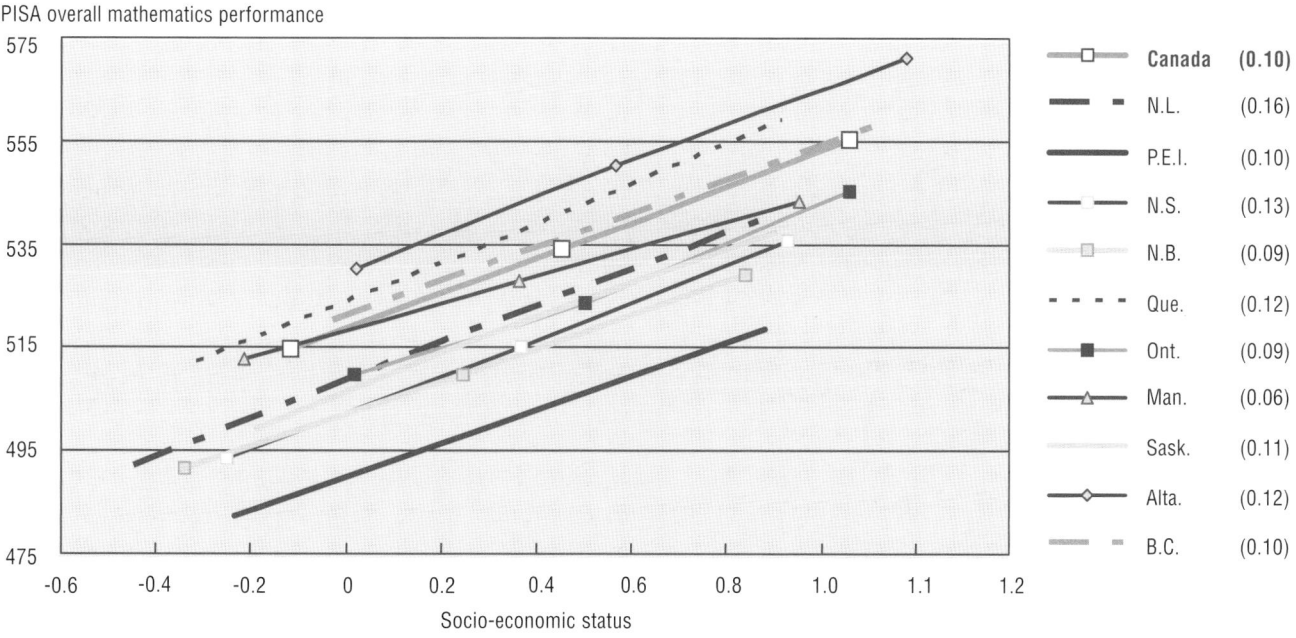

PISA overall mathematics performance

Canada	(0.10)
N.L.	(0.16)
P.E.I.	(0.10)
N.S.	(0.13)
N.B.	(0.09)
Que.	(0.12)
Ont.	(0.09)
Man.	(0.06)
Sask.	(0.11)
Alta.	(0.12)
B.C.	(0.10)

Socio-economic status

Earlier in this chapter, the importance of SES was discussed. However, schools play an important role in moderating the effects of individual SES. Figure 4.8 shows the typical range (25th to 75th percentiles) of mathematics scores of students in schools with different socio-economic composition after controlling for individual socio-economic background. Schools were grouped into the lowest, middle, and highest thirds of average SES. Even if all students had similar socio-economic backgrounds, students tended to perform better, on average, in schools with higher average SES. This tendency suggests that students are not only affected by the socio-economic circumstances of their own parents, but by those of their peers as well. This may have a positive effect for students surrounded by positive peer influences and role models, but it may also doubly-disadvantage students from lower SES families attending school with other students from similar backgrounds.

However, there is a great deal of overlap in the distributions, indicating that even if all students and schools had similar SES, there would still be differences in student performance.

Summary

The results from this chapter revealed that the home environment of a student is related to mathematics performance. In all provinces, students whose parents had a university education performed almost a full proficiency level higher than those whose parents had high school or less. However, there were still many Canadian students whose parents had high school or less with higher mathematics scores than students with university-educated parents. Parental education is associated with, but does not determine, performance for students.

Parental occupation was also related to the mathematics performance of students. Specifically, students whose parents had occupations requiring advanced mathematics skills performed over a full performance level higher than other students whose parents had occupations associated with similar education and income. These results suggest that the value of skills

modeled by parents through pursuit of education and occupations may have a greater influence on student performance than the income or prestige associated with the attainment of these goals.

Parents may also model the value of skills and learning by developing a positive home environment for their children. Such an environment includes role models who demonstrate the value of skills and learning as well as resources and opportunities to learn. Socio-economic status (SES) was used as a measure to describe the relative advantage associated with a student's home environment. Canadian students tend to be more advantaged than students in all OECD countries combined, but students in some provinces are more advantaged than others. In every province, students with higher SES tend to perform better in mathematics. Furthermore, students tend to have better performance when they attend schools with students from high SES backgrounds, regardless of their own families' SES.

Note

22.   Statistics Canada. 2003. Earnings of Canadians, 2001 Census. Catalogue no. 97F0019XCB2001000. Ottawa.

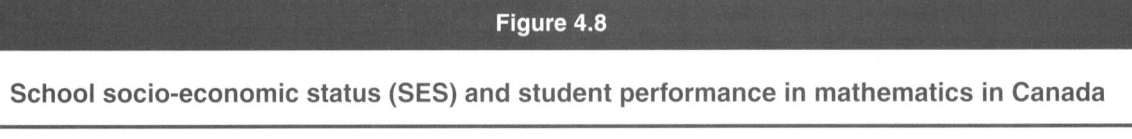

Figure 4.8

School socio-economic status (SES) and student performance in mathematics in Canada

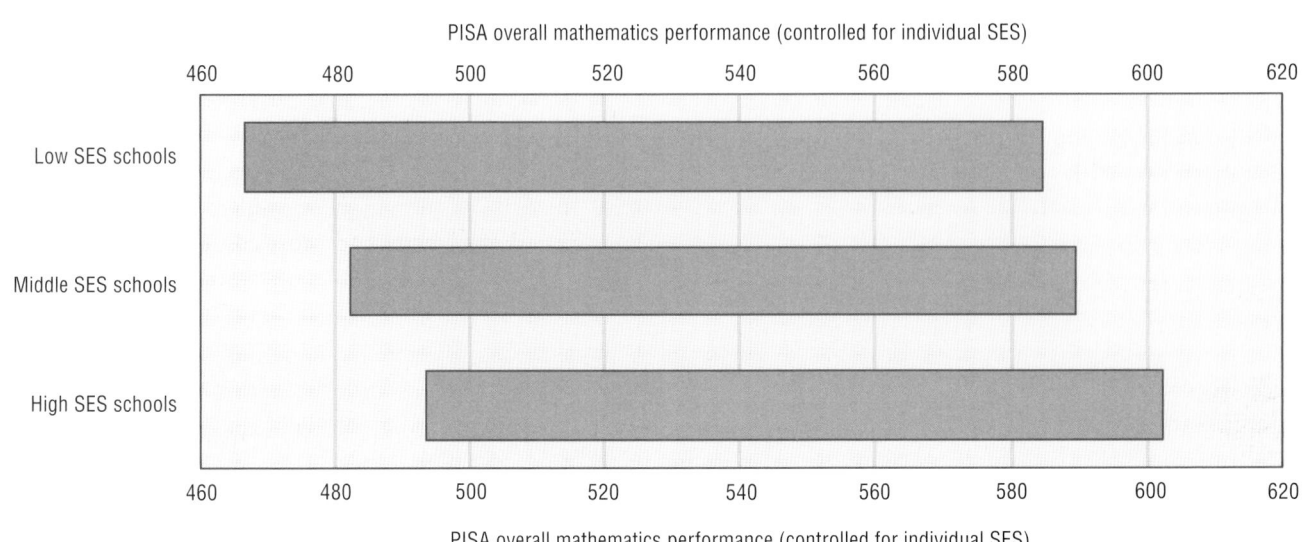

Conclusion

Ensuring that Canadian students acquire the skills and knowledge to participate fully in a knowledge-based economy and society is a goal shared by all levels of government and by the Canadian population. Will Canadian youth be well equipped to compete in tomorrow's economy? Have they developed a foundation of knowledge and skills for lifelong learning?

The OECD Programme for International Student Assessment (PISA) was first conducted in 2000. It compares how 15-year-old students from Canada perform in three domains - mathematics, reading, and science - in comparison with their peers from other countries. Each PISA assessment provides more detailed information on one of the three domains. Reading was the major domain in 2000 and mathematics in 2003. In addition to having reading and science as minor domains, the 2003 assessment also assessed problem-solving skills.

The PISA 2000 results were positive for Canada since the students' performances were among the highest and most equitably distributed. Results from this report on PISA 2003 also show that 15-year-old students in Canada performed well in all four domains assessed, relative to their international peers.

Canadian 15-year-olds performed well in mathematics

Students from only two countries (Hong Kong-China and Finland) outperformed Canada's 15-year-olds in mathematics. The PISA 2003 design allowed for an examination of four sub-domains corresponding to four content areas in mathematics: *space and shape; change and relationships, quantity*, and *uncertainty*. Canadian students performed less well in the *space and shape* sub-domain relative to their performance in the three other sub-

domains. They were outperformed by eight countries in *space and shape* compared to only one or two countries in the other sub-domains. Further study is needed to understand why the performance of Canadian students was lower in *space and shape* relative to the other three sub-domains.

The mathematical abilities of students are also described using six proficiency levels. A higher proportion of Canadian students performed at the two highest proficiency levels (Levels 5 and 6) compared to the OECD average. Furthermore, a lower proportion of 15-year-old Canadians performed at Level 1 or below. Using these proficiency levels, it is also possible to express the differences not only in terms of statistical significance, but also in terms of differences in mathematical abilities. The difference between the country with the highest overall mathematics result (Hong Kong-China) and the result for Canada is equivalent to less than a third of a proficiency level. On the other hand, Canadian 15-year-old students scored more than half a proficiency level above the OECD average.

It is possible to compare performance in the two mathematics sub-domains included in both PISA 2000 and 2003. For Canada and most countries for which a comparison is possible, there was no change in the performance on *space and shape* while there was an improvement in the performance on *change and relationships*.

At the provincial level, all provinces performed at or above the OECD average in mathematics. Furthermore, students from Alberta, British Columbia, and Quebec performed as well as those from the top performing countries. Examining provincial results in mathematics by proficiency levels reveals some important differences. Students from Alberta performed around half a proficiency level higher, or more, than students from Newfoundland and Labrador, Saskatchewan, Nova Scotia, New Brunswick, and Prince Edward Island on the combined mathematics scale. On the other hand, students from Prince Edward Island were outperformed by about half a proficiency level or more by students from Manitoba, Ontario, Quebec, British Columbia, and Alberta.

Between 2000 and 2003, Canadian students' performance remained unchanged in reading but was lower in science

Canadian 15-year-olds also performed well in the other domains measured by PISA. Only Finland outperformed Canada in reading, while four countries outperformed Canada in science and problem solving (Finland, Japan, Hong Kong-China, Korea).

Compared with PISA 2000, the average reading performance of Canadian 15-year-olds remained unchanged in PISA 2003. On the other hand, the average science performance was lower in PISA 2003. While this decrease cannot be seen as a trend, it warrants further analysis. Since science will be the major domain of PISA 2006, the third cycle of PISA will provide additional insight on how well equipped Canadian students are in this domain, will allow for a relative estimate of trend in performance, and will provide additional insight into the factors associated with science performance.

All provinces did well in the three minor domains of reading, science, and problem solving and performed at or above the OECD average with one exception: Prince Edward Island performed below the OECD average in science. In fact, students from Alberta performed equally well as students from the top performing countries in all three domains. Similarly, the performance of the students from British Columbia was as good as students from the top performing countries in reading. Although most provinces performed at or above the OECD average, differences in performance among the provinces in all four PISA domains raise interesting questions of equity across Canada.

Boys significantly outperformed girls in mathematics, but the magnitude of the difference is small

Another matter that warrants further analysis is the gender difference in performance. In 27 countries, including Canada, boys' outperformed girls in mathematics. However, it should be noted that the magnitude of the difference in Canada was small, representing only about a sixth of a proficiency level. Furthermore, there was no detectable difference between boys and girls in three provinces (Prince Edward Island, Quebec, and Saskatchewan).

As was the case in PISA 2000, there was a relatively large difference favouring girls in reading. This difference was significant in all but one country and in all provinces. As was the case with mathematics, boys performed significantly higher than girls in science in Canada overall. However, among the provinces, the difference was significant in Nova Scotia, Ontario and Manitoba. There was no gender difference in problem solving in Canada and in most provinces.

Differences in performance between students in the French-language and English-language school systems varied by province and subject

Except for Ontario, there was no difference in the mathematics performance between students in the English-language and French-language school systems.

In Ontario, students in the French-language school system performed lower than their peers in the English-language school system in mathematics as well as in reading, science, and problem solving. On the other hand, in Quebec there was no difference between the French-language and English-language school systems in any of the domains assessed.

The performance of students in the French-language school system from New Brunswick and Nova Scotia was lower in reading, science and problem solving as was the performance of students from the French-language school system in Manitoba in reading and science.

Mathematics confidence and anxiety are strongly related to achievement

The results presented in this report also reveal that student engagement in mathematics is related to achievement. In fact, students with high mathematics confidence performed around two proficiency levels higher than did students with low confidance. Furthermore, students with high mathematical anxiety performed the equivalent of one proficiency level lower than students with low anxiety. These results suggest that high Mathematics confidence and low mathematics anxiety may be important outcomes on their own.

Family background characteristics are related to student performance

Family background characteristics were also related to student performance in mathematics. In all provinces, 15-year-old students whose parents had a university degree performed about two-thirds of a proficiency level higher than those whose parents had high school education or less. Additionally, students whose parents had an occupation requiring advanced mathematics performed almost one proficiency level higher than other students whose parents had occupations associated with similar education and income but whose occupation did not require advanced mathematics.

Students from families with higher socio-economic status also tended to perform better in mathematics. However, socio-economic status had a smaller impact on mathematics achievement in Canada than in all OECD countries combined.

The socio-economic composition of schools influences mathematics achievement

Students who attended schools with students from higher socio-economic status (SES) backgrounds performed better in mathematics regardless of the SES of their family. This finding suggests that students are not only affected by the socio-economic circumstances of their own parents, but by those of their peers as well. However, there is a great deal of overlap in the distributions of student performance by the socio-economic composition of the schools they attend. This finding indicates that even if all students and schools had similar socio-economic status, there would still be differences in student performance.

The performance of Canadian 15-year-olds merits recognition yet also raises some concerns. Overall, when compared with their peers in other participating countries, Canadian students did well on the PISA 2003 assessment. However, significant provincial differences in many domains exist. Furthermore, the relatively lower performance in the *space and shape* sub-domain and the science domain as well as the lower performance in science between PISA 2000 and PISA 2003 are noteworthy. Nevertheless, the performance of Canadian youth in the PISA assessment is promising to their future and the future of Canada.

Appendix A

PISA sampling procedures and response rates

The accuracy of PISA survey results depends on the quality of the information on which the sample is based as well as the sampling procedures. The PISA sample for Canada was based on a two-stage stratified sample. The first stage consisted of sampling individual schools in which 15-year-old students were enrolled. Schools were sampled systematically with probabilities proportional to size, the measure of size being a function of the estimated number of eligible (15-year-old) students enrolled. A minimum of 150 schools were required to be selected in each country. In Canada, a much larger sample of schools was selected in order to produce reliable estimates for each province and for each of the language systems in the five provinces where these populations were separately sampled (Nova Scotia, New Brunswick, Quebec, Ontario and Manitoba).

The second stage of the selection process sampled students within sampled schools. Once schools were selected, a list of each sampled school's 15-year-old students was prepared. From this list, 35 students were then selected with equal probability. All 15-year old students were selected if fewer than 35 were enrolled. Additionally, in Prince Edward Island, Nova Scotia and New Brunswick and in the French-language school system in Manitoba, more than 35 students were selected in order to meet sample size requirements.

In order to minimize the potential for response bias, data quality standards in PISA require minimum participation rates for schools and students. At the national level, a minimum response rate of 85% was required for schools initially selected. School response rates were also considered acceptable where the initial school response rate was between 65% and 85% and replacement schools were used to achieve a school response rate of 85% or higher. Schools with student participation rates between 25% and 50% were not counted as participating schools, but data for these schools were included in the database. Schools with student participation rates of less than 25% were not counted as participating and their data were excluded from the database.

PISA also requires a minimum student participation rate of 80% within all participating schools combined (original sample and replacements) at the national level.

Table A1 shows the response rates for schools and students, before and after replacement, for Canada and the 10 provinces. At the national level 1,162 schools were selected to participate in PISA and 1,040 of these initially selected schools participated. Rather than calculating school participation rates by dividing the number of participating schools by the total number of schools, school response rates were weighted based on 15-year-old enrollment numbers in each school.

With the exception of Ontario, school response rates across the provinces were 95% or higher. In Ontario, the school response rate was 64.3% after replacement.

Table A1

PISA 2003 school and student response rates

Provinces	Total number of selected schools (participating and not participating)	School response rate before replacement		School response rate after replacement		Total number of students sampled (participating and not participating)		Total number of students participating		Weighted student participation rate after replacement (%)
		N	weighted %*	N	weighted %*	un-weighted	weighted	un-weighted	weighted	
Newfoundland and Labrador	111	108	98.8	108	98.8	2,606	5,913	2,301	5,215	88.2
Prince Edward Island	26	26	100.0	26	100.0	1,832	1,832	1,653	1,653	90.2
Nova Scotia	118	117	98.8	117	98.8	3,308	10,274	2,871	8,917	86.8
New Brunswick	76	76	100.0	76	100.0	4,209	8,341	3,781	7,480	89.7
Quebec	138	131	96.9	131	96.9	3,918	71,373	3,357	61,286	85.9
Ontario	202	116	53.2	138	64.3	4,055	81,701	3,230	63,673	77.9
Manitoba	126	117	93.7	120	95.9	3,108	12,217	2,778	10,605	86.8
Saskatchewan	122	112	95.2	112	95.2	2,657	11,939	2,350	10,478	87.8
Alberta	119	115	94.9	116	95.2	2,777	34,504	2,442	29,587	85.8
British Columbia	124	122	98.9	122	98.9	3,429	40,622	2,949	34,935	86.0
Canada	1,162	1,040	80.0	1,066	84.4	31,899	278,716	27,712	233,829	83.9

*   School response rates were weighted based on 15-year-old enrollment

As response rates were lower than anticipated in Ontario, a detailed analysis was undertaken in this province to detect whether non-participation of schools was concentrated in one specific area, i.e. if there appeared to be a bias. To do this, the distribution of the non-participating schools was examined by school size and sector (French and English), by urban/rural and by public/private sector. Information on these characteristics was available for all schools, whether they participated in PISA or not. There were no differences in the distribution of various characteristics between in-scope schools and participating schools. Further analysis revealed that the distribution of schools by school board was similar for both in-scope schools and responding schools and that non-response was not concentrated within particular school boards. Consequently, among the variables that were available for analysis, there was no evidence of bias between responding and non-responding schools.

This analysis was shared with the international PISA consortium that validated the quality of the Canadian database and concluded that the Canadian data were of good quality.

Appendix B

Tables

The enclosed tables are based on the Organisation for Economic Cooperation and Development Programme for International Student Assessment, 2003.

The *standard error* associated with the estimates presented is included in parenthesis. The *confidence interval*, when presented, represents the range within which the score for the population is likely to fall, with 95% probability.

Several tables in this publication present average scores along with standard errors for these averages. In order to estimate whether two means are significantly different, the following method explains how to use the published standard errors to approximate a 95% confidence interval.

Approximate Confidence Interval = average score +/- 1.96 x Standard Error

This rough confidence interval gives a range within which the true mean is likely to fall. If two confidence intervals overlap, then there is no significant difference between the means. It should be noted that this guide will allow you to determine significance with only **about** a 95% level of confidence. As a result, by using this rule of thumb, there is a small risk that cases where the difference is significant (but very small) are not identified.

In some tables the performance of countries and provinces relative to Canada has been indicated as being higher, the same, or lower using the following legend.

Performed significantly higher than Canada	Performed the same as Canada	Performed significantly lower than Canada

Table B1.1

Estimated average scores and confidence intervals for provinces and countries: COMBINED MATHEMATICS

Country and province	Estimated average score	Standard error	Confidence interval – 95% lower limit	Confidence interval – 95% upper limit
Hong Kong-China	550	(4.5)	541	559
Alberta	549	(4.3)	540	557
Finland	544	(1.9)	541	548
Korea	542	(3.2)	536	549
British Columbia	538	(2.4)	534	543
Netherlands	538	(3.1)	532	544
Quebec	537	(4.7)	528	546
Liechtenstein	536	(4.1)	528	544
Japan	534	(4.0)	526	542
Canada	**532**	**(1.8)**	**529**	**536**
Ontario	530	(3.6)	523	537
Belgium	529	(2.3)	525	534
Manitoba	528	(3.1)	522	534
Macao-China	527	(2.9)	522	533
Switzerland	527	(3.4)	520	533
Australia	524	(2.1)	520	528
New Zealand	523	(2.3)	519	528
Newfoundland and Labrador	517	(2.5)	512	522
Saskatchewan	516	(3.9)	509	524
Czech Republic	516	(3.5)	510	523
Nova Scotia	515	(2.2)	511	519
Iceland	515	(1.4)	512	518
Denmark	514	(2.7)	509	520
New Brunswick	512	(1.8)	508	515
France	511	(2.5)	506	516
Sweden	509	(2.6)	504	514
Austria	506	(3.3)	499	512
Germany	503	(3.3)	496	509
Ireland	503	(2.4)	498	508
Prince Edward Island	500	(2.0)	496	504
Slovak Republic	498	(3.3)	492	505
Norway	495	(2.4)	491	500
Luxembourg	493	(1.0)	491	495
Poland	490	(2.5)	485	495
Hungary	490	(2.8)	484	496
Spain	485	(2.4)	480	490
Latvia	483	(3.7)	476	491
United States	483	(2.9)	477	489
Russian Federation	468	(4.2)	460	477
Portugal	466	(3.4)	459	473
Italy	466	(3.1)	460	472
Greece	445	(3.9)	437	453
Serbia and Montenegro (Ser.)	437	(3.8)	430	444
Turkey	423	(6.7)	410	437
Uruguay	422	(3.3)	416	429
Thailand	417	(3.0)	411	423
Mexico	385	(3.6)	378	392
Indonesia	360	(3.9)	352	368
Tunisia	359	(2.5)	354	364
Brazil	356	(4.8)	347	365

Note: The OECD average is 500 with a standard error of 0.6.

Table B1.2

Estimated average scores and confidence intervals for provinces and countries: MATHEMATICS SPACE AND SHAPE

Country and province	Estimated average score	Standard error	Confidence interval – 95% lower limit	Confidence interval – 95% upper limit
Hong Kong-China	558	(4.8)	549	568
Japan	553	(4.3)	545	562
Korea	552	(3.8)	544	559
Switzerland	540	(3.5)	533	546
Finland	539	(2.0)	535	543
Liechtenstein	538	(4.6)	529	547
Alberta	534	(4.3)	526	543
Belgium	530	(2.3)	525	534
Macao-China	528	(3.3)	521	534
Quebec	528	(4.5)	519	537
Czech Republic	527	(4.1)	519	535
Netherlands	526	(2.9)	521	532
New Zealand	525	(2.3)	520	530
British Columbia	523	(2.6)	517	528
Australia	521	(2.3)	516	525
Canada	**518**	**(1.8)**	**514**	**521**
Austria	515	(3.5)	508	522
Manitoba	513	(3.5)	506	519
Denmark	512	(2.8)	507	518
Ontario	512	(3.6)	505	519
France	508	(3.0)	502	513
Slovak Republic	505	(4.0)	498	513
Iceland	504	(1.5)	501	506
Saskatchewan	500	(3.7)	493	507
Germany	500	(3.3)	493	506
Sweden	498	(2.6)	493	503
Newfoundland and Labrador	498	(2.7)	493	503
Nova Scotia	498	(2.4)	493	502
New Brunswick	498	(1.7)	494	501
Poland	490	(2.7)	485	496
Luxembourg	488	(1.4)	486	491
Latvia	486	(4.0)	478	494
Norway	483	(2.5)	478	488
Prince Edward Island	480	(2.5)	475	485
Hungary	479	(3.3)	473	486
Spain	476	(2.6)	471	482
Ireland	476	(2.4)	471	481
Russian Federation	474	(4.7)	465	484
United States	472	(2.8)	467	477
Italy	470	(3.1)	464	476
Portugal	450	(3.4)	444	457
Greece	437	(3.8)	430	445
Serbia and Montenegro (Ser.)	432	(3.9)	425	440
Thailand	424	(3.3)	417	430
Turkey	417	(6.3)	405	430
Uruguay	412	(3.0)	406	418
Mexico	382	(3.2)	375	388
Indonesia	361	(3.7)	354	368
Tunisia	359	(2.6)	354	364
Brazil	350	(4.1)	342	358

Note: The OECD average is 496 with a standard error of 0.7.

Table B1.3

Estimated average scores and confidence intervals for provinces and countries: MATHEMATICS CHANGE AND RELATIONSHIPS

Country and province	Estimated average score	Standard error	Confidence interval – 95% lower limit	Confidence interval – 95% upper limit
Alberta	554	(4.4)	546	563
Netherlands	551	(3.1)	545	558
Korea	548	(3.5)	541	554
British Columbia	543	(2.5)	538	548
Finland	543	(2.2)	539	547
Hong Kong-China	540	(4.7)	531	549
Liechtenstein	540	(3.7)	532	547
Quebec	538	(5.0)	528	547
Canada	**537**	**(1.9)**	**533**	**540**
Japan	536	(4.3)	528	545
Ontario	536	(3.8)	528	543
Belgium	535	(2.4)	530	540
Manitoba	532	(3.2)	526	538
New Zealand	526	(2.4)	521	530
Australia	525	(2.3)	521	530
Switzerland	523	(3.7)	516	530
Newfoundland and Labrador	521	(2.6)	516	526
Saskatchewan	520	(4.1)	512	528
France	520	(2.6)	515	525
Macao-China	519	(3.5)	512	526
Nova Scotia	517	(2.2)	513	522
Czech Republic	515	(3.5)	508	522
New Brunswick	513	(1.9)	509	517
Iceland	509	(1.4)	507	512
Denmark	509	(3.0)	503	515
Germany	507	(3.7)	500	514
Ireland	506	(2.4)	501	511
Sweden	505	(2.9)	499	511
Prince Edward Island	502	(2.0)	498	506
Austria	500	(3.6)	493	507
Hungary	495	(3.1)	489	501
Slovak Republic	494	(3.5)	488	501
Norway	488	(2.6)	483	493
Latvia	487	(4.4)	479	496
Luxembourg	487	(1.2)	485	489
United States	486	(3.0)	480	491
Poland	484	(2.7)	479	490
Spain	481	(2.8)	475	486
Russian Federation	477	(4.6)	468	486
Portugal	468	(4.0)	460	476
Italy	452	(3.2)	446	458
Greece	436	(4.3)	427	444
Turkey	423	(7.6)	408	438
Serbia and Montenegro (Ser.)	419	(4.0)	411	427
Uruguay	417	(3.6)	410	424
Thailand	405	(3.4)	398	412
Mexico	364	(4.1)	356	372
Tunisia	337	(2.8)	331	342
Indonesia	334	(4.6)	325	343
Brazil	333	(6.0)	321	345

Note: The OECD average is 499 with a standard error of 0.7.

Table B1.4

Estimated average scores and confidence intervals for provinces and countries: MATHEMATICS QUANTITY

Country and province	Estimated average score	Standard error	Confidence interval – 95% lower limit	Confidence interval – 95% upper limit
Finland	549	(1.8)	545	552
Hong Kong-China	545	(4.2)	537	553
Alberta	545	(4.0)	537	552
Korea	537	(3.0)	531	543
Liechtenstein	534	(4.1)	525	542
British Columbia	533	(2.3)	528	538
Macao-China	533	(3.0)	527	539
Switzerland	533	(3.1)	527	539
Quebec	531	(4.7)	522	541
Belgium	530	(2.3)	525	534
Netherlands	528	(3.1)	522	534
Canada	**528**	**(1.8)**	**524**	**532**
Czech Republic	528	(3.5)	521	535
Japan	527	(3.8)	519	534
Ontario	526	(3.8)	519	534
Manitoba	523	(3.2)	517	529
Australia	517	(2.1)	513	521
Denmark	516	(2.6)	510	521
Germany	514	(3.4)	507	520
Sweden	514	(2.5)	509	518
Iceland	513	(1.5)	510	516
Austria	513	(3.0)	507	519
Saskatchewan	513	(3.9)	505	520
Newfoundland and Labrador	512	(2.6)	507	517
Slovak Republic	513	(3.4)	506	519
New Zealand	511	(2.2)	507	515
Nova Scotia	511	(2.2)	506	515
France	507	(2.5)	502	512
New Brunswick	507	(2.1)	503	511
Ireland	502	(2.5)	497	507
Luxembourg	501	(1.1)	499	504
Hungary	496	(2.7)	491	502
Prince Edward Island	496	(2.2)	491	500
Norway	494	(2.2)	490	499
Spain	492	(2.5)	487	497
Poland	492	(2.5)	487	497
Latvia	482	(3.6)	475	489
United States	476	(3.2)	470	483
Italy	475	(3.4)	468	481
Russian Federation	472	(4.0)	465	480
Portugal	465	(3.5)	459	472
Serbia and Montenegro (Ser.)	456	(3.8)	449	464
Greece	446	(4.0)	438	454
Uruguay	430	(3.2)	423	436
Thailand	415	(3.1)	409	421
Turkey	413	(6.8)	400	426
Mexico	394	(3.9)	386	402
Tunisia	364	(2.8)	359	370
Brazil	360	(5.0)	350	370
Indonesia	357	(4.3)	349	366

Note: The OECD average is 501 with a standard error of 0.6.

Table B1.5

Estimated average scores and confidence intervals for provinces and countries: MATHEMATICS UNCERTAINTY

Country and province	Estimated average score	Standard error	Confidence interval – 95% lower limit	Confidence interval – 95% upper limit
Hong Kong-China	558	(4.6)	549	567
Alberta	556	(4.4)	547	565
British Columbia	550	(2.4)	545	555
Netherlands	549	(3.0)	543	555
Finland	545	(2.1)	541	549
Quebec	542	(4.8)	533	551
Canada	542	(1.8)	538	545
Ontario	540	(3.6)	533	547
Korea	538	(3.0)	532	544
Manitoba	538	(3.0)	532	544
New Zealand	532	(2.3)	528	537
Macao-China	532	(3.2)	525	538
Australia	531	(2.2)	527	535
Newfoundland and Labrador	530	(2.5)	525	535
Japan	528	(3.9)	520	535
Iceland	528	(1.5)	525	531
Nova Scotia	528	(2.2)	523	532
Saskatchewan	526	(4.0)	519	534
Belgium	526	(2.2)	521	530
Liechtenstein	523	(3.7)	516	531
New Brunswick	523	(1.8)	519	526
Ireland	517	(2.6)	512	522
Switzerland	517	(3.3)	510	523
Denmark	516	(2.8)	510	521
Prince Edward Island	515	(2.2)	510	519
Norway	513	(2.6)	508	518
Sweden	511	(2.7)	506	516
France	506	(2.4)	501	511
Czech Republic	500	(3.1)	494	506
Austria	494	(3.1)	488	500
Poland	494	(2.3)	489	498
Germany	493	(3.3)	486	499
Luxembourg	492	(1.1)	490	494
United States	491	(3.0)	486	497
Hungary	489	(2.6)	484	494
Spain	489	(2.4)	484	494
Slovak Republic	476	(3.2)	470	482
Latvia	474	(3.3)	467	480
Portugal	471	(3.4)	464	477
Italy	463	(3.0)	457	469
Greece	458	(3.5)	451	465
Turkey	443	(6.2)	430	455
Russian Federation	436	(4.0)	429	444
Serbia and Montenegro (Ser.)	428	(3.5)	421	435
Thailand	423	(2.5)	418	428
Uruguay	419	(3.1)	412	425
Mexico	390	(3.3)	383	396
Indonesia	385	(2.9)	379	390
Brazil	377	(3.9)	369	384
Tunisia	363	(2.3)	359	368

Note: The OECD average is 502 with a standard error of 0.6.

Table B1.6

Variation in combined mathematics performance, Canada and the provinces

	Variance	Standard error	Ratio
Canada	7,588.12	(169.70)	1.00
Newfoundland and Labrador	6,946.84	(295.04)	0.92
Prince Edward Island	7,379.07	(293.94)	0.97
Nova Scotia	7,069.40	(275.71)	0.93
New Brunswick	7,404.28	(196.55)	0.98
Quebec	8,670.44	(421.23)	1.14
Ontario	6,957.44	(313.30)	0.92
Manitoba	7,738.30	(360.13)	1.02
Saskatchewan	7,512.17	(386.47)	0.99
Alberta	7,576.65	(247.95)	1.00
British Columbia	7,181.90	(210.45)	0.95

Table B1.7

Percent of students at each level for provinces and countries COMBINED MATHEMATICS

Country and province	Below Level 1		Level 1		Level 2		Level 3		Level 4		Level 5		Level 6	
	%	(SE)	%	(SE)	%	(SE)	%	(SE)	%	(SE)	%	(SE)	%	(SE)
Finland	1.5	(0.2)	5.3	(0.4)	16.0	(0.6)	27.7	(0.7)	26.1	(0.9)	16.7	(0.6)	6.7	(0.5)
Alberta	1.7	(0.3)	5.7	(0.8)	15.0	(2.1)	24.6	(1.4)	26.0	(1.7)	18.5	(1.1)	8.5	(1.4)
British Columbia	1.7	(0.3)	6.9	(0.6)	17.6	(1.0)	25.8	(1.1)	26.3	(1.0)	15.8	(0.8)	5.9	(0.6)
Korea	2.5	(0.3)	7.1	(0.7)	16.6	(0.8)	24.1	(1.0)	25.0	(1.1)	16.7	(0.8)	8.1	(0.9)
Ontario	2.0	(0.4)	7.7	(0.8)	19.1	(1.1)	27.7	(1.3)	25.1	(1.3)	13.8	(1.2)	4.6	(0.8)
Canada	2.4	(0.3)	7.7	(0.4)	18.3	(0.6)	26.2	(0.7)	25.1	(0.6)	14.8	(0.5)	5.5	(0.4)
Hong Kong-China	3.9	(0.7)	6.5	(0.6)	13.9	(1.0)	20.0	(1.2)	25.0	(1.2)	20.2	(1.0)	10.5	(0.9)
Netherlands	2.6	(0.7)	8.4	(0.9)	18.0	(1.1)	23.0	(1.1)	22.6	(1.3)	18.2	(1.1)	7.3	(0.6)
Manitoba	2.8	(0.6)	8.2	(0.8)	19.2	(1.2)	26.3	(1.4)	24.5	(1.5)	14.2	(1.2)	4.8	(0.6)
Quebec	3.3	(0.6)	7.8	(0.9)	16.2	(1.3)	23.5	(1.5)	25.6	(1.5)	16.6	(1.2)	7.0	(0.8)
Macao-China	2.3	(0.6)	8.8	(1.3)	19.6	(1.4)	26.8	(1.8)	23.7	(1.7)	13.8	(1.6)	4.8	(1.0)
Liechtenstein	4.8	(1.3)	7.5	(1.7)	17.3	(2.8)	21.6	(2.5)	23.2	(3.1)	18.3	(3.2)	7.3	(1.7)
Newfoundland and Labrador	2.9	(0.6)	9.6	(0.9)	22.2	(1.6)	27.5	(1.5)	23.6	(1.4)	11.2	(1.1)	3.0	(0.5)
Japan	4.7	(0.7)	8.6	(0.7)	16.3	(0.8)	22.4	(1.0)	23.6	(1.2)	16.1	(1.0)	8.2	(1.1)
Nova Scotia	3.2	(0.5)	10.4	(0.7)	21.5	(1.1)	28.3	(1.1)	22.3	(1.4)	11.3	(1.1)	3.0	(0.6)
Saskatchewan	3.9	(1.0)	9.9	(0.9)	20.9	(1.5)	26.7	(1.5)	23.7	(1.5)	11.7	(1.1)	3.2	(0.5)
New Brunswick	3.7	(0.5)	10.6	(0.6)	22.8	(0.9)	27.4	(1.0)	22.0	(1.0)	10.1	(0.8)	3.4	(0.4)
Australia	4.3	(0.4)	10.0	(0.5)	18.6	(0.6)	24.0	(0.7)	23.3	(0.6)	14.0	(0.5)	5.8	(0.4)
Switzerland	4.9	(0.4)	9.6	(0.6)	17.5	(0.8)	24.3	(1.0)	22.5	(0.7)	14.2	(1.1)	7.0	(0.9)
Iceland	4.5	(0.4)	10.5	(0.6)	20.2	(1.0)	26.1	(0.9)	23.2	(0.8)	11.7	(0.6)	3.7	(0.4)
New Zealand	4.9	(0.4)	10.1	(0.6)	19.2	(0.7)	23.2	(0.9)	21.9	(0.8)	14.1	(0.6)	6.6	(0.4)
Denmark	4.7	(0.5)	10.7	(0.6)	20.6	(0.9)	26.2	(0.9)	21.9	(0.8)	11.8	(0.9)	4.1	(0.5)
Belgium	7.2	(0.6)	9.3	(0.5)	15.9	(0.6)	20.1	(0.7)	21.0	(0.6)	17.5	(0.7)	9.0	(0.5)
Czech Republic	5.0	(0.7)	11.6	(0.9)	20.1	(1.0)	24.3	(0.9)	20.8	(0.9)	12.9	(0.8)	5.3	(0.5)
France	5.6	(0.7)	11.0	(0.8)	20.2	(0.8)	25.9	(1.0)	22.1	(1.0)	11.6	(0.7)	3.5	(0.4)
Ireland	4.7	(0.6)	12.1	(0.8)	23.6	(0.8)	28.0	(0.8)	20.2	(1.1)	9.1	(0.8)	2.2	(0.3)
Sweden	5.6	(0.5)	11.7	(0.6)	21.7	(0.8)	25.5	(0.9)	19.8	(0.8)	11.6	(0.6)	4.1	(0.5)
Prince Edward Island	5.2	(0.5)	12.5	(1.0)	23.7	(1.6)	28.0	(1.8)	20.5	(1.2)	7.5	(0.8)	2.6	(0.7)
Austria	5.6	(0.7)	13.2	(0.8)	21.6	(0.9)	24.9	(1.1)	20.5	(0.8)	10.5	(0.9)	3.7	(0.5)
Slovak Republic	6.7	(0.8)	13.2	(0.9)	23.5	(0.9)	24.9	(1.1)	18.9	(0.8)	9.8	(0.7)	2.9	(0.4)
Norway	6.9	(0.5)	13.9	(0.8)	23.7	(1.2)	25.2	(1.0)	18.9	(1.0)	8.7	(0.6)	2.7	(0.3)
OECD average	8.2	(0.2)	13.2	(0.2)	21.1	(0.1)	23.7	(0.2)	19.1	(0.2)	10.6	(0.1)	4.0	(0.1)
Germany	9.2	(0.8)	12.4	(0.8)	19.0	(1.0)	22.6	(0.8)	20.6	(1.0)	12.2	(0.9)	4.1	(0.5)
Luxembourg	7.4	(0.4)	14.3	(0.6)	22.9	(0.9)	25.9	(0.8)	18.7	(0.8)	8.5	(0.6)	2.4	(0.3)
Poland	6.8	(0.6)	15.2	(0.8)	24.8	(0.7)	25.3	(0.9)	17.7	(0.9)	7.8	(0.5)	2.3	(0.3)
Spain	8.1	(0.7)	14.9	(0.9)	24.7	(0.8)	26.7	(1.0)	17.7	(0.6)	6.5	(0.6)	1.4	(0.2)
Hungary	7.8	(0.8)	15.2	(0.8)	23.8	(1.0)	24.3	(0.9)	18.2	(0.9)	8.2	(0.7)	2.5	(0.4)
Latvia	7.6	(0.9)	16.1	(1.1)	25.5	(1.2)	26.3	(1.2)	16.6	(1.2)	6.3	(0.7)	1.6	(0.4)
United States	10.2	(0.8)	15.5	(0.8)	23.9	(0.8)	23.8	(0.8)	16.6	(0.7)	8.0	(0.5)	2.0	(0.4)
Portugal	11.3	(1.1)	18.8	(1.0)	27.1	(1.0)	24.0	(1.0)	13.4	(0.9)	4.6	(0.5)	0.8	(0.2)
Russian Federation	11.4	(1.0)	18.8	(1.1)	26.4	(1.1)	23.1	(1.0)	13.2	(0.9)	5.4	(0.6)	1.6	(0.4)
Italy	13.2	(1.2)	18.7	(0.9)	24.7	(1.0)	22.9	(0.8)	13.4	(0.7)	5.5	(0.4)	1.5	(0.2)
Greece	17.8	(1.2)	21.2	(1.2)	26.3	(1.0)	20.2	(1.0)	10.6	(0.9)	3.4	(0.5)	0.6	(0.2)
Serbia and Montenegro (Ser.)	17.6	(1.3)	24.5	(1.1)	28.6	(1.2)	18.9	(1.1)	8.1	(0.9)	2.1	(0.4)	0.2	(0.1)
Uruguay	26.3	(1.3)	21.8	(0.8)	24.2	(0.9)	16.8	(0.7)	8.2	(0.7)	2.3	(0.3)	0.5	(0.2)
Turkey	27.7	(2.0)	24.6	(1.3)	22.1	(1.1)	13.5	(1.3)	6.8	(1.0)	3.1	(0.8)	2.4	(1.0)
Thailand	23.8	(1.3)	30.2	(1.2)	25.4	(1.1)	13.7	(0.8)	5.3	(0.5)	1.5	(0.3)	0.2	(0.1)
Mexico	38.1	(1.7)	27.9	(1.0)	20.8	(0.9)	10.1	(0.8)	2.7	(0.4)	0.4	(0.1)	0.0	(0.0)
Brazil	53.3	(1.9)	21.9	(1.1)	14.1	(0.9)	6.8	(0.8)	2.7	(0.5)	0.9	(0.4)	0.3	(0.2)
Tunisia	51.1	(1.4)	26.9	(1.0)	14.7	(0.8)	5.7	(0.6)	1.4	(0.3)	0.2	(0.1)	0.0	
Indonesia	50.5	(2.1)	27.6	(1.1)	14.8	(1.1)	5.5	(0.7)	1.4	(0.4)	0.2	(0.1)	0.0	

Note: Countries and provinces have been sorted by the total percentage of students who attained level 2 or higher.

Table B1.8

Gender differences by country and province: COMBINED MATHEMATICS

	Gender differences					
	Females		Males		Difference (M - F)[1]	
Country and province	Estimated average score	Standard error	Estimated average score	Standard error	Score difference	Standard error
Liechtenstein	521	(6.3)	550	(7.2)	**29**	(10.9)
Korea	528	(5.3)	552	(4.4)	**23**	(6.8)
Macao-China	517	(3.3)	538	(4.8)	**21**	(5.8)
Greece	436	(3.8)	455	(4.8)	**19**	(3.6)
Slovak Republic	489	(3.6)	507	(3.9)	**19**	(3.7)
Italy	457	(3.8)	475	(4.6)	**18**	(5.9)
Luxembourg	485	(1.5)	502	(1.9)	**17**	(2.8)
Switzerland	518	(3.6)	535	(4.7)	**17**	(4.9)
Denmark	506	(3.0)	523	(3.4)	**17**	(3.2)
Brazil	348	(4.4)	365	(6.1)	**16**	(4.1)
Turkey	415	(6.7)	430	(7.9)	**15**	(6.2)
Czech Republic	509	(4.4)	524	(4.3)	**15**	(5.1)
Ireland	495	(3.4)	510	(3.0)	**15**	(4.2)
New Zealand	516	(3.2)	531	(2.8)	**14**	(3.9)
Manitoba	521	(3.9)	535	(4.1)	14	(5.0)
Portugal	460	(3.4)	472	(4.2)	**12**	(3.3)
Tunisia	353	(2.9)	365	(2.7)	**12**	(2.5)
Uruguay	416	(3.8)	428	(4.0)	**12**	(4.2)
OECD average	494	(0.8)	506	(0.8)	11	(0.8)
Nova Scotia	509	(2.9)	521	(3.0)	11	(3.9)
Canada	530	(1.9)	541	(2.1)	11	(2.1)
Ontario	524	(3.6)	536	(4.6)	11	(4.0)
Mexico	380	(4.1)	391	(4.3)	**11**	(3.9)
Newfoundland and Labrador	512	(3.0)	522	(3.5)	10	(4.2)
Russian Federation	463	(4.2)	473	(5.3)	10	(4.4)
Alberta	544	(4.2)	554	(5.3)	10	(4.4)
Germany	499	(3.9)	508	(4.0)	9	(4.4)
Spain	481	(2.2)	490	(3.4)	9	(3.0)
France	507	(2.9)	515	(3.6)	9	(4.2)
Japan	530	(4.0)	539	(5.8)	8	(5.9)
British Columbia	534	(2.2)	542	(3.4)	8	(3.2)
Hungary	486	(3.3)	494	(3.3)	8	(3.5)
Austria	502	(4.0)	509	(4.0)	8	(4.4)
Belgium	525	(3.2)	533	(3.4)	8	(4.8)
Finland	541	(2.1)	548	(2.5)	7	(2.7)
Quebec	534	(4.7)	541	(5.7)	7	(4.6)
Sweden	506	(3.1)	512	(3.0)	7	(3.3)
United States	480	(3.2)	486	(3.3)	6	(2.9)
Norway	492	(2.9)	498	(2.8)	6	(3.2)
New Brunswick	509	(1.9)	515	(2.7)	6	(2.9)
Poland	487	(2.9)	493	(3.0)	6	(3.1)
Australia	522	(2.7)	527	(3.0)	5	(3.8)
Netherlands	535	(3.5)	540	(4.1)	5	(4.3)
Hong Kong-China	548	(4.6)	552	(6.5)	4	(6.6)
Indonesia	358	(4.6)	362	(3.9)	3	(3.4)
Latvia	482	(3.6)	485	(4.8)	3	(4.0)
Serbia and Montenegro (Ser.)	436	(4.5)	437	(4.2)	1	(4.4)
Prince Edward Island	501	(2.7)	500	(3.3)	-1	(4.5)
Saskatchewan	518	(4.2)	515	(4.4)	-3	(3.7)
Thailand	419	(3.4)	415	(4.0)	-4	(4.2)
Iceland	523	(2.2)	508	(2.3)	**-15**	(3.5)

1. Significant differences are marked in bold. Difference is significant when the score difference +/-(1.96*SE) does not include zero.

Table B1.9

Gender differences by country and province: MATHEMATICS SPACE AND SHAPE

Country and province	Gender differences					
	Females		Males		Difference (M - F)[1]	
	Estimated average score	Standard error	Estimated average score	Standard error	Score difference	Standard error
Liechtenstein	518	(7.1)	557	(7.9)	**39**	(12.1)
Slovak Republic	487	(4.1)	522	(4.7)	**35**	(4.5)
Czech Republic	512	(5.1)	542	(4.8)	**30**	(5.7)
Luxembourg	474	(2.0)	503	(2.2)	**28**	(3.3)
Korea	536	(6.2)	563	(5.1)	**27**	(8.0)
Ireland	463	(3.4)	489	(3.0)	**25**	(4.3)
Switzerland	526	(3.7)	552	(5.3)	**25**	(5.6)
Macao-China	517	(4.3)	540	(5.1)	**23**	(6.8)
Manitoba	501	(4.6)	524	(4.3)	**23**	(5.7)
Uruguay	402	(3.4)	423	(3.6)	**21**	(3.6)
Russian Federation	464	(5.0)	485	(5.8)	**21**	(5.0)
Ontario	503	(4.2)	523	(4.4)	**20**	(4.6)
Canada	511	(2.2)	530	(2.1)	**20**	(2.5)
Greece	428	(3.8)	447	(4.7)	**19**	(4.0)
Austria	506	(4.3)	525	(4.4)	**19**	(5.2)
Spain	467	(2.4)	486	(3.5)	**18**	(3.0)
Italy	462	(4.1)	480	(4.7)	**18**	(6.3)
Alberta	525	(4.2)	543	(5.5)	**18**	(5.0)
New Zealand	516	(3.3)	534	(2.7)	**18**	(3.9)
Belgium	520	(3.3)	538	(3.2)	**18**	(4.6)
France	499	(3.2)	517	(4.3)	**18**	(4.7)
OECD average	488	(0.8)	505	(0.8)	17	(0.9)
British Columbia	513	(2.7)	531	(3.5)	17	(3.7)
Nova Scotia	489	(3.2)	506	(3.0)	**16**	(4.1)
Denmark	504	(3.3)	521	(3.4)	**16**	(3.7)
Tunisia	351	(3.2)	367	(2.8)	**16**	(3.0)
Indonesia	353	(4.2)	369	(3.7)	**16**	(2.9)
Mexico	374	(3.5)	390	(4.1)	**16**	(3.8)
United States	464	(3.1)	480	(3.3)	**15**	(3.2)
Newfoundland and Labrador	491	(3.4)	506	(3.9)	**15**	(4.9)
Portugal	443	(3.5)	458	(4.2)	**15**	(3.5)
Hungary	471	(3.9)	486	(3.8)	**15**	(4.0)
Brazil	343	(4.0)	358	(5.2)	**15**	(4.1)
New Brunswick	490	(2.2)	505	(2.7)	**15**	(3.4)
Latvia	480	(3.9)	494	(5.2)	**14**	(4.2)
Quebec	522	(4.5)	535	(5.6)	14	(4.9)
Poland	484	(3.3)	497	(3.2)	**13**	(3.7)
Australia	515	(2.9)	526	(3.2)	**12**	(3.9)
Turkey	411	(6.2)	423	(7.6)	12	(6.0)
Germany	494	(4.0)	506	(4.0)	**11**	(4.7)
Sweden	493	(3.2)	503	(3.0)	**10**	(3.5)
Japan	549	(4.2)	558	(6.3)	9	(6.3)
Prince Edward Island	476	(3.7)	485	(4.0)	9	(5.8)
Netherlands	522	(3.4)	530	(3.7)	8	(4.3)
Norway	479	(3.5)	486	(3.1)	7	(4.3)
Saskatchewan	497	(4.4)	503	(4.1)	6	(4.3)
Thailand	422	(3.8)	426	(4.3)	5	(4.7)
Hong Kong-China	556	(5.0)	560	(6.8)	4	(6.8)
Serbia and Montenegro (Ser.)	431	(4.9)	434	(4.3)	3	(4.9)
Finland	538	(2.4)	540	(2.6)	2	(3.0)
Iceland	511	(2.3)	496	(2.4)	**-15**	(3.7)

1. Significant differences are marked in bold. Difference is significant when the score difference +/- (1.96*SE) does not include zero.

Table B1.10

Gender differences by country and province: MATHEMATICS CHANGE AND RELATIONSHIPS

| Country and province | Gender differences | | | | | |
| | Females | | Males | | Difference (M - F)[1] | |
	Estimated average score	Standard error	Estimated average score	Standard error	Score difference	Standard error
Liechtenstein	526	(6.5)	552	(7.4)	**26**	(12.1)
Korea	532	(5.8)	558	(4.7)	**25**	(7.3)
Italy	442	(4.0)	463	(4.9)	**21**	(6.3)
Denmark	499	(3.3)	520	(3.7)	**21**	(3.5)
Macao-China	509	(4.6)	529	(5.0)	**20**	(6.6)
Brazil	324	(5.5)	344	(7.3)	**20**	(4.7)
Greece	427	(4.4)	445	(5.2)	**18**	(4.2)
New Zealand	517	(3.4)	534	(2.8)	**17**	(4.1)
Slovak Republic	486	(3.9)	502	(4.1)	**16**	(4.2)
Manitoba	524	(3.9)	540	(4.4)	**16**	(5.3)
Switzerland	515	(3.9)	530	(5.1)	**15**	(5.3)
Ontario	529	(3.8)	544	(4.9)	**15**	(4.0)
Luxembourg	480	(1.8)	494	(2.5)	**14**	(3.7)
Canada	532	(2.0)	546	(2.2)	**13**	(2.3)
Portugal	462	(4.0)	475	(4.8)	**13**	(3.8)
Czech Republic	508	(4.0)	521	(4.5)	**13**	(4.9)
Ireland	500	(3.5)	512	(3.0)	**13**	(4.4)
Nova Scotia	511	(3.1)	524	(3.1)	**13**	(4.3)
Germany	502	(4.4)	514	(4.3)	**12**	(4.4)
OECD average	493	(0.8)	504	(0.8)	11	(0.9)
Finland	537	(2.4)	549	(2.8)	**11**	(2.8)
Tunisia	331	(3.3)	342	(3.0)	**11**	(3.0)
Alberta	549	(4.9)	560	(5.3)	**11**	(5.3)
Newfoundland and Labrador	516	(3.2)	526	(3.7)	**10**	(4.5)
British Columbia	538	(2.4)	548	(3.6)	**10**	(3.7)
Hungary	490	(3.6)	499	(3.6)	**10**	(3.9)
Spain	477	(2.6)	485	(3.8)	**8**	(3.3)
Quebec	534	(4.9)	542	(6.0)	8	(4.7)
New Brunswick	509	(2.0)	517	(2.8)	**8**	(3.0)
Mexico	360	(4.6)	368	(4.9)	8	(4.4)
Poland	481	(3.4)	488	(3.1)	**8**	(3.6)
Belgium	531	(3.5)	539	(3.6)	8	(5.1)
Japan	533	(4.3)	539	(6.4)	6	(6.6)
Turkey	419	(7.4)	425	(9.1)	6	(7.2)
Netherlands	548	(3.7)	554	(3.8)	6	(4.3)
United States	483	(3.3)	488	(3.4)	6	(2.9)
Uruguay	414	(4.2)	420	(4.2)	5	(4.4)
Austria	497	(4.4)	502	(4.4)	5	(5.0)
Australia	523	(2.8)	527	(3.2)	4	(3.8)
France	518	(3.2)	522	(4.0)	4	(5.0)
Norway	486	(3.1)	490	(3.2)	4	(3.3)
Indonesia	332	(5.4)	336	(4.4)	4	(3.4)
Russian Federation	475	(4.5)	479	(6.0)	3	(5.1)
Serbia and Montenegro (Ser.)	418	(4.9)	420	(4.5)	1	(4.9)
Sweden	504	(3.9)	506	(3.4)	1	(4.3)
Hong Kong-China	539	(4.8)	540	(6.8)	1	(7.2)
Prince Edward Island	502	(2.7)	501	(3.7)	-1	(5.0)
Latvia	488	(4.3)	487	(5.3)	-1	(4.0)
Saskatchewan	521	(4.4)	519	(4.7)	-2	(3.9)
Iceland	514	(2.3)	505	(2.4)	**-10**	(3.8)
Thailand	409	(4.0)	400	(4.5)	-10	(5.1)

1. Significant differences are marked in bold. Difference is significant when the score difference +/- (1.96*SE) does not include zero.

Table B1.11

Gender differences by country and province: MATHEMATICS QUANTITY

	Gender differences					
	Females		Males		Difference (M - F)[1]	
Country and province	Estimated average score	Standard error	Estimated average score	Standard error	Score difference	Standard error
Greece	435	(4.0)	458	(4.9)	**23**	(4.0)
Korea	524	(4.9)	546	(4.0)	**22**	(6.2)
Liechtenstein	523	(5.6)	544	(7.0)	**21**	(9.9)
Brazil	351	(4.8)	370	(6.3)	**18**	(4.5)
Turkey	404	(6.6)	421	(8.0)	**18**	(6.3)
Macao-China	525	(4.2)	542	(4.3)	**17**	(6.0)
Tunisia	357	(3.3)	372	(2.9)	**16**	(2.7)
Portugal	459	(3.7)	473	(4.1)	**14**	(3.3)
Italy	469	(4.4)	481	(5.0)	13	(6.5)
Slovak Republic	506	(3.6)	519	(4.0)	**13**	(3.6)
Mexico	388	(4.3)	400	(4.8)	**12**	(4.5)
Uruguay	424	(3.8)	436	(3.9)	**12**	(4.1)
New Zealand	505	(3.2)	517	(2.7)	**12**	(3.9)
Denmark	511	(2.9)	520	(3.2)	**9**	(3.1)
Ireland	497	(3.5)	506	(3.1)	**9**	(4.3)
Luxembourg	497	(1.6)	506	(2.2)	**9**	(3.2)
Manitoba	519	(4.2)	527	(4.2)	8	(5.3)
Ontario	523	(3.8)	530	(4.8)	7	(4.2)
Switzerland	529	(3.2)	536	(4.4)	7	(4.6)
OECD average	498	(0.8)	504	(0.8)	6	(0.8)
Russian Federation	469	(4.2)	476	(5.0)	6	(4.4)
Czech Republic	525	(4.5)	531	(4.2)	6	(5.1)
Spain	490	(2.2)	495	(3.6)	5	(3.1)
Canada	528	(1.9)	533	(2.2)	5	(2.2)
Alberta	542	(3.8)	547	(5.5)	5	(5.1)
United States	474	(3.6)	478	(3.6)	4	(3.4)
Sweden	512	(3.2)	515	(2.9)	3	(3.6)
Finland	547	(2.1)	550	(2.3)	3	(2.3)
Japan	525	(3.7)	528	(5.6)	3	(5.7)
Austria	512	(3.7)	515	(3.7)	3	(4.2)
Latvia	480	(3.6)	483	(4.4)	3	(3.4)
Newfoundland and Labrador	511	(3.2)	514	(3.9)	3	(4.8)
France	506	(2.9)	508	(3.8)	2	(4.4)
Indonesia	356	(5.0)	359	(4.0)	2	(3.1)
Hungary	495	(3.2)	497	(3.3)	2	(3.6)
Poland	491	(3.0)	493	(2.9)	2	(3.3)
Nova Scotia	510	(3.2)	511	(3.1)	1	(4.4)
Australia	516	(2.7)	518	(2.9)	1	(3.7)
Belgium	529	(3.3)	530	(3.3)	1	(4.7)
Germany	514	(3.8)	515	(4.2)	1	(4.4)
Quebec	531	(4.6)	532	(5.7)	1	(4.5)
Norway	494	(2.7)	494	(2.8)	0	(3.3)
British Columbia	533	(2.6)	533	(3.2)	0	(3.6)
New Brunswick	508	(2.2)	506	(3.0)	-2	(3.1)
Hong Kong-China	546	(4.1)	544	(6.0)	-3	(6.1)
Serbia and Montenegro (Ser.)	458	(4.7)	455	(4.2)	-3	(4.7)
Netherlands	530	(3.6)	526	(4.2)	-4	(4.7)
Thailand	417	(3.8)	412	(4.1)	-5	(4.9)
Saskatchewan	517	(4.2)	509	(4.6)	-8	(4.3)
Prince Edward Island	500	(2.9)	491	(3.7)	-9	(4.9)
Iceland	528	(2.3)	500	(2.5)	**-28**	(3.9)

1. Significant differences are marked in bold. Difference is significant when the score difference +/- (1.96*SE) does not include zero.

Table B1.12

Gender differences by country and province: MATHEMATICS UNCERTAINTY

| | Gender differences | | | | | |
| | Females | | Males | | Difference (M - F)[1] | |
Country and province	Estimated average score	Standard error	Estimated average score	Standard error	Score difference	Standard error
Liechtenstein	508	(5.6)	538	(6.9)	**31**	(10.5)
Italy	451	(3.8)	475	(4.5)	**24**	(5.9)
Korea	525	(5.2)	547	(4.1)	**22**	(6.6)
Luxembourg	481	(1.8)	503	(2.2)	**22**	(3.5)
Denmark	505	(3.0)	527	(3.4)	**22**	(3.2)
Switzerland	506	(3.7)	526	(4.7)	**20**	(5.2)
Greece	449	(3.7)	469	(4.3)	**20**	(3.7)
Turkey	432	(6.1)	451	(7.3)	**19**	(5.7)
Germany	484	(3.8)	502	(3.9)	**18**	(4.0)
Macao-China	523	(4.2)	541	(4.5)	**18**	(5.9)
Slovak Republic	467	(3.4)	484	(3.8)	**17**	(3.5)
Czech Republic	492	(3.8)	509	(3.9)	**17**	(4.6)
Ireland	509	(3.7)	525	(3.2)	**15**	(4.6)
Manitoba	531	(3.7)	546	(3.8)	15	(4.5)
Brazil	369	(3.7)	385	(4.9)	**15**	(3.4)
Japan	521	(3.8)	535	(5.6)	14	(5.7)
OECD average	496	(0.8)	508	(0.7)	13	(0.8)
Ontario	534	(3.5)	547	(4.8)	13	(4.3)
Alberta	549	(4.3)	563	(5.5)	13	(4.7)
Canada	538	(1.9)	551	(2.2)	13	(2.3)
Finland	539	(2.3)	551	(2.6)	**12**	(2.6)
Hong Kong-China	552	(4.6)	564	(6.6)	12	(6.7)
New Zealand	526	(3.3)	538	(2.7)	**12**	(3.9)
Nova Scotia	522	(2.9)	533	(3.0)	11	(4.0)
France	501	(2.8)	512	(3.5)	**11**	(4.2)
Norway	508	(3.2)	518	(3.0)	10	(3.3)
Newfoundland and Labrador	525	(3.0)	535	(3.5)	10	(4.3)
Portugal	466	(3.5)	476	(4.1)	**10**	(3.1)
Netherlands	544	(3.7)	554	(3.6)	9	(4.1)
British Columbia	545	(2.3)	554	(3.5)	9	(3.5)
Quebec	538	(4.6)	547	(5.9)	9	(4.4)
Sweden	506	(3.4)	515	(3.2)	9	(3.7)
Russian Federation	432	(3.9)	441	(5.1)	8	(4.2)
Uruguay	415	(3.6)	423	(3.9)	8	(4.1)
Spain	485	(2.2)	493	(3.3)	8	(2.8)
Hungary	485	(3.0)	493	(3.2)	8	(3.3)
Austria	490	(4.0)	498	(3.8)	8	(4.6)
Belgium	522	(3.2)	529	(3.2)	7	(4.7)
Australia	527	(2.7)	535	(3.0)	7	(3.7)
New Brunswick	520	(1.9)	527	(2.6)	7	(2.8)
Tunisia	360	(2.8)	367	(2.5)	**7**	(2.6)
Serbia and Montenegro (Ser.)	425	(4.2)	431	(4.0)	5	(4.2)
Mexico	388	(3.6)	392	(3.8)	4	(3.5)
United States	490	(3.1)	493	(3.4)	3	(2.8)
Poland	492	(2.8)	495	(2.8)	3	(3.2)
Latvia	474	(3.1)	474	(4.2)	0	(3.3)
Prince Edward Island	515	(2.7)	514	(3.6)	-1	(4.6)
Saskatchewan	527	(4.3)	526	(4.6)	-2	(3.7)
Indonesia	387	(3.4)	382	(2.8)	**-5**	(2.4)
Thailand	425	(3.0)	420	(3.4)	-5	(4.0)
Iceland	532	(2.4)	524	(2.4)	**-8**	(3.8)

1. Significant differences are marked in bold. Difference is significant when the score difference +/- (1.96*SE) does not include zero.

Table B2.6

Gender differences for provinces and countries: PROBLEM SOLVING

Country and province	Gender differences					
	Females		Males		Difference (M - F)[1]	
	Estimated average score	Standard error	Estimated average score	Standard error	Score difference	Standard error
Liechtenstein	524	(5.9)	535	(6.6)	12	(9.8)
Macao-China	527	(3.2)	538	(4.3)	**11**	(5.5)
Korea	546	(4.8)	554	(4.0)	8	(6.1)
Slovak Republic	488	(3.6)	495	(4.1)	7	(3.7)
Czech Republic	513	(4.3)	520	(4.1)	7	(5.0)
Brazil	368	(4.3)	374	(6.0)	5	(3.7)
Mexico	382	(4.7)	387	(5.0)	5	(4.5)
Denmark	514	(2.9)	519	(3.1)	5	(3.2)
Netherlands	518	(3.6)	522	(3.6)	4	(4.1)
Manitoba	525	(3.7)	529	(4.4)	3	(5.7)
Uruguay	409	(4.2)	412	(4.6)	3	(4.8)
Tunisia	343	(2.5)	346	(2.5)	3	(2.6)
Luxembourg	492	(1.9)	495	(2.4)	2	(3.3)
Russian Federation	477	(4.4)	480	(5.9)	2	(4.9)
Turkey	406	(5.8)	408	(7.3)	2	(5.8)
Greece	448	(4.1)	449	(4.9)	2	(4.4)
Alberta	546	(4.4)	547	(5.3)	1	(4.8)
Ontario	527	(3.4)	528	(4.3)	1	(3.9)
Ireland	498	(3.5)	499	(2.8)	1	(4.2)
Canada	532	(1.8)	533	(2.0)	0	(2.1)
Portugal	470	(3.9)	470	(4.6)	0	(3.5)
France	520	(2.9)	519	(3.8)	-1	(4.1)
United States	478	(3.5)	477	(3.4)	-1	(3.0)
Poland	487	(3.0)	486	(3.4)	-1	(3.1)
OECD average	501	(0.8)	499	(0.7)	**-2**	(0.8)
Newfoundland and Labrador	518	(3.9)	516	(4.2)	-2	(4.8)
British Columbia	537	(2.2)	535	(3.5)	-2	(3.5)
Nova Scotia	515	(3.3)	513	(3.0)	-2	(4.2)
Japan	548	(4.1)	546	(5.7)	-2	(5.7)
Switzerland	523	(3.3)	520	(4.0)	-2	(4.1)
Latvia	484	(4.0)	481	(5.1)	-3	(4.6)
Quebec	532	(4.2)	530	(5.4)	-3	(4.4)
Austria	508	(3.8)	505	(3.9)	-3	(4.3)
New Zealand	534	(3.1)	531	(2.6)	-3	(3.8)
Belgium	527	(3.2)	524	(3.1)	-3	(4.5)
Hungary	503	(3.4)	499	(3.4)	-4	(3.7)
Italy	471	(3.5)	467	(5.0)	-4	(6.0)
Hong Kong-China	550	(4.0)	545	(6.2)	-5	(6.3)
Germany	517	(3.7)	511	(3.9)	-6	(3.9)
Spain	485	(2.6)	479	(3.6)	-6	(3.1)
Australia	533	(2.5)	527	(2.7)	-6	(3.3)
New Brunswick	511	(2.1)	504	(3.3)	-6	(3.3)
Indonesia	365	(4.0)	358	(3.1)	**-7**	(3.0)
Serbia and Montenegro (Ser.)	424	(3.9)	416	(3.8)	-7	(4.1)
Norway	494	(3.2)	486	(3.1)	**-8**	(3.6)
Sweden	514	(2.8)	504	(3.0)	**-10**	(3.1)
Finland	553	(2.2)	543	(2.5)	**-10**	(3.0)
Thailand	431	(3.1)	418	(3.9)	**-12**	(4.3)
Prince Edward Island	503	(2.8)	491	(3.7)	**-13**	(4.8)
Saskatchewan	524	(4.4)	508	(4.6)	**-16**	(4.2)
Iceland	520	(2.5)	490	(2.2)	**-30**	(3.9)

1. Significant differences are marked in bold. Difference is significant when the score difference +/- (1.96*SE) does not include zero.

Table B3.1

Average score for indices of student engagement in mathematics, Canada and the provinces

	Index average	Standard error	Confidence interval – 95% lower limit	Confidence interval – 95% upper limit
Interest and enjoyment in mathematics				
Alberta	0.05	(0.02)	0.00	0.10
Newfoundland and Labrador	0.05	(0.03)	0.00	0.10
Quebec	0.02	(0.03)	-0.03	0.08
Nova Scotia	0.01	(0.02)	-0.04	0.06
New Brunswick	-0.01	(0.02)	-0.05	0.03
Canada	**-0.01**	**(0.01)**	**-0.04**	**0.02**
Ontario	-0.02	(0.04)	-0.09	0.05
Saskatchewan	-0.05	(0.03)	-0.11	0.01
Prince Edward Island	-0.09	(0.03)	-0.14	-0.03
Manitoba	-0.09	(0.03)	-0.14	-0.03
British Columbia	-0.12	(0.03)	-0.17	-0.07
Belief in the usefulness of mathematics				
Quebec	0.36	(0.03)	0.31	0.42
Nova Scotia	0.32	(0.03)	0.27	0.38
Newfoundland and Labrador	0.27	(0.02)	0.22	0.32
Alberta	0.27	(0.02)	0.23	0.31
Saskatchewan	0.24	(0.03)	0.18	0.29
Prince Edward Island	0.23	(0.03)	0.18	0.28
Canada	**0.23**	**(0.01)**	**0.20**	**0.26**
Manitoba	0.20	(0.02)	0.16	0.25
New Brunswick	0.15	(0.02)	0.12	0.19
Ontario	0.13	(0.03)	0.07	0.18
British Columbia	0.11	(0.02)	0.07	0.16
Mathematics confidence				
Quebec	0.38	(0.04)	0.31	0.45
Alberta	0.37	(0.04)	0.29	0.46
Newfoundland and Labrador	0.27	(0.03)	0.22	0.32
Canada	**0.25**	**(0.02)**	**0.22**	**0.28**
British Columbia	0.24	(0.03)	0.19	0.29
Manitoba	0.16	(0.02)	0.11	0.21
Nova Scotia	0.14	(0.02)	0.09	0.19
New Brunswick	0.14	(0.02)	0.10	0.18
Ontario	0.14	(0.03)	0.07	0.20
Saskatchewan	0.05	(0.03)	0.00	0.10
Prince Edward Island	-0.02	(0.03)	-0.07	0.04
Perceived ability in mathematics				
Quebec	0.32	(0.02)	0.27	0.37
Alberta	0.27	(0.02)	0.22	0.31
New Brunswick	0.23	(0.02)	0.20	0.27
Newfoundland and Labrador	0.20	(0.03)	0.14	0.25
Prince Edward Island	0.19	(0.03)	0.14	0.24
Canada	**0.19**	**(0.01)**	**0.17**	**0.21**
Nova Scotia	0.18	(0.02)	0.13	0.23
Saskatchewan	0.17	(0.03)	0.11	0.24
Manitoba	0.09	(0.02)	0.04	0.14
British Columbia	0.07	(0.02)	0.03	0.12
Ontario	0.07	(0.03)	0.02	0.13

Table B3.1 – Concluded

Average score for indices of student engagement in mathematics, Canada and the provinces

	Index average	Standard error	Confidence interval – 95% lower limit	Confidence interval – 95% upper limit
Mathematics anxiety				
Ontario	0.03	(0.03)	-0.02	0.09
British Columbia	0.00	(0.02)	-0.04	0.05
Manitoba	-0.03	(0.03)	-0.08	0.02
Canada	**-0.04**	**(0.01)**	**-0.07**	**-0.02**
Quebec	-0.07	(0.02)	-0.12	-0.02
Saskatchewan	-0.07	(0.03)	-0.12	-0.01
New Brunswick	-0.10	(0.02)	-0.14	-0.06
Alberta	-0.11	(0.03)	-0.16	-0.05
Nova Scotia	-0.13	(0.03)	-0.18	-0.07
Newfoundland and Labrador	-0.16	(0.02)	-0.21	-0.11
Prince Edward Island	-0.18	(0.03)	-0.23	-0.12

Note: The OECD average for all indices is 0. Provinces are sorted by average score.

Table B3.2

Difference in mathematics performance between students with high mathematics engagement compared to students with low mathematics engagement, Canada and the provinces

	Average combined mathematics score for students who are low* on the index	Average combined mathematics score for students who are high* on the index	Difference in scores (high-low)	Standard error
Belief in the usefulness of mathematics				
Prince Edward Island	457	536	79	(8.6)
British Columbia	500	575	76	(5.2)
New Brunswick	474	548	74	(5.0)
Alberta	514	587	72	(7.9)
Nova Scotia	481	551	70	(6.9)
Ontario	495	562	67	(7.3)
Canada	**504**	**567**	**62**	**(3.2)**
Saskatchewan	490	552	62	(6.5)
Manitoba	496	557	61	(8.7)
Newfoundland and Labrador	490	545	56	(8.3)
Quebec	517	560	44	(5.9)
Interest and enjoyment in mathematics				
Nova Scotia	485	566	81	(7.4)
Prince Edward Island	460	540	80	(6.9)
British Columbia	503	576	73	(5.3)
Ontario	498	569	71	(7.6)
New Brunswick	482	552	70	(6.8)
Canada	**503**	**573**	**70**	**(3.9)**
Newfoundland and Labrador	489	550	62	(7.8)
Alberta	521	582	61	(7.1)
Saskatchewan	498	549	52	(7.9)
Manitoba	503	555	52	(8.4)
Quebec	513	563	49	(8.3)

Table B3.2 – Concluded

Difference in mathematics performance between students with high mathematics engagement compared to students with low mathematics engagement, Canada and the provinces

	Average combined mathematics score for students who are low* on the index	Average combined mathematics score for students who are high* on the index	Difference in scores (high-low)	Standard error
Perceived ability in mathematics				
Prince Edward Island	449	582	134	(6.5)
New Brunswick	457	585	128	(4.7)
Manitoba	479	604	125	(8.4)
Nova Scotia	466	589	123	(6.4)
British Columbia	487	609	123	(5.5)
Alberta	502	622	120	(8.4)
Saskatchewan	472	588	116	(6.2)
Canada	**492**	**603**	**111**	**(3.0)**
Newfoundland and Labrador	468	579	111	(6.3)
Quebec	488	598	110	(5.9)
Ontario	485	586	102	(7.5)
Mathematics confidence				
Prince Edward Island	428	584	156	(8.4)
Newfoundland and Labrador	440	596	156	(8.1)
Quebec	461	612	150	(7.7)
Alberta	472	622	149	(8.1)
New Brunswick	437	583	146	(5.8)
Nova Scotia	441	585	144	(7.4)
British Columbia	471	614	143	(6.9)
Manitoba	458	599	141	(9.9)
Ontario	462	597	134	(10.0)
Canada	**478**	**611**	**133**	**(4.0)**
Saskatchewan	455	589	133	(9.6)
Mathematics anxiety				
Canada	**554**	**483**	**-71**	**(4.3)**
Newfoundland and Labrador	567	479	-88	(8.1)
Ontario	577	485	-92	(7.5)
Prince Edward Island	543	450	-93	(7.7)
British Columbia	587	491	-96	(6.7)
Saskatchewan	563	462	-101	(6.8)
Manitoba	582	480	-102	(9.7)
Nova Scotia	570	467	-103	(6.8)
Quebec	581	477	-104	(9.3)
New Brunswick	566	459	-107	(5.3)
Alberta	607	495	-112	(7.1)

* Students low on a given index are defined as those falling one standard deviation below the average.
Students high on a given index are defined as those falling one standard deviation above the average.

Table B3.3

Student engagement regression coefficients for females relative to males controlling for mathematics ability, Canada and the provinces

	Regression coefficient (females relative to males)	Standard error	Confidence interval – 95% lower limit	Confidence interval – 95% upper limit
Interest and enjoyment in mathematics				
Manitoba	0.09	(0.01)	0.06	0.12
Prince Edward Island	0.08	(0.03)	0.02	0.14
Saskatchewan	0.03	(0.01)	0.01	0.04
Nova Scotia	0.02	(0.01)	0.01	0.04
Newfoundland and Labrador	-0.03	(0.02)	-0.06	0.00
British Columbia	-0.06	(0.01)	-0.09	-0.03
Alberta	-0.07	(0.02)	-0.10	-0.03
Quebec	-0.10	(0.03)	-0.16	-0.05
New Brunswick	-0.11	(0.01)	-0.12	-0.09
Canada	**-0.12**	**(0.04)**	**-0.20**	**-0.04**
Ontario	-0.15	(0.02)	-0.19	-0.10
Belief in the usefulness of mathematics				
Newfoundland and Labrador	0.00	(0.05)	-0.10	0.10
Canada	**-0.06**	**(0.01)**	**-0.08**	**-0.04**
Alberta	-0.06	(0.01)	-0.08	-0.05
Manitoba	-0.07	(0.02)	-0.10	-0.03
Saskatchewan	-0.09	(0.01)	-0.12	-0.06
Nova Scotia	-0.10	(0.01)	-0.11	-0.08
Prince Edward Island	-0.10	(0.04)	-0.17	-0.03
British Columbia	-0.12	(0.04)	-0.19	-0.05
Quebec	-0.14	(0.01)	-0.16	-0.13
Ontario	-0.22	(0.01)	-0.24	-0.19
New Brunswick	-0.25	(0.02)	-0.29	-0.21
Mathematics confidence				
Quebec	-0.24	(0.04)	-0.31	-0.17
Newfoundland and Labrador	-0.25	(0.02)	-0.29	-0.20
Nova Scotia	-0.25	(0.02)	-0.29	-0.22
Ontario	-0.26	(0.04)	-0.33	-0.19
Canada	**-0.26**	**(0.01)**	**-0.28**	**-0.24**
New Brunswick	-0.27	(0.01)	-0.30	-0.25
British Columbia	-0.29	(0.01)	-0.32	-0.27
Saskatchewan	-0.31	(0.02)	-0.35	-0.27
Alberta	-0.35	(0.03)	-0.40	-0.30
Prince Edward Island	-0.36	(0.02)	-0.39	-0.32
Manitoba	-0.37	(0.02)	-0.42	-0.32
Perceived ability in mathematics				
Newfoundland and Labrador	-0.17	(0.02)	-0.21	-0.14
Saskatchewan	-0.23	(0.01)	-0.25	-0.20
Manitoba	-0.23	(0.02)	-0.27	-0.20
Prince Edward Island	-0.25	(0.01)	-0.28	-0.22
British Columbia	-0.26	(0.01)	-0.28	-0.23
Nova Scotia	-0.27	(0.03)	-0.33	-0.22
Canada	**-0.29**	**(0.01)**	**-0.31**	**-0.27**
Quebec	-0.31	(0.01)	-0.34	-0.29
Alberta	-0.31	(0.02)	-0.35	-0.28
Ontario	-0.32	(0.01)	-0.35	-0.30
New Brunswick	-0.34	(0.02)	-0.37	-0.31

Table B3.3 – Concluded

Student engagement regression coefficients for females relative to males controlling for mathematics ability, Canada and the provinces

	Regression coefficient (females relative to males)	Standard error	Confidence interval – 95% lower limit	Confidence interval – 95% upper limit
Mathematics anxiety				
New Brunswick	0.39	(0.02)	0.36	0.42
Nova Scotia	0.37	(0.03)	0.31	0.43
Saskatchewan	0.35	(0.02)	0.31	0.38
Ontario	0.32	(0.02)	0.29	0.35
Manitoba	0.30	(0.03)	0.25	0.36
Newfoundland and Labrador	0.29	(0.01)	0.28	0.31
Quebec	0.28	(0.01)	0.26	0.30
Alberta	0.28	(0.03)	0.22	0.34
Canada	**0.27**	**(0.01)**	**0.25**	**0.29**
Prince Edward Island	0.27	(0.01)	0.25	0.29
British Columbia	0.27	(0.01)	0.24	0.29

Note: Positive regression coefficients indicate that females score higher on a given index while negative regression coefficients indicate that males score higher on a given index.

Table B3.4

Average scores on indices of learning strategies and preferences for learning situations in mathematics, Canada and the provinces

	Index average	Standard error	Confidence interval – 95% lower limit	Confidence interval – 95% upper limit
Memorization/rehearsal learning strategies				
Newfoundland and Labrador	0.30	(0.02)	0.26	0.34
Alberta	0.25	(0.03)	0.19	0.31
Ontario	0.17	(0.02)	0.13	0.21
Nova Scotia	0.16	(0.02)	0.12	0.20
Saskatchewan	0.16	(0.03)	0.10	0.22
Canada	**0.16**	**(0.01)**	**0.14**	**0.18**
New Brunswick	0.14	(0.02)	0.10	0.18
Manitoba	0.13	(0.03)	0.07	0.19
British Columbia	0.12	(0.02)	0.08	0.16
Quebec	0.11	(0.03)	0.05	0.17
Prince Edward Island	0.08	(0.03)	0.02	0.14
Control strategies				
Quebec	0.33	(0.03)	0.27	0.39
Newfoundland and Labrador	0.15	(0.02)	0.11	0.19
Canada	**0.06**	**(0.01)**	**0.04**	**0.08**
Alberta	-0.01	(0.02)	-0.05	0.03
Ontario	-0.03	(0.03)	-0.09	0.03
British Columbia	-0.05	(0.03)	-0.11	0.01
New Brunswick	-0.06	(0.02)	-0.10	-0.02
Nova Scotia	-0.07	(0.02)	-0.11	-0.03
Saskatchewan	-0.08	(0.03)	-0.14	-0.02
Manitoba	-0.09	(0.03)	-0.15	-0.03
Prince Edward Island	-0.13	(0.03)	-0.19	-0.07

Table B3.4 – Concluded

Average scores on indices of learning strategies and preferences for learning situations in mathematics, Canada and the provinces

	Index average	Standard error	Confidence interval – 95% lower limit	Confidence interval – 95% upper limit
Elaboration strategies				
Nova Scotia	0.13	(0.02)	0.09	0.17
Quebec	0.12	(0.03)	0.06	0.18
New Brunswick	0.11	(0.02)	0.07	0.15
Alberta	0.11	(0.02)	0.07	0.15
Canada	**0.08**	**(0.01)**	**0.06**	**0.10**
Ontario	0.07	(0.03)	0.01	0.13
Newfoundland and Labrador	0.06	(0.02)	0.02	0.10
Prince Edward Island	0.04	(0.03)	-0.02	0.10
Manitoba	0.03	(0.02)	-0.01	0.07
Saskatchewan	0.02	(0.03)	-0.04	0.08
British Columbia	-0.02	(0.02)	-0.06	0.02
Preferences for cooperative learning situations				
Newfoundland and Labrador	0.27	(0.02)	0.23	0.31
New Brunswick	0.21	(0.02)	0.17	0.25
Ontario	0.21	(0.03)	0.15	0.27
Nova Scotia	0.18	(0.02)	0.14	0.22
Manitoba	0.16	(0.02)	0.12	0.20
Canada	**0.14**	**(0.01)**	**0.12**	**0.16**
Prince Edward Island	0.13	(0.03)	0.07	0.19
Alberta	0.12	(0.03)	0.06	0.18
British Columbia	0.10	(0.02)	0.06	0.14
Quebec	0.08	(0.02)	0.04	0.12
Saskatchewan	0.08	(0.03)	0.02	0.14
Preferences for competitive learning situations				
Alberta	0.29	(0.02)	0.25	0.33
Quebec	0.23	(0.03)	0.17	0.29
British Columbia	0.20	(0.02)	0.16	0.24
Canada	**0.19**	**(0.01)**	**0.17**	**0.21**
Newfoundland and Labrador	0.17	(0.02)	0.13	0.21
Ontario	0.17	(0.03)	0.11	0.23
New Brunswick	0.16	(0.02)	0.12	0.20
Nova Scotia	0.14	(0.03)	0.08	0.20
Saskatchewan	0.13	(0.03)	0.07	0.19
Prince Edward Island	0.08	(0.02)	0.04	0.12
Manitoba	0.06	(0.03)	0.00	0.12

Note: The OECD average for all indices is 0. Provinces are sorted by average score.

Table B3.5

Difference in mathematics performance between students with high levels of mathematics learning strategies and preferences for learning compared to students with low levels, Canada and the provinces

	Average mathematics score for students who are low* on the index	Average mathematics score for students who are high* on the index	Difference in scores (high-low)	Standard error
Memorization strategies				
Newfoundland and Labrador	505	535	30	(11.3)
Prince Edward Island	467	513	46	(13.4)
Nova Scotia	491	538	47	(7.0)
New Brunswick	490	519	29	(6.0)
Quebec	550	525	-25	(8.0)
Ontario	497	548	51	(7.4)
Manitoba	505	552	47	(9.3)
Saskatchewan	502	541	39	(9.2)
Alberta	524	569	45	(11.1)
British Columbia	518	559	41	(6.4)
Canada	513	548	34	(3.8)
Control strategies				
Newfoundland and Labrador	479	538	58	(9.3)
Prince Edward Island	462	519	56	(9.2)
Nova Scotia	481	536	54	(6.5)
New Brunswick	482	529	47	(6.6)
Quebec	514	548	33	(6.7)
Ontario	494	543	49	(9.3)
Manitoba	507	547	40	(8.8)
Saskatchewan	490	540	50	(7.6)
Alberta	529	585	56	(9.6)
British Columbia	511	563	51	(6.6)
Canada	505	553	49	(3.7)
Elaboration strategies				
Newfoundland and Labrador	496	543	47	(9.6)
Prince Edward Island	466	525	58	(11.3)
Nova Scotia	491	541	50	(7.6)
New Brunswick	483	533	50	(6.5)
Quebec	523	539	16	(8.5)
Ontario	504	550	46	(8.2)
Manitoba	513	544	30	(11.3)
Saskatchewan	503	527	25	(11.8)
Alberta	548	576	28	(12.7)
British Columbia	517	563	46	(8.9)
Canada	509	552	43	(4.0)
Preferences for cooperative learning				
Newfoundland and Labrador	518	509	-9	(8.4)
Prince Edward Island	491	500	9	(10.9)
Nova Scotia	530	504	-26	(7.5)
New Brunswick	507	508	1	(6.4)
Quebec	537	535	-3	(6.9)
Ontario	532	519	-14	(6.9)
Manitoba	530	533	3	(10.5)
Saskatchewan	519	518	-1	(7.8)
Alberta	571	551	-20	(10.4)
British Columbia	541	540	-1	(8.3)
Canada	524	529	5	(4.0)

Table B3.5 – Concluded

Difference in mathematics performance between students with high levels of mathematics learning strategies and preferences for learning compared to students with low levels, Canada and the provinces

	Average mathematics score for students who are low* on the index	Average mathematics score for students who are high* on the index	Difference in scores (high-low)	Standard error
Preferences for competitive learning				
Newfoundland and Labrador	500	540	40	(7.1)
Prince Edward Island	453	540	87	(10.3)
Nova Scotia	487	557	70	(9.5)
New Brunswick	487	538	51	(6.6)
Quebec	530	548	18	(8.3)
Ontario	507	562	55	(10.0)
Manitoba	501	566	65	(10.6)
Saskatchewan	504	550	47	(8.8)
Alberta	536	588	52	(10.4)
British Columbia	517	582	65	(6.3)
Canada	**516**	**568**	**52**	**(4.1)**

* Students low on a given index are defined as those falling one standard deviation below the mean.

Students high on a given index are defined as those falling one standard deviation above the mean.

Table B3.6

Average scores for learning strategies and preferences for learning: low achievers versus high achievers, Canada and the provinces

	Low performers on the combined mathematics scale		High performers on the combined mathematics scale	
	Index average	Standard error	Index average	Standard error
Memorization strategies				
Newfoundland and Labrador	0.26	(0.07)	0.39	(0.08)
Prince Edward Island	-0.14	(0.08)	0.20	(0.11)
Nova Scotia	-0.13	(0.06)	0.33	(0.05)
New Brunswick	0.00	(0.06)	0.17	(0.04)
Quebec	0.28	(0.05)	-0.10	(0.04)
Ontario	-0.09	(0.08)	0.39	(0.04)
Manitoba	-0.01	(0.07)	0.29	(0.06)
Saskatchewan	-0.03	(0.09)	0.33	(0.08)
Alberta	-0.07	(0.07)	0.42	(0.08)
British Columbia	-0.25	(0.08)	0.23	(0.04)
Canada	**0.00**	**(0.04)**	**0.24**	**(0.02)**
Control strategies				
Newfoundland and Labrador	-0.08	(0.06)	0.40	(0.07)
Prince Edward Island	-0.43	(0.07)	0.08	(0.09)
Nova Scotia	-0.39	(0.06)	0.14	(0.06)
New Brunswick	-0.32	(0.05)	0.11	(0.05)
Quebec	0.13	(0.06)	0.44	(0.04)
Ontario	-0.37	(0.08)	0.18	(0.05)
Manitoba	-0.32	(0.07)	0.09	(0.06)
Saskatchewan	-0.38	(0.07)	0.11	(0.07)
Alberta	-0.36	(0.07)	0.19	(0.05)
British Columbia	-0.44	(0.07)	0.18	(0.05)
Canada	**-0.25**	**(0.04)**	**0.24**	**(0.03)**

Table B3.6 – Concluded

Average scores for learning strategies and preferences for learning: low achievers versus high achievers, Canada and the provinces

	Low performers on the combined mathematics scale		High performers on the combined mathematics scale	
	Index average	Standard error	Index average	Standard error
Elaboration strategies				
Newfoundland and Labrador	0.07	(0.06)	0.29	(0.09)
Prince Edward Island	-0.05	(0.07)	0.37	(0.08)
Nova Scotia	0.05	(0.05)	0.42	(0.06)
New Brunswick	0.03	(0.06)	0.41	(0.05)
Quebec	0.33	(0.05)	0.19	(0.05)
Ontario	0.01	(0.07)	0.31	(0.05)
Manitoba	0.11	(0.07)	0.11	(0.05)
Saskatchewan	0.05	(0.08)	0.17	(0.06)
Alberta	0.06	(0.07)	0.22	(0.05)
British Columbia	-0.12	(0.07)	0.14	(0.05)
Canada	**0.09**	**(0.03)**	**0.23**	**(0.02)**
Preferences for cooperative learning				
Newfoundland and Labrador	0.34	(0.07)	0.21	(0.07)
Prince Edward Island	0.03	(0.08)	-0.03	(0.08)
Nova Scotia	0.36	(0.06)	-0.10	(0.06)
New Brunswick	0.22	(0.05)	0.02	(0.06)
Quebec	0.24	(0.06)	-0.04	(0.04)
Ontario	0.24	(0.08)	0.02	(0.04)
Manitoba	0.12	(0.07)	0.00	(0.06)
Saskatchewan	0.08	(0.07)	-0.03	(0.06)
Alberta	0.14	(0.07)	-0.04	(0.05)
British Columbia	-0.02	(0.08)	-0.06	(0.05)
Canada	**0.19**	**(0.04)**	**-0.02**	**(0.02)**
Preferences for competitive learning				
Newfoundland and Labrador	0.10	(0.05)	0.39	(0.07)
Prince Edward Island	-0.10	(0.07)	0.53	(0.09)
Nova Scotia	-0.12	(0.05)	0.58	(0.07)
New Brunswick	0.10	(0.04)	0.44	(0.06)
Quebec	0.28	(0.05)	0.27	(0.05)
Ontario	0.06	(0.08)	0.47	(0.06)
Manitoba	0.03	(0.06)	0.40	(0.06)
Saskatchewan	-0.01	(0.06)	0.44	(0.07)
Alberta	0.13	(0.07)	0.54	(0.08)
British Columbia	-0.11	(0.06)	0.53	(0.05)
Canada	**0.09**	**(0.03)**	**0.44**	**(0.03)**

Note: Low performers are defined as those who score below 420 points on the combined mathematics scale which corresponds to a proficiency level of 1 or less. High performers are defined as those who score above 606 points on the combined mathematics scale which corresponds to a proficiency level of 5 or higher.

Table B4.1

Parental educational attainment, Canada and the provinces

	High school or less	Standard error	College	Standard error	University	Standard error
Canada	0.37	(0.01)	0.25	(0.00)	0.38	(0.01)
Newfoundland and Labrador	0.53	(0.01)	0.18	(0.01)	0.29	(0.01)
Prince Edward Island	0.34	(0.01)	0.27	(0.01)	0.39	(0.01)
Nova Scotia	0.44	(0.01)	0.20	(0.01)	0.37	(0.01)
New Brunswick	0.41	(0.01)	0.23	(0.01)	0.36	(0.01)
Quebec	0.40	(0.01)	0.25	(0.01)	0.35	(0.01)
Ontario	0.31	(0.02)	0.29	(0.01)	0.40	(0.02)
Manitoba	0.43	(0.02)	0.17	(0.01)	0.40	(0.02)
Saskatchewan	0.45	(0.02)	0.17	(0.01)	0.38	(0.02)
Alberta	0.36	(0.02)	0.22	(0.01)	0.42	(0.02)
British Columbia	0.38	(0.01)	0.23	(0.01)	0.39	(0.02)

Note: Data are presented as proportions. For example, 0.37 is equivalent to 37%.

Table B4.2

Parental education and student performance in mathematics, Canada and the provinces

	Percentiles of overall mathematics performance					
	25	Standard error	50	Standard error	75	Standard error
Canada						
High School or less	460	(2.40)	514	(2.72)	573	(3.17)
College	475	(2.79)	533	(2.99)	589	(2.72)
University	497	(3.57)	558	(3.22)	616	(2.95)
Newfoundland and Labrador						
High School or less	449	(3.50)	501	(4.24)	555	(4.59)
College	477	(7.95)	532	(6.29)	580	(7.12)
University	484	(8.87)	550	(9.31)	606	(6.69)
Prince Edward Island						
High School or less	430	(5.18)	487	(5.94)	544	(4.86)
College	438	(9.14)	494	(6.23)	543	(5.70)
University	466	(5.22)	528	(4.99)	581	(5.32)
Nova Scotia						
High School or less	441	(4.83)	497	(4.74)	553	(3.94)
College	459	(5.46)	509	(5.11)	564	(6.23)
University	485	(5.77)	544	(5.55)	601	(5.88)
New Brunswick						
High School or less	438	(3.18)	493	(3.55)	552	(3.63)
College	463	(4.80)	515	(4.36)	571	(4.37)
University	471	(3.75)	531	(4.82)	588	(2.92)
Quebec						
High School or less	461	(7.47)	519	(5.53)	580	(5.65)
College	484	(9.70)	550	(7.05)	606	(6.44)
University	500	(9.41)	568	(6.13)	628	(7.49)
Ontario						
High School or less	460	(4.57)	506	(4.94)	565	(5.97)
College	471	(5.39)	525	(5.00)	580	(5.62)
University	497	(6.87)	554	(5.97)	611	(5.56)

Table B4.2 – Concluded

Parental education and student performance in mathematics, Canada and the provinces

	Percentiles of overall mathematics performance					
	25	Standard error	50	Standard error	75	Standard error
Manitoba						
High School or less	459	(6.08)	519	(4.78)	579	(6.18)
College	479	(7.49)	531	(6.35)	588	(8.35)
University	482	(6.24)	543	(5.34)	602	(5.38)
Saskatchewan						
High School or less	448	(7.17)	505	(6.10)	566	(5.38)
College	464	(10.63)	527	(6.90)	588	(9.32)
University	474	(5.59)	535	(4.78)	588	(4.49)
Alberta						
High School or less	473	(8.35)	531	(8.89)	592	(8.76)
College	493	(7.79)	547	(6.48)	606	(9.30)
University	516	(7.12)	572	(5.87)	632	(6.40)
British Columbia						
High School or less	469	(4.34)	523	(4.72)	582	(4.67)
College	477	(4.60)	534	(5.14)	593	(5.31)
University	503	(7.02)	563	(4.72)	617	(4.11)

Table B4.3

Distribution of parental education for Canadian students with high and low overall mathematics performance

	Level of parental education					
	High school or less	Standard error	College	Standard error	University	Standard error
Lowest 15% in mathematics	0.46	(0.01)	0.26	(0.01)	0.28	(0.01)
Highest 15% in mathematics	0.25	(0.01)	0.23	(0.01)	0.52	(0.01)

Note: Data are presented as proportions. For example, 0.46 is equivalent to 46%.

Table B4.4

Parental educational attainment and occupation, Canada

	High school or less	Standard error	College	Standard error	University	Standard error
Higher service	0.13	(0.01)	0.21	(0.01)	0.41	(0.01)
Lower service	0.18	(0.01)	0.31	(0.01)	0.38	(0.01)
Routine clerical/sales	0.29	(0.01)	0.26	(0.01)	0.11	(0.01)
Skilled-manual	0.18	(0.01)	0.11	(0.01)	0.05	(0.00)
Semi-unskilled manual	0.20	(0.01)	0.09	(0.01)	0.04	(0.00)
Farmers/Farm managers	0.03	(0.00)	0.02	(0.00)	0.01	(0.00)

Note: Data are presented as proportions. For example, 0.13 is equivalent to 13%.

Table B4.5

Parental occupation and student mathematics performance, Canada and the provinces

			Percentiles for overall mathematics performance			
	25	Standard error	50	Standard error	75	Standard error
Canada						
Higher service	502	(3.56)	564	(3.35)	621	(3.12)
Lower service	487	(3.34)	544	(2.51)	601	(2.69)
Routine clerical / sales	471	(3.26)	528	(3.13)	584	(3.01)
Skilled-manual	446	(4.05)	512	(3.95)	570	(3.78)
Semi-unskilled manual	445	(4.12)	498	(3.64)	555	(3.99)
Farmers / Farm managers	484	(9.62)	545	(6.73)	608	(11.12)
Newfoundland and Labrador						
Higher service	497	(8.16)	561	(8.16)	609	(9.25)
Lower service	487	(7.46)	537	(5.45)	590	(8.19)
Routine clerical / sales	462	(5.75)	510	(6.96)	564	(7.56)
Skilled-manual	439	(7.88)	500	(7.95)	553	(6.41)
Semi-unskilled manual	433	(7.73)	484	(8.36)	539	(9.38)
Farmers / Farm managers	534	(35.15)	548	(38.40)	585	(46.37)
Prince Edward Island						
Higher service	477	(10.23)	540	(9.30)	592	(8.48)
Lower service	462	(6.45)	517	(5.62)	569	(6.22)
Routine clerical / sales	444	(7.42)	500	(5.93)	549	(5.73)
Skilled-manual	415	(11.64)	477	(9.85)	534	(7.47)
Semi-unskilled manual	424	(9.65)	475	(9.55)	533	(11.32)
Farmers / Farm managers	449	(16.20)	511	(11.86)	561	(17.73)
Nova Scotia						
Higher service	488	(7.34)	545	(5.80)	599	(7.42)
Lower service	480	(4.82)	535	(5.79)	593	(6.27)
Routine clerical / sales	455	(5.22)	506	(4.94)	556	(6.47)
Skilled-manual	427	(6.92)	482	(8.38)	533	(8.67)
Semi-unskilled manual	421	(8.96)	479	(8.50)	538	(9.51)
Farmers / Farm managers	476	(34.16)	542	(34.48)	619	(68.26)
New Brunswick						
Higher service	491	(5.92)	544	(4.39)	596	(5.41)
Lower service	469	(4.90)	524	(5.19)	581	(4.44)
Routine clerical / sales	452	(4.91)	506	(4.83)	563	(6.40)
Skilled-manual	435	(6.34)	491	(6.18)	551	(6.41)
Semi-unskilled manual	423	(5.29)	477	(4.89)	535	(7.75)
Farmers / Farm managers	419	(16.89)	481	(30.25)	535	(21.04)
Quebec						
Higher service	515	(9.13)	578	(8.10)	634	(6.42)
Lower service	489	(7.94)	555	(7.88)	611	(5.98)
Routine clerical / sales	469	(9.55)	532	(7.90)	588	(6.20)
Skilled-manual	441	(10.27)	517	(9.48)	582	(8.27)
Semi-unskilled manual	448	(8.89)	503	(7.80)	559	(9.30)
Farmers / Farm managers	495	(35.05)	572	(22.96)	637	(37.12)
Ontario						
Higher service	490	(6.61)	551	(7.64)	611	(8.56)
Lower service	485	(5.56)	539	(5.88)	595	(6.60)
Routine clerical / sales	477	(5.72)	532	(6.63)	584	(5.34)
Skilled-manual	450	(8.48)	510	(6.54)	561	(7.68)
Semi-unskilled manual	447	(8.34)	496	(6.94)	552	(9.12)
Farmers / Farm managers	480	(18.63)	530	(24.39)	597	(53.13)

Table B4.5 – Concluded

Parental occupation and student mathematics performance, Canada and the provinces

	Percentiles for overall mathematics performance					
	25	Standard error	50	Standard error	75	Standard error
Manitoba						
Higher service	495	(7.58)	555	(7.50)	612	(8.52)
Lower service	479	(7.45)	539	(6.71)	594	(5.45)
Routine clerical / sales	467	(9.38)	528	(5.89)	585	(6.49)
Skilled-manual	449	(9.67)	514	(9.87)	572	(10.31)
Semi-unskilled manual	440	(8.60)	490	(9.83)	537	(9.09)
Farmers / Farm managers	473	(9.28)	525	(13.36)	585	(16.52)
Saskatchewan						
Higher service	488	(8.10)	546	(6.98)	603	(7.49)
Lower service	475	(8.03)	533	(6.16)	585	(5.56)
Routine clerical / sales	449	(11.00)	511	(8.05)	570	(8.88)
Skilled-manual	421	(11.73)	480	(10.11)	539	(15.39)
Semi-unskilled manual	416	(11.30)	471	(14.54)	537	(12.60)
Farmers / Farm managers	475	(9.84)	530	(11.77)	584	(11.36)
Alberta						
Higher service	527	(7.51)	585	(4.53)	639	(8.20)
Lower service	500	(7.84)	550	(7.55)	610	(8.47)
Routine clerical / sales	479	(10.43)	532	(11.29)	594	(10.57)
Skilled-manual	457	(16.07)	528	(14.09)	585	(11.80)
Semi-unskilled manual	446	(14.42)	510	(16.31)	568	(9.03)
Farmers / Farm managers	516	(15.26)	574	(12.93)	622	(13.29)
British Columbia						
Higher service	513	(7.23)	570	(5.57)	619	(4.76)
Lower service	491	(5.21)	549	(5.05)	605	(5.23)
Routine clerical / sales	470	(6.25)	527	(6.86)	586	(5.54)
Skilled-manual	460	(8.28)	517	(6.29)	578	(6.75)
Semi-unskilled manual	457	(9.78)	508	(8.14)	565	(8.79)
Farmers / Farm managers	499	(45.65)	560	(24.65)	602	(26.15)

Table B4.6

School socio-economic status (SES) and student performance in mathematics in Canada

	Percentiles of PISA overall mathematics performance after conditioning on individual SES					
	25	Standard error	50	Standard error	75	Standard error
Low SES schools	466	(3.61)	525	(3.40)	585	(3.53)
Middle SES schools	482	(2.38)	535	(2.50)	589	(2.71)
High SES schools	494	(3.49)	548	(3.27)	602	(3.21)